BOOK 3 – FINANCIAL STATEMENT ANALYSIS

READINGS AND LEARNING OUTCOME STATEMENTS

READINGS

The following material is a review of the Financial Statement Analysis principles designed to address the learning outcome statements set forth by CFA Institute.

STUDY SESSION 7

Reading Assignments
Financial Statement Analysis, CFA Program Curriculum, Volume 3 (CFA Institute, 2008)

STUDY SESSION 8

Reading Assignments
Financial Statement Analysis, CFA Program Curriculum, Volume 3 (CFA Institute, 2008)

STUDY SESSION 9

Reading Assignments
Financial Statement Analysis, CFA Program Curriculum, Volume 3 (CFA Institute, 2008)

STUDY SESSION 10

Reading Assignments
Financial Statement Analysis, CFA Program Curriculum, Volume 3 (CFA Institute, 2008)

LEARNING OUTCOME STATEMENTS (LOS)

STUDY SESSION 7

The topical coverage corresponds with the following CFA Institute assigned reading:

29. **Financial Statement Analysis: An Introduction**

The candidate should be able to:

a. discuss the roles of financial reporting and financial statement analysis. (page 10)

b. discuss the role of key financial statements (income statement, balance sheet, cash flow statement and statement of changes in owners' equity) in evaluating a company's performance and financial position. (page 11)

c. discuss the importance of financial statement notes and supplementary information (including disclosures of accounting methods, estimates and assumptions), and management's discussion and analysis. (page 12)

d. discuss the objective of audits of financial statements, the types of audit reports, and the importance of effective internal controls. (page 13)

e. identify and explain information sources other than annual financial statements and supplementary information that analysts use in financial statement analysis. (page 14)

f. describe the steps in the financial statement analysis framework. (page 15)

The topical coverage corresponds with the following CFA Institute assigned reading:

30. **Financial Reporting Mechanics**

The candidate should be able to:

a. identify the groups (operating, investing, and financing activities) into which business activities are categorized for financial reporting purposes and classify any business activity into the appropriate group. (page 19)

b. explain the relationship of financial statement elements and accounts, and classify accounts into the financial statement elements. (page 20)

c. explain the accounting equation in its basic and expanded forms. (page 21)

d. explain the process of recording business transactions using an accounting system based on the accounting equations. (page 22)

e. explain the need for accruals and other adjustments in preparing financial statements. (page 22)

f. prepare financial statements, given account balances or other elements in the relevant accounting equation, and explain the relationships among the income statement, balance sheet, statement of cash flows, and statement of owners' equity. (page 23)

g. describe the flow of information in an accounting system. (page 26)

h. explain the use of the results of the accounting process in security analysis. (page 26)

The topical coverage corresponds with the following CFA Institute assigned reading:

31. **Financial Reporting Standards**

The candidate should be able to:

a. explain the objective of financial statements and the importance of reporting standards in security analysis and valuation. (page 33)

b. explain the role of standard-setting bodies, such as the International Accounting Standards Board and the U.S. Financial Accounting Standards Board, and regulatory authorities such as the International Organization of Securities Commissions, the U.K. Financial Services Authority, and the U.S. Securities and Exchange Commission in establishing and enforcing financial reporting standards. (page 33)

c. discuss the ongoing barriers to developing one universally accepted set of financial reporting standards. (page 35)

d. describe the International Financial Reporting Standards (IFRS) framework, including the objective of financial statements, their qualitative characteristics, required reporting elements, and the constraints and assumptions in preparing financial statements. (page 35)

e. explain the general requirements for financial statements. (page 37)

f. compare and contrast key concepts of financial reporting standards under IFRS and alternative reporting systems, and discuss the implications for financial analysis of differing financial reporting systems. (page 38)

g. identify the characteristics of a coherent financial reporting framework and barriers to creating a coherent financial reporting network. (page 39)

h. discuss the importance of monitoring developments in financial reporting standards and evaluate company disclosures of significant accounting policies. (page 40)

STUDY SESSION 8

The topical coverage corresponds with the following CFA Institute assigned reading:

32. **Understanding the Income Statement**
The candidate should be able to:

a. describe the components of the income statement and construct an income statement using the alternative presentation formats of that statement. (page 46)

b. explain the general principles of revenue recognition and accrual accounting, demonstrate specific revenue recognition applications (including accounting for long-term contracts, installment sales, barter transactions, and gross and net reporting of revenue), and discuss the implications of revenue recognition principles for financial analysis. (page 48)

c. discuss the general principles of expense recognition, such as the matching principle, specific expense recognition applications (including depreciation of long-term assets and inventory methods), and the implications of expense recognition principles for financial analysis. (page 53)

d. determine which method of depreciation, accounting for inventory, or amortizing intangibles is appropriate, based on facts that might influence the decision. (page 54)

e. demonstrate the depreciation of long-term assets using each approved method, accounting for inventory using each approved method, and amortization of intangibles. (page 55)

f. distinguish between the operating and nonoperating components of the income statement. (page 59)

g. discuss the financial reporting treatment and analysis of nonrecurring items (including discontinued operations, extraordinary items, and unusual or infrequent items), and changes in accounting standards. (page 59)

h. describe the components of earnings per share and calculate a company's earnings per share (both basic and diluted earnings per share) for both a simple and complex capital structure. (page 61)

i. distinguish between dilutive and antidilutive securities, and discuss the implications of each for the earnings per share calculation. (page 61)

j. evaluate a company's financial performance using common-size income statements and financial ratios based on the income statement. (page 71)

k. state the accounting classification for items that are excluded from the income statement but affect owners' equity, and list the major types of items receiving that treatment. (page 73)

l. describe and calculate comprehensive income. (page 74)

The topical coverage corresponds with the following CFA Institute assigned reading:

33. **Understanding the Balance Sheet**

The candidate should be able to:

a. illustrate and interpret the components of the assets, liabilities, and equity sections of the balance sheet, and discuss the uses of the balance sheet in financial analysis. (page 84)

b. describe the various formats of balance sheet presentation. (page 86)

c. explain how assets and liabilities arise from the accrual process. (page 86)

d. compare and contrast current and noncurrent assets and liabilities. (page 87)

e. explain the measurement bases (e.g., historical cost and fair value) of assets and liabilities, including current assets, current liabilities, tangible assets, and intangible assets. (page 88)

f. discuss off-balance-sheet disclosures. (page 93)

g. demonstrate the appropriate classifications and related accounting treatments for marketable and non-marketable financial instruments held as assets or owed by the company as liabilities. (page 93)

h. list and explain the components of owners' equity. (page 95)

i. interpret balance sheets, common-size balance sheets, the statement of changes in equity, and commonly used balance sheet ratios. (page 96)

The topical coverage corresponds with the following CFA Institute assigned reading:

34. **Understanding the Cash Flow Statement**

The candidate should be able to:

a. compare and contrast cash flows from operating, investing, and financing activities, and classify cash flow items as relating to one of these three categories, given a description of the items. (page 107)

b. describe how noncash investing and financing activities are reported. (page 108)

c. compare and contrast the key differences in cash flow statements prepared under international financial reporting standards and U.S. generally accepted accounting principles. (page 108)

d. demonstrate the difference between the direct and indirect methods of presenting cash from operating activities and explain the arguments in favor of each. (page 109)

e. demonstrate how the cash flow statement is linked to the income statement and balance sheet. (page 111)

f. demonstrate the steps in the preparation of direct and indirect cash flow statements, including how cash flows can be computed using income statement and balance sheet data. (page 112)

g. describe the process of converting a statement of cash flows from the indirect to the direct method of presentation. (page 119)

h. analyze and interpret a cash flow statement using both total currency amounts and common-size cash flow statements. (page 121)

i. explain and calculate free cash flow to the firm, free cash flow to equity, and other cash flow ratios. (page 123)

STUDY SESSION 9

The topical coverage corresponds with the following CFA Institute assigned reading:

35. **Analysis of Inventories**

The candidate should be able to:

a. compute ending inventory balances and cost of goods sold using the LIFO, FIFO, and average cost methods to account for product inventory. (page 137)

b. explain the relationship among and the usefulness of inventory and cost of goods sold data provided by the LIFO, FIFO, and average cost methods when prices are (1) stable or (2) changing. (page 139)

c. compare and contrast the effect of the different methods on cost of goods sold and inventory balances and discuss how a company's choice of inventory accounting method affects other financial items such as income, cash flow, and working capital. (page 142)

d. compare and contrast the effects of the choice of inventory method on profitability, liquidity, activity, and solvency ratios. (page 147)

e. indicate the reasons that a LIFO reserve might decline during a given period and evaluate the implications of such a decline for financial analysis. (page 151)

f. illustrate how inventories are reported in the financial statements and how the lower-of-cost-or-market principle is used and applied. (page 151)

The topical coverage corresponds with the following CFA Institute assigned reading:

36. **Analysis of Long-Lived Assets: Part I—The Capitalization Decision**
The candidate should be able to:
a. demonstrate the effects of capitalizing versus expensing on net income, shareholders' equity, cash flow from operations, and financial ratios. (page 163)
b. determine which intangible assets, including software development costs and research and development costs, should be capitalized, according to U.S. GAAP and international accounting standards. (page 185)

The topical coverage corresponds with the following CFA Institute assigned reading:

37. **Analysis of Long-Lived Assets: Part II—Analysis of Depreciation and Impairment**
The candidate should be able to:
a. demonstrate the different depreciation methods and explain how the choice of depreciation method affects a company's financial statements, ratios, and taxes. (page 178)
b. demonstrate how modifying the depreciation method, the estimated useful life, and/or the salvage value used in accounting for long-lived assets affect financial statements and ratios. (page 185)
c. determine the average age and average depreciable life of a company's assets using the company's fixed asset disclosures. (page 186)
d. explain and illustrate the use of impairment charges on long-lived assets, and analyze the effects of taking such impairment charges on a company's financial statements and ratios. (page 188)
e. discuss accounting requirements related to remedying environmental damage caused by operating assets and explain the financial statement and ratio effects that result from the application of those requirements. (page 190)

The topical coverage corresponds with the following CFA Institute assigned reading:

38. **Analysis of Income Taxes**
The candidate should be able to:
a. explain the key terms related to income tax accounting and the origin of deferred tax liabilities and assets. (page 200)
b. demonstrate the liability method of accounting for deferred taxes. (page 203)
c. discuss the use of valuation allowances for deferred tax assets, and their implications for financial statement analysis. (page 203)
d. explain the factors that determine whether a company's deferred tax liabilities should be treated as a liability or as equity for purposes of financial analysis. (page 204)
e. distinguish between temporary and permanent items in pretax financial income and taxable income. (page 205)
f. calculate and interpret income tax expense, income taxes payable, deferred tax assets, and deferred tax liabilities. (page 207)
g. calculate and interpret the adjustment(s) to the deferred tax accounts related to a change in the tax rate. (page 210)

h. interpret a deferred tax footnote disclosure that reconciles the effective and statutory tax rates. (page 212)

i. analyze disclosures relating to, and the effect of, deferred taxes on a company's financial statements and financial ratios. (page 215)

j. compare and contrast a company's deferred tax items and effective tax rate reconciliation (1) between reporting periods and (2) with the comparable items reported by other companies. (page 215)

The topical coverage corresponds with the following CFA Institute assigned reading:

39. **Analysis of Financing Liabilities**
The candidate should be able to:

a. distinguish between operating and trade debt related to operating activities and debt generated by financing activities, and discuss the analytical implications of a shift between the two types of liabilities. (page 227)

b. determine the effects of debt issuance and amortization of bond discounts and premiums on financial statements and financial ratios. (page 228)

c. analyze the effect on financial statements and financial ratios of issuing zero-coupon debt. (page 232)

d. classify a debt security with equity features as a debt or equity security and demonstrate the effect of issuing debt with equity features on the financial statements and ratios. (page 234)

e. describe the disclosures relating to financing liabilities, and discuss the advantages/disadvantages to the company of selecting a given financing instrument and the effect of the selection on a company's financial statements and ratios. (page 235)

f. determine the effects of changing interest rates on the market value of debt and on financial statements and ratios. (page 237)

g. calculate and describe the accounting treatment of, and economic gains and losses resulting from, the various methods of retiring debt prior to its maturity. (page 238)

h. analyze the implications of debt covenants for creditors and the issuing company. (page 239)

The topical coverage corresponds with the following CFA Institute assigned reading:

40. **Leases and Off-Balance-Sheet Debt**
The candidate should be able to:

a. discuss the incentives for leasing assets instead of purchasing them, and the incentives for reporting the leases as operating leases rather than capital leases. (page 247)

b. contrast the effects of capital and operating leases on the financial statements and ratios of lessees and lessors. (page 249)

c. describe the types of off-balance-sheet financing and analyze their effects on selected financial ratios. (page 253)

d. distinguish between sales-type leases and direct financing leases and explain the effects of these types of leases on the financial statements of lessors. (page 255)

STUDY SESSION 10

The topical coverage corresponds with the following CFA Institute assigned reading:

41. **Financial Analysis Techniques**
The candidate should be able to:

a. evaluate and compare companies using ratio analysis, common-size financial statements, and charts in financial analysis. (page 267)

b. describe the limitations of ratio analysis. (page 272)

c. explain and demonstrate the classification of financial ratios. (page 273)

d. calculate and interpret activity, liquidity, solvency, profitability, and valuation ratios. (page 273)

e. demonstrate how ratios are related and how to evaluate a company using a combination of different ratios. (page 282)

f. demonstrate the application of DuPont analysis (the decomposition of return on equity). (page 286)

g. calculate and interpret the ratios used in equity analysis, credit analysis, and segment analysis. (page 291)

h. describe how the results of common-size and ratio analysis can be used to model and forecast earnings. (page 295)

The topical coverage corresponds with the following CFA Institute assigned reading:

42. **Financial Statement Analysis: Applications**
The candidate should be able to:

a. evaluate a company's past financial performance and explain how a company's strategy is reflected in past financial performance. (page 306)

b. prepare a basic projection of a company's future net income and cash flow. (page 307)

c. describe the role of financial statement analysis in assessing the credit quality of a potential debt investment. (page 308)

d. discuss the use of financial statement analysis in screening for potential equity investments. (page 309)

e. determine and justify appropriate analyst adjustments to a company's financial statements to facilitate comparison with another company. (page 309)

The topical coverage corresponds with the following CFA Institute assigned reading:

43. **International Standards Convergence**
The candidate should be able to:

a. identify and explain the major international accounting standards for each asset and liability category on the balance sheet and the key differences from U.S. generally accepted accounting principles (GAAP). (page 315)

b. identify and explain the major international accounting standards for major revenue and expense categories on the income statement, and the key differences from U.S. GAAP. (page 320)

c. identify and explain the major differences between international and U.S. GAAP accounting standards concerning the treatment of interest and dividends on the cash flow statement. (page 321)

d. interpret the effect of differences between international and U.S. GAAP accounting standards on the balance sheet, income statement, and the statement of changes in equity for some commonly used financial ratios. (page 322)

The following is a review of the Financial Statement Analysis principles designed to address the learning outcome statements set forth by CFA Institute®. This topic is also covered in:

FINANCIAL STATEMENT ANALYSIS: AN INTRODUCTION

Study Session 7

EXAM FOCUS

This introduction may be useful to those with no previous experience with financial statements. While the income statement, balance sheet, and statement of cash flows are covered in detail in subsequent readings, candidates should pay special attention here to the other sources of information for financial analysis. The nature of the audit report is important, as is the information that is contained in the footnotes to financial statements, proxy statements, Management's Discussion and Analysis, and the supplementary schedules. A useful framework enumerating the steps in financial statement analysis is presented.

LOS 29.a: Discuss the roles of financial reporting and financial statement analysis.

Financial reporting refers to the way companies show their financial performance to investors, creditors, and other interested parties by preparing and presenting financial statements. The role of financial reporting is described by the International Accounting Standards Board (IASB) in its "Framework for the Preparation and Presentation of Financial Statements":

> "The objective of financial statements is to provide information about the financial position, performance and changes in financial position of an entity that is useful to a wide range of users in making economic decisions."

The role of **financial statement analysis** is to use the information in a company's financial statements, along with other relevant information, to make economic decisions. Examples of such decisions include whether to invest in the company's securities or recommend them to investors, and whether to extend trade or bank credit to the company. Analysts use financial statement data to evaluate a company's past performance and current financial position in order to form opinions about the company's ability to earn profits and generate cash flow in the future.

LOS 29.b: Discuss the role of key financial statements (income statement, balance sheet, cash flow statement and statement of changes in owners' equity) in evaluating a company's performance and financial position.

The **income statement** reports on the financial performance of the firm over a period of time. The elements of the income statement include revenues, expenses, and gains and losses.

- *Revenues* are inflows from delivering or producing goods, rendering services, or other activities that constitute the entity's ongoing major or central operations.
- *Expenses* are outflows from delivering or producing goods or services that constitute the entity's ongoing major or central operations.
- *Gains and losses* are increases and decreases in equity or net assets from peripheral or incidental transactions.

The **balance sheet** reports the firm's financial position at a point in time. The balance sheet consists of three elements:

1. *Assets* are probable current and future economic benefits obtained or controlled by a particular entity as a result of past transactions or events. Assets are a firm's economic resources.

2. *Liabilities* are probable future economic costs. They arise from present obligations of a particular entity to transfer assets or provide services to other entities in the future as a result of past transactions or events.

3. *Owners' equity* is the residual interest in the net assets of an entity that remains after deducting its liabilities.

Transactions are measured so that the fundamental **accounting equation** holds:

assets = liabilities + owners' equity

The **cash flow statement** reports the company's cash receipts and payments. These cash flows are classified as follows:

- *Operating cash flows* include the cash effects of transactions that involve the normal business of the firm.
- *Investing cash flows* are those resulting from the acquisition or sale of property, plant, and equipment, of a subsidiary or segment, of securities, and of investments in other firms.
- *Financing cash flows* are those resulting from issuance or retirement of the firm's debt and equity securities, and include dividends paid to stockholders.

The **statement of changes in owners' equity** reports the amounts and sources of changes in equity investors' investment in the firm over a period of time.

LOS 29.c: Discuss the importance of financial statement notes and supplementary information (including disclosures of accounting methods, estimates and assumptions), and management's discussion and analysis.

Financial statement notes (footnotes) include disclosures that provide further details about the information summarized in the financial statements. Footnotes allow users to improve their assessments of the amount, timing, and uncertainty of the estimates reported in the financial statements. Footnotes:

- Provide information about accounting methods, assumptions, and estimates used by management.
- Are audited, whereas other disclosures, such as supplementary schedules, are not audited.
- Provide additional information on items such as business acquisitions or disposals, legal actions, employee benefit plans, contingencies and commitments, significant customers, sales to related parties, and segments of the firm.

Supplementary schedules contain additional information. Examples of such disclosures include:

- Operating income or sales by region or business segment.
- Reserves for an oil and gas company.
- Information about hedging activities and financial instruments.

Management's Discussion and Analysis (MD&A) provides an assessment of the financial performance and condition of a company from the perspective of its management. For publicly held companies in the United States, the MD&A is required to discuss:

- Results from operations, with a discussion of trends in sales and expenses.
- Capital resources and liquidity, with a discussion of trends in cash flows.
- A general business overview based on known trends.

Management's Discussion and Analysis can also include:

- Discussion of accounting policies that require significant judgements by management.
- Discussion of significant effects of currently known trends, events, and uncertainties (may voluntarily disclose forward-looking data).
- Liquidity and capital resource issues, and transactions or events with liquidity implications.
- Discontinued operations, extraordinary items, and other unusual or infrequent events.
- Extensive disclosures in interim financial statements.
- Disclosures of a segment's need for cash flows or its contribution to revenues or profit.

LOS 29.d: Discuss the objective of audits of financial statements, the types of audit reports, and the importance of effective internal controls.

An **audit** is an independent review of an entity's financial statements. Public accountants conduct audits and examine the financial reports and supporting records. The objective of an audit is to enable the auditor to provide an opinion on the fairness and reliability of the financial statements.

The independent certified public accounting firm employed by the board of directors is responsible for seeing that the financial statements conform to the applicable accounting standards. The auditor examines the company's accounting and internal control systems, confirms assets and liabilities, and generally tries to determine that there are no material errors in the financial statements. The auditor's report is an important source of information.

The **standard auditor's opinion** contains three parts and states that:

1. Whereas the financial statements are prepared by management and are its responsibility, the auditor has performed an independent review.

2. Generally accepted auditing standards were followed, thus providing *reasonable assurance* that the financial statements contain no material errors.

3. The auditor is satisfied that the statements were prepared in accordance with accepted accounting principles, and that the principles chosen and estimates made are reasonable. The auditor's report must also contain additional explanation when accounting methods have not been used consistently between periods.

An *unqualified opinion* indicates that the auditor believes the statements are free from material omissions and errors. If the statements make any exceptions to the accounting principles, the auditor may issue a *qualified opinion* and explain these exceptions in the audit report. The auditor can issue an *adverse opinion* if the statements are not presented fairly or are materially nonconforming with accounting standards.

The auditor's opinion will also contain an explanatory paragraph when a material loss is probable but the amount cannot be reasonably estimated. These "uncertainties" may relate to the *going concern assumption* (the assumption that the firm will continue to operate for the foreseeable future), the valuation or realization of asset values, or to litigation. This type of disclosure may be a signal of serious problems and may call for close examination by the analyst.

Under U.S. Generally Accepted Accounting Principles (GAAP), the auditor must state its opinion on the company's **internal controls**, which are the processes by which the company ensures that it presents accurate financial statements. The auditor can provide this opinion separately or as the fourth element of the standard auditor's opinion.

Internal controls are the responsibility of the firm's management. Under the Sarbanes-Oxley Act, management is required to provide a report on the company's internal control system that includes the following elements:

- A statement that the firm's management is responsible for implementing and maintaining effective internal controls.
- A description of how management evaluates the internal control system.
- An assessment by management of the effectiveness over the most recent year of the firm's internal controls.
- A statement that the firm's auditors have assessed management's report on internal controls.
- A statement certifying that the firm's financial statements are presented fairly.

LOS 29.e: Identify and explain information sources other than annual financial statements and supplementary information that analysts use in financial statement analysis.

Besides the annual financial statements, an analyst should examine a company's *quarterly or semiannual reports*. These interim reports typically update the major financial statements and footnotes, but are not necessarily audited.

Securities and Exchange Commission (SEC) filings are available from EDGAR (Electronic Data Gathering, Analysis, and Retrieval System, www.sec.gov). These include Form 8-K, which a company must file to report events such as acquisitions and disposals of major assets or changes in its management or corporate governance. Companies' annual and quarterly financial statements are also filed with the SEC (Form 10-K and Form 10-Q, respectively).

Proxy statements are issued to shareholders when there are matters that require a shareholder vote. These statements, which are also filed with the SEC and available from EDGAR, are a good source of information about the election of (and qualifications of) board members, compensation, management qualifications, and the issuance of stock options.

Corporate reports and press releases are written by management and are often viewed as public relations or sales materials. Not all of the material is independently reviewed by outside auditors. Such information can often be found on the company's web site.

An analyst should also review pertinent information on economic conditions and the company's industry and compare the company to its competitors. The necessary information can be acquired from trade journals, statistical reporting services, and government agencies.

LOS 29.f: Describe the steps in the financial statement analysis framework.

The **financial statement analysis framework**[1] consists of six steps:

1. *State the objective and context.* Determine what questions the analysis seeks to answer, the form in which this information needs to be presented, and what resources and how much time are available to perform the analysis.

2. *Gather data.* Acquire the company's financial statements and other relevant data on its industry and the economy. Ask questions of the company's management, suppliers, and customers, and visit company sites.

3. *Process the data.* Make any appropriate adjustments to the financial statements. Calculate ratios. Prepare exhibits such as graphs and common-size balance sheets.

4. *Analyze and interpret the data.* Use the data to answer the questions stated in the first step. Decide what conclusions or recommendations the information supports.

5. *Report the conclusions or recommendations.* Prepare a report and communicate it to its intended audience. Be sure the report and its dissemination comply with the Code and Standards that relate to investment analysis and recommendations.

6. *Update the analysis.* Repeat these steps periodically and change the conclusions or recommendations when necessary.

---

1. Hennie van Greuning and Sonja Brajovic Bratanovic, *Analyzing and Managing Banking Risk: Framework for Assessing Corporate Governance and Financial Risk*, International Bank for Reconstruction and Development, April 2003, p. 300.

KEY CONCEPTS

1. The role of financial reporting is to provide decision makers with useful information about a company's performance and financial position.

2. The role of financial statement analysis is to use the data from financial statements to support economic decisions.

3. The income statement shows the effects of transactions completed over the period; the balance sheet shows assets, liabilities, and owners' equity at a point in time; and the cash flow statement shows the sources and uses of cash over the period. The statement of changes in owners' equity reports the amount and sources of changes in owners' investment in the firm.

4. Important sources of information in a company's financial statements are the financial statement notes (footnotes), supplementary schedules, and Management's Discussion and Analysis.

5. A company's management is responsible for maintaining an effective internal control system to ensure the accuracy of its financial statements.

6. The auditor's opinion gives evidence of an independent review of the financial statements that verifies that appropriate accounting principles were used, that standard auditing procedures were used to establish reasonable assurance that the statements contain no material errors, and that management's report on the company's internal controls has been reviewed.

7. Along with the annual financial statements, important information sources for an analyst include a company's quarterly and semiannual reports, proxy statements, and press releases.

8. The framework for financial analysis has six steps:
   • State the objective of the analysis.
   • Gather data.
   • Process the data.
   • Analyze and interpret the data.
   • Report the conclusions or recommendations.
   • Update the analysis.

CONCEPT CHECKERS

1. Which of the following statements *least accurately* describes a role of financial statement analysis?
    A. Use the information in financial statements to make economic decisions.
    B. Make decisions about whether to invest in or recommend investing in an entity.
    C. Provide reasonable assurance that the financial statements are free of material errors.
    D. Evaluate an entity's financial position and past performance to form opinions about its future ability to earn profits and generate cash flow.

2. A firm's financial position at a specific point in time is reported in the:
    A. balance sheet.
    B. income statement.
    C. cash flow statement.
    D. statement of changes in owners' equity.

3. Information about accounting estimates, assumptions, and methods chosen for reporting is *most likely* found in:
    A. Management's Discussion and Analysis.
    B. the auditor's opinion.
    C. financial statement notes.
    D. supplementary schedules.

4. If an auditor finds that a company's financial statements have made a specific exception to applicable accounting principles, she is *most likely* to issue a:
    A. qualification letter.
    B. dissenting opinion.
    C. cautionary note.
    D. qualified opinion.

5. Information about elections of members to a company's Board of Directors is *most likely* found in:
    A. a 10-Q filing.
    B. a proxy statement.
    C. an auditor's report.
    D. footnotes to the financial statements.

6. Which of these steps is *least likely* to be a part of the financial statement analysis framework?
    A. State the purpose and context of the analysis.
    B. Determine whether the company's securities are suitable for the client.
    C. Report the conclusions or recommendations based on analysis of the data.
    D. Adjust the financial statement data and compare the company to its industry peers.

ANSWERS – CONCEPT CHECKERS

1. **C** This statement describes the role of an auditor, rather than the role of an analyst. The other responses describe the role of financial statement analysis.

2. **A** The balance sheet reports a company's financial position as of a specific date. The income statement, cash flow statement, and statement of changes in owners' equity show the company's performance during a specific period.

3. **C** Information about accounting methods and estimates is contained in the footnotes to the financial statements.

4. **D** An auditor will issue a qualified opinion if the financial statements make any exceptions to applicable accounting standards and will explain the effect of these exceptions in the auditor's report.

5. **B** Proxy statements contain information related to matters that come before shareholders for a vote, such as elections of board members.

6. **B** Determining the suitability of an investment for a client is not one of the six steps in the financial statement analysis framework. The analyst would only perform this function if he also had an advisory relationship with the client. Stating the objective, processing the data, and reporting the conclusions are three of the six steps in the framework. The others are gathering the data, analyzing the data, and updating the analysis.

The following is a review of the Financial Statement Analysis principles designed to address the learning outcome statements set forth by CFA Institute®. This topic is also covered in:

FINANCIAL REPORTING MECHANICS

Study Session 7

EXAM FOCUS

The analysis of financial statements requires an understanding of how a company's transactions are recorded in the various accounts. Candidates should focus on the financial statement elements (assets, liabilities, equity, revenues, and expenses) and be able to classify any account into its appropriate element. Candidates should also learn the basic and expanded accounting equations and why every transaction must be recorded in at least two accounts. Knowing the four types of accruals and when each of them is used, and understanding how changes in accounts affect the financial statements and the relationships among the financial statements, are all important topics.

LOS 30.a: Identify the groups (operating, investing, and financing activities) into which business activities are categorized for financial reporting purposes and classify any business activity into the appropriate group.

Business transactions can be classified for financial reporting as operating activities, investing activities, or financing activities.

Operating activities are transactions that involve the firm's primary activities of production and trade. Sales and their related costs are typically a firm's primary operating activities. Other examples of operating activities include paying taxes, buying short-term assets, and taking on short-term liabilities to support the firm's ordinary business.

Investing activities are transactions to acquire or dispose of long-term assets. Purchases and sales of property, plant, and equipment are investing activities, as are purchases and sales of securities issued by others.

Financing activities are transactions through which the firm raises or repays capital. These include issuing or repaying debt, issuing or repurchasing stock, and paying dividends to shareholders.

How a transaction is classified depends on the nature of the firm, rather than the nature of the transaction. For example, holding long-term securities is an investing activity for most firms, but is an operating activity for a company whose primary business is making such investments.

LOS 30.b: Explain the relationship of financial statement elements and accounts, and classify accounts into the financial statement elements.

Financial statement elements are the major classifications of assets, liabilities, owners' equity, revenues, and expenses. **Accounts** are the specific records within each element where various transactions are entered. On the financial statements, accounts are typically presented in groups such as "inventory" or "accounts payable." A company's **chart of accounts** is a detailed list of the accounts that make up the five financial statement elements and the line items presented in the financial statements.

Contra accounts are used for entries that offset some part of the value of another account. For example, equipment is typically valued on the balance sheet at acquisition (historical) cost, and the estimated decrease in its value over time is recorded in a contra account titled "accumulated depreciation."

Classifying Accounts Into the Financial Statement Elements

Assets are the firm's economic resources. Examples of assets include:

- *Cash and cash equivalents.* Liquid securities with maturities of 90 days or less are considered cash equivalents.
- *Accounts receivable.* Accounts receivable often have an "allowance for bad debt expense" or "allowance for doubtful accounts" as a contra account.
- *Inventory.*
- *Financial assets* such as marketable securities.
- *Prepaid expenses.* Items that will be expenses on future income statements.
- *Property, plant, and equipment.* Includes a contra-asset account for accumulated depreciation.
- *Investment in affiliates* accounted for using the equity method.
- *Deferred tax assets.*
- *Intangible assets.* Economic resources of the firm that do not have a physical form, such as patents, trademarks, licenses, and goodwill. Except for goodwill, these values may be reduced by "accumulated amortization."

Liabilities are creditor claims on the company's resources. Examples of liabilities include:

- *Accounts payable* and *trade payables.*
- *Financial liabilities* such as short-term notes payable.
- *Unearned revenue.* Items that will show up on future income statements as revenues.
- *Income taxes payable.* The taxes accrued during the past year but not yet paid.
- *Long-term debt* such as bonds payable.
- *Deferred tax liabilities.*

Owners' equity is the owners' residual claim on a firm's resources, which is the amount by which assets exceed liabilities. Owners' equity includes:

- *Capital.* Par value of common stock.
- *Additional paid-in capital.* Proceeds from common stock sales in excess of par value. (Share repurchases that the company has made are represented in the contra account, *treasury stock*.)
- *Retained earnings.* Cumulative net income that has not been distributed as dividends.
- *Other comprehensive income.* Changes resulting from foreign currency translation, minimum pension liability adjustments, or unrealized gains and losses on investments.

Revenue represents inflows of economic resources and includes:

- *Sales.* Revenue from the firm's day-to-day activities.
- *Gains.* Increases in assets or equity from transactions incidental to the firm's day-to-day activities.
- *Investment income* such as interest and dividend income.

Expenses are outflows of economic resources and include:

- *Cost of goods sold.*
- *Selling, general and administrative expenses.* These include such expenses as advertising, management salaries, rent and utilities.
- *Depreciation* and *amortization.* To reflect the "using up" of tangible and intangible assets.
- *Tax expense.*
- *Interest expense.*
- *Losses.* Decreases in assets or equity from transactions incidental to the firm's day-to-day activities.

LOS 30.c: Explain the accounting equation in its basic and expanded forms.

The **basic accounting equation** is the relationship among the three balance sheet elements:

assets = liabilities + owners' equity

Owners' equity consists of capital contributed by the firm's owners and the cumulative earnings the firm has retained. With that in mind, we can state the **expanded accounting equation**:

assets = liabilities + contributed capital + ending retained earnings

Ending retained earnings for an accounting period is the result of adding that period's retained earnings (revenues minus expenses minus dividends) to beginning retained earnings. So the expanded accounting equation can also be stated as:

Assets =   Liabilities
            + Contributed Capital
            + Beginning Retained Earnings
            + Revenue
            – Expenses
            – Dividends

LOS 30.d: Explain the process of recording business transactions using an accounting system based on the accounting equations.

Keeping the accounting equation in balance requires **double-entry accounting**, in which a transaction has to be recorded in at least two accounts. An increase in an asset account, for example, must be balanced by a decrease in another asset account or by an increase in a liability or owners' equity account.

Some typical examples of double entry accounting include:

- *Purchase equipment for $10,000 cash.* Property, plant and equipment (an asset) increases by $10,000. Cash (an asset) decreases by $10,000.
- *Borrow $10,000 to purchase equipment.* PP&E increases by $10,000. Notes payable (a liability) increases by $10,000.
- *Buy office supplies for $100 cash.* Cash decreases by $100. Supply expense increases by $100. An expense reduces retained earnings, so owners' equity decreases by $100.
- *Buy inventory for $8,000 cash and sell it for $10,000 cash.* The purchase decreases cash by $8,000 and increases inventory (an asset) by $8,000. The sale increases cash by $10,000 and decreases inventory by $8,000, so assets increase by $2,000. At the same time, sales (a revenue account) increase by $10,000 and "cost of goods sold" (an expense) increases by the $8,000 cost of inventory. The $2,000 difference is an increase in net income and, therefore, in retained earnings and owners' equity (ignoring taxes).

LOS 30.e: Explain the need for accruals and other adjustments in preparing financial statements.

Revenues and expenses are not always recorded at the same time that cash receipts and payments are made. The principle of **accrual accounting** requires that revenue is recorded when the firm earns it and expenses are recorded as the firm incurs them, regardless of whether cash has actually been paid. Accruals fall into four categories:

1. *Unearned revenue.* The firm receives cash before it provides a good or service to customers. Cash increases and unearned revenue, a liability, increases by the same amount. When the firm provides the good or service, revenue increases and the liability decreases. For example, a newspaper or magazine subscription is typically

paid in advance. The publisher records the cash received and increases the unearned revenue liability account. The firm recognizes revenues and decreases the liability as it fulfills the subscription obligation.

2. *Accrued revenue.* The firm provides goods or services before it receives cash payment. Revenue increases and accounts receivable (an asset) increases. When the customer pays cash, accounts receivable decreases. A typical example would be a manufacturer that sells goods to retail stores "on account." The manufacturer records revenue when it delivers the goods, but does not receive cash until after the retailers sell the goods to consumers.

3. *Prepaid expenses.* The firm pays cash ahead of time for an anticipated expense. Cash (an asset) decreases and prepaid expense (also an asset) increases. Prepaid expense decreases and expenses increase when the expense is actually incurred. For example, a retail store that rents space in a shopping mall will often pay its rent in advance.

4. *Accrued expenses.* The firm owes cash for expenses it has incurred. Expenses increase and a liability for accrued expenses increases as well. The liability decreases when the firm pays cash to satisfy it. Wages payable are a common example of an accrued expense, as companies typically pay their employees at a later date for work they performed in the prior week or month.

Accruals require an accounting entry when the earliest event occurs (paying or receiving cash, providing a good or service, or incurring an expense) and require one or more offsetting entries as the exchange is completed. With unearned revenue and prepaid expenses, cash changes hands first and the revenue or expense is recorded later. With accrued revenue and accrued expenses, the revenue or expense is recorded first and cash is exchanged later. In all these cases, the effect of accrual accounting is to recognize revenues or expenses in the appropriate period.

Other Adjustments

Most assets are recorded on the financial statements at their historical costs. However, accounting standards require balance sheet values of certain assets to reflect their current market values. Accounting entries that update these assets' values are called **valuation adjustments**. To keep the accounting equation in balance, changes in asset values also change owners' equity, through gains or losses recorded on the income statement or in "other comprehensive income."

LOS 30.f: Prepare financial statements, given account balances or other elements in the relevant accounting equation, and explain the relationships among the income statement, balance sheet, statement of cash flows, and statement of owners' equity.

Figures 1 through 4 contain the financial statements for a sample corporation. The balance sheet summarizes the company's financial position at the end of the current accounting period (and in this example, it also shows the company's position at the end of the previous fiscal period). The income statement, cash flow statement, and statement of owners' equity show changes that occurred during the most recent accounting period.

Note these key relationships among the financial statements:

- The income statement shows that net income was $37,500 in 20X8. The company declared $8,500 of that income as dividends to its shareholders. The remaining $29,000 is an increase in retained earnings. Retained earnings on the balance sheet increased by $29,000, from $30,000 in 20X7 to $59,000 in 20X8.
- The cash flow statement shows a $24,000 net increase in cash. On the balance sheet, cash increased by $24,000, from $9,000 in 20X7 to $33,000 in 20X8.
- One of the uses of cash shown on the cash flow statement is a repurchase of stock for $10,000. The balance sheet shows this $10,000 repurchase as a decrease in common stock, from $50,000 in 20X7 to $40,000 in 20X8.
- The statement of owners' equity reflects the changes in retained earnings and contributed capital (common stock). Owners' equity increased by $19,000, from $80,000 in 20X7 to $99,000 in 20X8. This equals the $29,000 increase in retained earnings less the $10,000 decrease in common stock.

Figure 1: Income Statement for 20X8

Sales	$100,000
Expenses	
Cost of goods sold	40,000
Wages	5,000
Depreciation	7,000
Interest	500
Total expenses	$52,500
Income from continuing operations	47,500
Gain from sale of land	10,000
Pretax income	$57,500
Provision for taxes	20,000
Net income	$37,500
Common dividends declared	8,500

Figure 2: Balance Sheet for 20X7 and 20X8

	20X8	20X7
Assets		
Current assets		
Cash	$33,000	$9,000
Accounts receivable	10,000	9,000
Inventory	5,000	7,000
Noncurrent assets		
Land	$35,000	$40,000
Gross plant and equipment	85,000	60,000
less: Accumulated depreciation	(16,000)	(9,000)
Net plant and equipment	$69,000	$51,000
Goodwill	10,000	10,000
Total assets	$162,000	$126,000
Liabilities and Equity		
Current liabilities		
Accounts payable	$9,000	$5,000
Wages payable	4,500	8,000
Interest payable	3,500	3,000
Taxes payable	5,000	4,000
Dividends payable	6,000	1,000
Noncurrent liabilities		
Bonds	$15,000	$10,000
Deferred taxes	20,000	15,000
Stockholders' equity		
Common stock	$40,000	$50,000
Retained earnings	59,000	30,000
Total liabilities & stockholders' equity	$162,000	$126,000

Figure 3: Cash Flow Statement for 20X8

Cash collections	$99,000
cash inputs	(34,000)
cash expenses	(8,500)
cash interest	0
cash taxes	(14,000)
Cash flow from operations	$42,500
Cash from sale of land	$15,000
Purchase of plant and equipment	(25,000)
Cash flow from investments	($10,000)
Sale of bonds	$5,000
Repurchase of stock	(10,000)
Cash dividends	(3,500)
Cash flow from financing	($8,500)
Total cash flow	$24,000

Figure 4: Statement of Owners' Equity for 20X8

	Contributed Capital	Retained Earnings	Total
Balance, 12/31/20X7	$50,000	$30,000	$80,000
Repurchase of stock	($10,000)		($10,000)
Net income		$37,500	$37,500
Distributions		($8,500)	($8,500)
Balance, 12/31/20X8	$40,000	$59,000	$99,000

LOS 30.g: Describe the flow of information in an accounting system.

Information flows through an accounting system in four steps:

1. *Journal entries* record every transaction, showing which accounts are changed and by what amounts. A listing of all the journal entries in order of their dates is called the "general journal."

2. The *general ledger* sorts the entries in the general journal by account.

3. At the end of the accounting period, an *initial trial balance* is prepared that shows the balances in each account. If any adjusting entries are needed, they will be recorded and reflected in an *adjusted trial balance*.

4. The account balances from the adjusted trial balance are presented in the *financial statements*.

LOS 30.h: Explain the use of the results of the accounting process in security analysis.

An analyst does not have access to the detailed information that flows through a company's accounting system, but sees only the end product, the financial statements. An analyst needs to understand the various accruals, adjustments, and management assumptions that go into the financial statements. Much of this detail is contained in the footnotes to the statements and Management's Discussion and Analysis, so it is crucial for an analyst to review these parts of the financial statements. With this information, the analyst can better judge how well the financial statements reflect the company's true performance and what adjustments to the data are necessary for appropriate analysis.

Because adjustments and assumptions within the financial statements are, at least to some extent, at the discretion of management, the possibility exists that management may attempt to manipulate or misrepresent the company's financial performance. A good understanding of the accounting process can help an analyst identify financial statement entries that appear to be out of line.

KEY CONCEPTS

1. Business transactions can be categorized as *operating activities*, the firm's ordinary business; *investing activities*, purchasing, selling, and disposing of long-term assets; and *financing activities*, raising and repaying capital.

2. Transactions are recorded in accounts that form the financial statement elements of assets, liabilities, owners' equity, revenues, and expenses.

3. Assets are the firm's economic resources. Liabilities are creditors' claims on the firm's resources.

4. Owners' equity includes paid-in capital (common and preferred stock), retained earnings, and cumulative other comprehensive income.

5. Revenue includes sales, investment income, and gains. Expenses include the cost of goods sold, selling and administrative expenses, depreciation, interest expense, tax expense, and losses.

6. The basic accounting equation is:

    assets = liabilities + owners' equity

    The expanded accounting equation is:

    assets = liabilities + contributed capital + ending retained earnings

7. To keep the accounting equation in balance, each transaction has to be recorded in at least two accounts.

8. A firm must recognize revenues when they are earned and expenses when they are incurred. Accruals are required when the timing of cash payments does not match the timing of the revenue or expense.

9. The balance sheet shows a company's financial position at a point in time. Changes in the balance sheet during an accounting period are reflected in the income statement, the cash flow statement, and the statement of owners' equity.

10. Information enters an accounting system as journal entries, which are sorted by account into a general ledger. Trial balances are formed at the end of an accounting period. Accounts are then adjusted and presented in financial statements.

11. A security analyst must understand the accounting process used to produce the financial statements, including management's adjustments and assumptions, in order to determine whether the data are reasonable.

CONCEPT CHECKERS

1. Richland Paper is a manufacturer of folding cartons for packaging retail items. This year the company acquired a new cutting machine that it expects to use for the next eight years. This purchase should be classified as a(n):
   A. operating activity.
   B. investing activity.
   C. financing activity.
   D. economic activity.

2. Sparta Distributors, a wholesaler, has obtained a $5 million 10-year loan from Stoddard National Bank. How should each firm *best* classify this transaction?

	Sparta Distributors	Stoddard Nat'l Bank
A.	Investing activity	Financing activity
B.	Investing activity	Operating activity
C.	Financing activity	Financing activity
D.	Financing activity	Operating activity

3. Accounts receivable and accounts payable are *most likely* classified as which financial statement elements?

	Accounts receivable	Accounts payable
A.	Assets	Liabilities
B.	Assets	Expenses
C.	Revenues	Liabilities
D.	Revenues	Expenses

4. Annual depreciation and accumulated depreciation are *most likely* classified as which financial statement elements?

	Depreciation	Accumulated depreciation
A.	Expenses	Contra liabilities
B.	Expenses	Contra assets
C.	Liabilities	Contra liabilities
D.	Liabilities	Contra assets

5. The accounting equation is *least accurately* stated as:
   A. owners' equity = liabilities − assets.
   B. liabilities = assets − contributed capital − ending retained earnings.
   C. ending retained earnings = assets − contributed capital − liabilities.
   D. assets = liabilities + contributed capital + beginning retained earnings + revenue − expenses − dividends.

6. A decrease in assets would *least likely* be consistent with a(n):
   A. increase in expenses.
   B. decrease in revenues.
   C. decrease in liabilities.
   D. increase in contributed capital.

7. An electrician repaired the light fixtures in a retail shop on October 24 and
    sent the bill to the shop on November 3. If both the electrician and the shop
    prepare financial statements under the accrual method on October 31, how
    will they each record this transaction?

	Electrician	Retail shop
A.	Accrued revenue	Accrued expense
B.	Accrued revenue	Prepaid expense
C.	Unearned revenue	Accrued expense
D.	Unearned revenue	Prepaid expense

8. If a firm raises $10 million by issuing new common stock, which of its
    financial statements will reflect the transaction?
    A. Income statement and statement of owners' equity.
    B. Balance sheet, income statement, and cash flow statement.
    C. Balance sheet, cash flow statement, and statement of owners' equity.
    D. Balance sheet, income statement, cash flow statement, and statement of
        owners' equity.

9. An auditor needs to review all of a company's transactions that took place
    between August 15 and August 17 of the current year. To find this
    information, she would *most likely* consult the company's:
    A. general ledger.
    B. general journal.
    C. financial statements.
    D. adjusted trial balance.

10. Paul Schmidt, a representative for Westby Investments, is explaining how
    security analysts use the results of the accounting process. He states, "Analysts
    do not have access to all the entries that went into creating a company's
    financial statements. If the analyst carefully reviews the auditor's report for any
    instances where the financial statements deviate from the appropriate
    accounting principles, he can then be confident that management is not
    manipulating earnings." Schmidt is:
    A. correct.
    B. incorrect, because the entries that went into creating a company's financial
        statements are publicly available.
    C. incorrect, because management can manipulate earnings even within the
        confines of generally accepted accounting principles.
    D. incorrect, because the entries that went into creating a company's financial
        statements are publicly available and because management can manipulate
        earnings even within the confines of the accounting principles.

COMPREHENSIVE PROBLEMS

For each account listed, indicate whether the account should be classified as Assets (A), Liabilities (L), Owners' Equity (O), Revenues (R), or Expenses (X).

Account		Financial statement element				
Accounts payable	L	A	(L)	O	R	X
Accounts receivable	A	(A)	L	O	R	X
Accumulated depreciation	A	(A)	L	O	R	X
Additional paid-in capital	O	A	L	(O)	R	X
Allowance for bad debts	A	(A)	(L)	O	R	X
Bonds payable	L	A	(L)	O	R	X
Cash equivalents	A	(A)	L	O	R	X
Common stock	O	A	L	(O)	R	X
Cost of goods sold	X	A	L	O	R	(X)
Current portion of long-term debt	L	(A)	(L)	O	R	X
Deferred tax items	A/L	(A)	(L)	O	R	X
Depreciation	X	A	L	O	R	(X)
Dividends payable	L	A	(L)	O	R	X
Dividends received	R	(A)	L	O	R	X
Gain on sale of assets	R	(A)	L	O	R	X
Goodwill	A	A	L	O	R	X
Inventory	A	A	L	O	R	X
Investment securities	A	A	L	O	R	X
Loss on sale of assets	X	A	L	O	R	X
Notes payable	L	A	L	O	R	X
Other comprehensive income	O	A	L	O	R	X
Prepaid expenses	A	A	L	O	R	X
Property, plant and equipment	A	A	L	O	R	X
Retained earnings	O	A	L	O	R	X
Sales	R	A	L	O	R	X
Unearned revenue	L	A	L	O	R	X

ANSWERS – CONCEPT CHECKERS °

1. **B**   Purchasing property, plant and equipment is an investing activity.

2. **D**   Obtaining a long-term loan is a financing activity for the wholesaler. For a bank, however, providing loans is its primary business, so making the loan would be best classified as an operating activity.

3. **A**   Accounts receivable are an asset and accounts payable are a liability.

4. **B**   Annual depreciation is an expense. Accumulated depreciation is a contra asset account that typically offsets the historical cost of property, plant, and equipment.

5. **A**   Owners' equity is equal to assets minus liabilities.

6. **D**   The expanded accounting equation shows that assets = liabilities + contributed capital + beginning retained earnings + revenue – expenses – dividends. A decrease in assets is consistent with an increase in expenses, a decrease in revenues, or a decrease in liabilities, but not with an increase in contributed capital.

7. **A**   The service is performed before cash is paid. This transaction represents accrued revenue to the electrician and an accrued expense to the retail shop. Since the invoice has not been sent as of the statement date, it is not shown in accounts receivable or accounts payable.

8. **C**   The $10 million raised appears on the cash flow statement as a cash inflow from financing and on the statement of owners' equity as an increase in contributed capital. Both assets (cash) and equity (common stock) increase on the balance sheet. The income statement is unaffected by stock issuance.

9. **B**   The general journal lists all of the company's transactions by date. The general ledger lists them by account.

10. **C**   Schmidt is correct in stating that analysts do not have access to the detailed accounting entries that went into a company's financial statements. However, he is incorrect in stating that an analyst can be sure management is not manipulating earnings if the audit report does not list deviations from accounting principles. Because accruals and many valuations require management's judgment, there is considerable room within the accounting standards for management to manipulate earnings.

ANSWERS – COMPREHENSIVE PROBLEMS

Account	Financial statement element
Accounts payable	L
Accounts receivable	A
Accumulated depreciation	A
Contra to the asset being depreciated.	
Additional paid-in capital	O
Allowance for bad debts	A
Contra to accounts receivable.	
Bonds payable	L
Cash equivalents	A
Common stock	O
Cost of goods sold	X
Current portion of long-term debt	L
Deferred tax items	A L
Both deferred tax assets and deferred tax liabilities are recorded.	
Depreciation	X
Dividends payable	L
Dividends received	R
Gain on sale of assets	R
Goodwill	A
Intangible asset.	
Inventory	A
Investment securities	A
Loss on sale of assets	X
Notes payable	L
Other comprehensive income	O
Prepaid expenses	A
Accrual account.	
Property, plant and equipment	A
Retained earnings	O
Sales	R
Unearned revenue	L
Accrual account.	

FINANCIAL REPORTING STANDARDS

EXAM FOCUS

This topic review covers accounting standards: why they exist, who issues them, and who enforces them. Know the difference between the roles of private standard-setting bodies and government regulatory authorities and be able to name the most important organizations of both kinds. Become familiar with the framework for International Financial Reporting Standards, including qualitative characteristics, constraints and assumptions, and principles for preparing and presenting financial statements. Be able to identify barriers to convergence of national accounting standards (such as U.S. GAAP) with IFRS, key differences between the IFRS and GAAP frameworks, and elements of and barriers to creating a coherent financial reporting network.

LOS 31.a: Explain the objective of financial statements and the importance of reporting standards in security analysis and valuation.

The objective of financial statements is to provide economic decision makers with useful information about a firm's financial performance and changes in financial position.

Given the variety and complexity of possible transactions and the estimates and assumptions a firm must make when presenting its performance, financial statements could potentially take any form if reporting standards didn't exist. Reporting standards ensure that the information is "useful to a wide range of users," including security analysts, by making financial statements comparable to one another and narrowing the range of management's "reasonable" estimates.

LOS 31.b: Explain the role of standard-setting bodies, such as the International Accounting Standards Board and the U.S. Financial Accounting Standards Board, and regulatory authorities such as the International Organization of Securities Commissions, the U.K. Financial Services Authority, and the U.S. Securities and Exchange Commission in establishing and enforcing financial reporting standards.

Standard-setting bodies are professional organizations of accountants and auditors that establish financial reporting standards. **Regulatory authorities are government** agencies that have the legal authority to enforce compliance with financial reporting standards.

The two primary standard-setting bodies are the *Financial Accounting Standards Board* (FASB) and the *International Accounting Standards Board* (IASB). In the United States, the FASB sets forth Generally Accepted Accounting Principles (GAAP). Outside the United States, the IASB establishes International Financial Reporting Standards (IFRS). Other national standard-setting bodies exist as well. Many of them (including the FASB) are working toward convergence with IFRS. Some of the older IASB standards are referred to as International Accounting Standards (IAS).

The IASB has four stated goals:[1]

1. Develop global accounting standards requiring transparency, comparability, and high quality in financial statements.

2. Promote the use of global accounting standards.

3. Account for the needs of emerging markets and small firms when implementing global accounting standards.

4. Achieve convergence between various national accounting standards and global accounting standards.

Regulatory authorities, such as the *Securities and Exchange Commission* (SEC) in the U.S. and the *Financial Services Authority* (FSA) in the United Kingdom, are established by national governments. Figure 1 summarizes the SEC's filing requirements for publicly traded companies in the United States. These filings, which are available from the SEC web site (www.sec.gov), are arguably the most important source of information for the analysis of publicly traded firms.

Most national authorities belong to the *International Organization of Securities Commissions* (IOSCO). The three objectives of financial market regulation according to IOSCO[2] are to (1) protect investors, (2) ensure the fairness, efficiency, and transparency of markets, and (3) reduce systemic risk. Because of the increasing globalization of securities markets, the IOSCO has a goal of uniform financial regulations across countries.

Figure 1: Securities and Exchange Commission Required Filings

Form S-1. Registration statement filed prior to the sale of new securities to the public.

Form 10-K. Required annual filing that includes information about the business and its management, audited financial statements and disclosures, and disclosures about legal matters involving the firm. Information required in Form 10-K is similar to that which a firm typically provides in its annual report to shareholders. However, a firm's annual report is not a substitute for the required 10-K filing. Equivalent SEC forms for foreign issuers in the U.S. markets are Form 40-F for Canadian companies and Form 20-F for other foreign issuers.

---

1. International Accounting Standards Committee Foundation Constitution, July 2005.
2. International Organization of Securities Commissions, "Objectives and Principles of Securities Regulation," May 2003.

Form 10-Q. U.S. firms are required to file this form quarterly, with updated financial statements (unlike Form 10-K, these statements do not have to be audited) and disclosures about certain events such as significant legal proceedings or changes in accounting policy. Non-U.S. companies are typically required to file the equivalent Form 6-K semiannually.

Form DEF-14A. When a company prepares a proxy statement for its shareholders prior to the annual meeting or other shareholder vote, it also files the statement with the SEC as Form DEF-14A.

Form 8-K. Companies must file this form to disclose material events including significant asset acquisitions and disposals, changes in management or corporate governance, or matters related to its accountants, its financial statements, or the markets in which its securities trade.

Form 144. A company can issue securities to certain qualified buyers without registering the securities with the SEC, but must notify the SEC that it intends to do so.

Forms 3, 4, and 5 involve the beneficial ownership of securities by a company's officers and directors. Analysts can use these filings to learn about purchases and sales of company securities by corporate insiders.

LOS 31.c: Discuss the ongoing barriers to developing one universally accepted set of financial reporting standards.

One barrier to developing one universally accepted set of accounting standards (referred to as "convergence") is simply that different standard-setting bodies and the regulatory authorities of different countries can and do disagree on the best treatment of a particular item or issue. Other barriers result from the political pressures that regulatory bodies face from business groups and others who will be affected by changes in reporting standards.

LOS 31.d: Describe the International Financial Reporting Standards (IFRS) framework, including the objective of financial statements, their qualitative characteristics, required reporting elements, and the constraints and assumptions in preparing financial statements.

The ideas on which the IASB bases its standards are expressed in the IFRS "Framework for the Preparation and Presentation of Financial Statements" that the organization adopted in 2001. The IFRS framework details the objective of financial statements, defines the qualitative characteristics necessary to meet that objective, and specifies the required reporting elements. The framework also notes certain constraints and assumptions that are involved in financial statement preparation.

The objective of financial statements, according to the IFRS framework, is "to provide information about the financial position, performance, and changes in financial position of an entity; this information should be useful to a wide range of users for the

---

purpose of making economic decisions." Stated another way, the objective of financial statements is the fair presentation of a company's financial performance.

Qualitative Characteristics

To meet the objectives of fairness and usefulness, financial statements should be understandable, relevant, reliable, and comparable. The IFRS framework describes each of these qualities.

Understandability. Users with a basic knowledge of business and accounting and who make a reasonable effort to study the financial statements should be able to readily understand the information the statements present.

Comparability. Financial statement presentation should be consistent among firms and across time periods.

Relevance. Financial statements are relevant if the information in them can influence users' economic decisions or affect users' evaluations of past events or forecasts of future events. To be relevant, information should be timely and sufficiently detailed (meaning no material omissions or misstatements).

Reliability. Information is reliable if it reflects economic reality, is unbiased, and is free of material errors. Specific factors that support reliability include:

- *Faithful representation* of transactions and events.
- *Substance over form,* presenting not only the legal form of a transaction or event, but its economic reality.
- *Neutrality,* an absence of bias.
- *Prudence* and conservatism in making estimates.
- *Completeness*, within the limits of cost and materiality.

Required Reporting Elements

The elements of financial statements are the by now familiar groupings of assets, liabilities, and owners' equity (for measuring financial position) and income and expenses (for measuring performance). The IFRS framework describes each of these elements:

- Assets are the resources the entity controls and from which it expects to derive economic benefits in the future.
- Liabilities are obligations that are expected to require an outflow of resources.
- Equity is the owners' residual interest in the assets after deducting the liabilities.
- Income is an increase in economic benefits, either increasing assets or decreasing liabilities in a way that increases owners' equity (but not including contributions by owners). Income includes revenues and gains.
- Expenses are decreases in economic benefits, either decreasing assets or increasing liabilities in a way that decreases owners' equity (but not including distributions to owners). Losses are included in expenses.

An item should be *recognized* in its financial statement element if a future economic benefit from the item (flowing to or from the firm) is probable and if the item's value or cost can be measured reliably. The amounts at which items are reported in the financial statement elements depend on their measurement base. Bases of measurement used in financial statements include *historical cost* (the amount originally paid for the asset), *current cost* (the amount the firm would have to pay today for the same asset), *realizable value* (the amount for which the firm could sell the asset), *present value* (the discounted value of the asset's expected future cash flows), and *fair value* (the amount at which two parties in an arm's-length transaction would exchange the asset).

 Professor's Note: In Study Session 8, we will discuss these measurement bases and the situations in which each is appropriate.

Constraints and Assumptions

Some of the qualitative characteristics of financial statements can be at cross-purposes. One of the constraints on financial statement preparation is the need to balance reliability, in the sense of being free of error, with the timeliness that makes the information relevant. Cost is also a constraint; the benefit that users gain from the information should be greater than the cost of presenting it. A third constraint is the fact that intangible and non-quantifiable information about a company (its reputation, brand loyalty, capacity for innovation, etc.) cannot be captured directly in financial statements.

The two primary assumptions that underlie financial statements are the *accrual basis* and the *going concern* assumption. The accrual basis means that financial statements should reflect transactions at the time they actually occur, not necessarily when cash is paid. The going concern assumption means there is an assumption that the company will continue to exist for the foreseeable future. If this is not the case, then presenting the company's financial position fairly requires a number of adjustments (for example, its inventory or other assets may only be worth their liquidation values).

LOS 31.e: Explain the general requirements for financial statements.

International Accounting Standard (IAS) No. 1 defines which financial statements are required and how they must be presented. The **required financial statements** are:

- Balance sheet.
- Income statement.
- Cash flow statement.
- Statement of changes in owners' equity.
- Explanatory notes, including a summary of accounting policies.

The fundamental **principles for preparing financial statements** are stated in IAS No. 1:

- *Fair presentation,* defined as faithfully representing the effects of the entity's transactions and events according to the standards for recognizing assets, liabilities, revenues, and expenses.
- *Going concern basis,* meaning the financial statements are based on the assumption that the firm will continue to exist unless its management intends to (or must) liquidate it.

- *Accrual basis* of accounting is used to prepare the financial statements other than the statement of cash flows.
- *Consistency* between periods in how items are presented and classified, with prior-period amounts disclosed for comparison.
- *Materiality,* meaning the financial statements should be free of misstatements or omissions that could influence the decisions of users of financial statements.

Also stated in IAS No. 1 are **principles for presenting financial statements:**

- *Aggregation* of similar items and separation of dissimilar items.
- *No offsetting* of assets against liabilities or income against expenses unless a specific standard permits or requires it.
- Most entities should present a *classified balance sheet* showing current and noncurrent assets and liabilities.
- *Minimum information* is required on the face of each financial statement and in the notes. For example, the face of the balance sheet must show specific items such as cash and cash equivalents, plant, property and equipment, and inventories. Items listed on the face of the income statement must include revenue, profit or loss, tax expense, and finance costs, among others.
- *Comparative information* for prior periods should be included unless a specific standard states otherwise.

LOS 31.f: Compare and contrast key concepts of financial reporting standards under IFRS and alternative reporting systems, and discuss the implications for financial analysis of differing financial reporting systems.

 Professor's Note: The "alternative reporting system" this LOS refers to is U.S. GAAP.

U.S. GAAP consists of standards issued by the FASB, along with numerous other pronouncements and interpretations. Like the IASB, the FASB has a framework for preparing and presenting financial statements. The two organizations are working toward a common framework, but at present the two frameworks differ in several respects.

- *Purpose of the framework.* Both frameworks are meant to help develop and revise standards, but the FASB framework, unlike the IASB framework, is not at the top of the "GAAP hierarchy." The IASB requires management to consider the framework if no explicit standard exists on an issue, but the FASB does not.
- *Objectives of financial statements.* The FASB framework presents different objectives for business and non-business financial statement reporting; the IASB framework has one objective for both.
- *Assumptions.* The IASB framework places more emphasis on the going concern assumption.
- *Qualitative characteristics.* In the FASB framework, relevance and reliability are the primary characteristics, while the IASB framework also lists comparability and understandability as primary characteristics.
- *Financial statement elements.* Differences here include: (1) The IASB framework lists income and expenses as the elements related to performance, while the FASB

framework uses revenues, expenses, gains, losses, and comprehensive income. (2) The FASB defines an asset as a future economic benefit, whereas the IASB defines it as a resource from which a future economic benefit is expected. (3) The word "probable" is used by the FASB to define assets and liabilities and by the IASB to define the criteria for recognition. (4) The FASB framework does not allow the values of most assets to be adjusted upward.

Until these frameworks converge, analysts will need to interpret financial statements that are prepared under different standards. In many cases, however, a company will present a **reconciliation statement** showing what its financial results would have been under an alternative reporting system. The SEC requires foreign firms that issue securities in the U.S. to include the information necessary to reconcile their financial statements to U.S. GAAP.

Even when a unified framework emerges, special reporting standards that apply to particular industries (e.g., insurance and banking) will continue to exist.

LOS 31.g: Identify the characteristics of a coherent financial reporting framework and barriers to creating a coherent financial reporting network.

A coherent financial reporting framework is one that fits together logically. Such a framework should be transparent, comprehensive, and consistent.

- *Transparency*—full disclosure and fair presentation reveal the underlying economics of the company to the financial statement user.
- *Comprehensiveness*—all types of transactions that have financial implications should be part of the framework, including new types of transactions that emerge.
- *Consistency*—similar transactions should be accounted for in similar ways across companies, geographic areas, and time periods.

Barriers to creating a coherent financial reporting framework include issues related to valuation, standard setting, and measurement.

- *Valuation*—The different measurement bases for valuation involve a trade-off between relevance and reliability. Bases that require little judgment, such as historical cost, tend to be more reliable, but may be less relevant than a basis like fair value that requires more judgment.
- *Standard setting*—Three approaches to standard setting are a "principles-based" approach that relies on a broad framework, a "rules-based" approach that gives specific guidance about how to classify transactions, and an "objectives oriented" approach that blends the other two approaches. IFRS is largely a principles-based approach. U.S. GAAP has traditionally been more rules-based, but FASB is moving toward an objectives oriented approach.
- *Measurement*—Another trade-off in financial reporting is between properly valuing the elements at one point in time (as on the balance sheet) and properly valuing the changes between points in time (as on the income statement). An "asset/liability" approach, which standard setters have largely used, focuses on balance sheet valuation. A "revenue/expense" approach would tend to place more significance on the income statement.

LOS 31.h: Discuss the importance of monitoring developments in financial reporting standards and evaluate company disclosures of significant accounting policies.

As financial reporting standards continue to evolve, analysts need to monitor how these developments will affect the financial statements they use. An analyst should be aware of new products and innovations in the financial markets that generate new types of transactions. These might not fall neatly into the existing financial reporting standards. The analyst can use the financial reporting framework as a guide for evaluating what effect new products or transactions might have on financial statements.

To keep up to date on the evolving standards, an analyst can monitor professional journals and other sources such as the IASB (www.iasb.org) and FASB (www.fasb.org) Web sites. CFA Institute produces position papers on financial reporting issues through the CFA Centre for Financial Market Integrity (www.cfainstitute.org/cfacentre).

Companies that prepare financial statements under IFRS or U.S. GAAP must disclose their accounting policies and estimates in the footnotes and in Management's Discussion and Analysis. An analyst should use these disclosures to evaluate what policies are discussed, whether they cover all the relevant data in the financial statements, which policies required management to make estimates, and whether the disclosures and estimates have changed since the prior period.

Another disclosure that is required for public companies is the likely impact of implementing recently issued accounting standards. Management can discuss the impact of adopting a new standard, conclude that the standard does not apply or will not affect the financial statements materially, or state that they are still evaluating the effects of the new standards. Analysts should be aware of the uncertainty this last statement implies.

KEY CONCEPTS

1. Reporting standards are designed to ensure that different firms' statements are comparable to one another and to narrow the range of reasonable estimates on which financial statements are based.

2. Standard-setting bodies are private-sector organizations that establish financial reporting standards. Regulatory authorities are government agencies that enforce compliance with financial reporting standards.

3. The two primary standard-setting bodies are the International Accounting Standards Board (IASB) and, in the U.S., the Financial Accounting Standards Board (FASB).

4. The IASB has four goals:
   - Develop global accounting standards requiring transparency, comparability, and high quality in financial statements.
   - Promote the use of global accounting standards.
   - Account for the needs of emerging markets and small firms when implementing global accounting standards.
   - Converge various national accounting principles with global accounting standards.

5. Regulatory authorities include the Securities and Exchange Commission (SEC) in the U.S. and the Financial Services Authority (FSA) in the United Kingdom. Many national regulatory authorities belong to the International Organization of Securities Commissions (IOSCO).

6. Three objectives of financial market regulation according to IOSCO are to:
   - Protect investors.
   - Ensure the fairness, efficiency, and transparency of markets.
   - Reduce systemic risk.

7. Barriers to developing one universally accepted set of financial reporting standards include disagreements among standard-setting bodies and regulatory authorities from different countries and political pressure from groups affected by changes in reporting standards.

8. The IFRS "Framework for the Preparation and Presentation of Financial Statements" document begins with the objective of financial statements, defines the qualitative characteristics they should have, specifies the required reporting elements, and notes the constraints and assumptions involved in preparing financial statements.

9. The qualitative characteristics of financial statements include understandability, relevance, reliability, and comparability.

10. Elements of financial statements are assets, liabilities, and owners' equity (for measuring financial position) and income and expenses (for measuring performance).

11. Constraints on financial statement preparation include cost, the need to balance reliability with timeliness, and the difficulty of capturing non-quantifiable information in financial statements.

12. The two primary assumptions that underlie the preparation of financial statements are the accrual basis and the going concern assumption.

13. Required financial statements are the balance sheet, income statement, cash flow statement, statement of changes in owners' equity, and explanatory notes.

14. Principles for *preparing* financial statements stated in IAS No. 1 are:
    - Fair presentation.
    - Going concern basis.
    - Accrual basis.
    - Consistency between periods.
    - Materiality.

15. Principles for *presenting* financial statements stated in IAS No. 1 are:
    - Aggregation.
    - No offsetting.
    - Classified balance sheet.
    - Minimum required information.
    - Comparative information.

16. The IASB and FASB frameworks differ in the purpose of the framework, objectives for business and non-business reporting, emphasis on the going concern assumption, qualitative characteristics, and financial statement elements.

17. A reconciliation statement shows a company's financial results under an alternative reporting system. The SEC requires foreign firms that issue securities in the U.S. to reconcile their financial statements to U.S. GAAP.

18. A coherent financial reporting framework should exhibit transparency, comprehensiveness, and consistency. Barriers to creating a coherent framework include issues of valuation, standard setting, and measurement.

19. An analyst should be aware of evolving financial reporting standards and new products and innovations that generate new types of transactions.

20. Under IFRS and U.S. GAAP, companies must disclose their accounting policies and estimates in the footnotes and MD&A. Public companies are also required to disclose the likely impact of recently issued accounting standards on their financial statements.

CONCEPT CHECKERS

1. Standard-setting bodies are responsible for:
    A. establishing financial reporting standards only.
    B. establishing and enforcing standards for financial reporting.
    C. enforcing compliance with financial reporting standards only.
    D. determining the information that must be disclosed by securities issuers.

2. Which of the following organizations is *least likely* involved with enforcing compliance with financial reporting standards?
    A. Financial Services Authority (FSA).
    B. Securities and Exchange Commission (SEC).
    C. International Accounting Standards Board (IASB).
    D. International Organization of Securities Commissions (IOSCO).

3. Dawn Czerniak is writing an article about international financial reporting standards. In her article she states, "Despite strong support from business groups for a universally accepted set of financial reporting standards, disagreements among the standard-setting bodies and regulatory authorities of various countries remain a barrier to developing one." Czerniak's statement is:
    A. correct.
    B. incorrect, because business groups have not supported a uniform set of financial reporting standards.
    C. incorrect, because disagreements among national standard-setting bodies and regulatory agencies have not been a barrier to developing a universal set of standards.
    D. incorrect, because business groups have not supported a uniform set of financial reporting standards, but disagreements among national standard-setting bodies and regulatory agencies have not been a barrier to developing one.

4. Which of the following characteristics *least likely* contributes to the reliability of financial statements?
    A. Prudence.
    B. Neutrality.
    C. Timeliness.
    D. Completeness.

5. Which of the following *most accurately* lists a required reporting element that is used to measure a company's financial position, and one that is used to measure a company's performance?

	Position	Performance
A.	Assets	Liabilities
B.	Income	Expenses
C.	Expenses	Assets
D.	Liabilities	Income

6. International Accounting Standard (IAS) No. 1 *least likely* requires which of the following?

   A. Neither assets and liabilities, nor income and expenses, may be offset unless required or permitted by a financial reporting standard.
   B. Audited financial statements and disclosures, along with updated information about the firm and its management, must be filed annually.
   C. Required financial statements include a balance sheet, income statement, cash flow statement, statement of owners' equity, and explanatory notes.
   D. Fair presentation of financial statements means faithfully representing the firm's events and transactions according to the financial reporting standards.

7. Compared to the International Financial Reporting Standards (IFRS) framework, does the Financial Accounting Standards Board (FASB) framework for U.S. GAAP place more emphasis on:

	Comparability and understandability?	The going concern assumption?
A.	Yes	Yes
B.	Yes	No
C.	No	Yes
D.	No	No

8. Which is *least likely* one of the conclusions about the impact of a change in financial reporting standards that might appear in management's discussion and analysis?

   A. The new standard does not apply to the company.
   B. Management is currently evaluating the impact of the new standard.
   C. Management has chosen not to implement the new standard.
   D. The new standard will not have a material impact on the company's financial statements.

ANSWERS – CONCEPT CHECKERS

1. **A** Standard-setting bodies are private sector organizations that establish financial reporting standards. Enforcement and determination of the information that must be disclosed by securities issuers are responsibilities and goals of regulatory authorities.

2. **C** The IASB is a standard-setting body. The SEC (in the United States) and the FSA (in the United Kingdom) are regulatory authorities, and IOSCO is an organization composed of national regulatory authorities.

3. **B** Political pressure from business groups and other interest groups who are affected by financial reporting standards has been a barrier to developing a universally accepted set of financial reporting standards. Disagreements among national standard-setting bodies and regulatory agencies have also been a barrier.

4. **C** Timeliness contributes to the relevance of financial statements, but there is often a trade-off between timeliness and reliability.

5. **D** Balance sheet reporting elements (assets, liabilities, and owners' equity) measure a company's financial position. Income statement reporting elements (income, expenses) measure its financial performance.

6. **B** It is the Securities and Exchange Commission's requirement that publicly traded companies file Form 10-K annually. The required financial statements are specified in IAS No. 1. Fair presentation is one of the IAS No. 1 principles for preparing financial statements. The ban against offsetting is one of the IAS No. 1 principles for presenting financial statements.

7. **D** Comparability, understandability, reliability and relevance are qualitative characteristics of financial statements in the IFRS framework, but only reliability and relevance are primary qualitative characteristics in the FASB framework. The IFRS framework places more emphasis on the going concern assumption.

8. **C** Management can discuss the impact of adopting the new standard, conclude that it does not apply or will have no material impact, or state that they are still evaluating the potential impact.

UNDERSTANDING THE INCOME STATEMENT

EXAM FOCUS

Now we're getting to the heart of the matter. Since forecasts of future earnings, and therefore estimates of firm value, depend crucially on understanding a firm's income statement, everything in this topic review is important. At least some questions requiring calculation of depreciation, COGS, and inventory under different cash flow assumptions, as well as basic and diluted EPS, are very likely to be included in your exam. The separation of items into operating and non-operating categories is important when estimating recurring income, as a first step in forecasting future firm earnings. Note well that questions regarding the effect on financial ratios of the choice of accounting method and of accounting estimates are one common way to test your understanding of the material on those topics presented here.

INCOME STATEMENT COMPONENTS AND FORMAT

The income statement reports the revenues and expenses of the firm over a period of time. The income statement is sometimes referred to as the "statement of operations," the "statement of earnings," or the "profit and loss statement." The income statement equation is:

revenues − expenses = net income

Investors examine a firm's income statement for valuation purposes while lenders examine the income statement for information about the firm's ability to make the promised interest and principal payments on its debt.

LOS 32.a: Describe the components of the income statement and construct an income statement using the alternative presentation formats of that statement.

Revenues are the amounts reported from the sale of goods and services in the normal course of business. Revenue less adjustments for estimated returns and allowances is known as **net revenue**.

> *Professor's Note: The terms "revenue" and "sales" are sometimes used synonymously. However, sales is just one component of revenue in many firms. In some countries, revenues are referred to as "turnover."*

Expenses are the amounts incurred to generate revenue and include cost of goods sold, operating expenses, interest, and taxes. Expenses are grouped together by their nature or function. Presenting all depreciation expense from manufacturing and administration together in one line of the income statement is an example of grouping by nature of the expense. Combining all costs associated with manufacturing (e.g., raw materials, depreciation, labor, etc.) as cost of goods sold is an example of grouping by function.

> *Professor's Note: Some firms present expenses as negative numbers while other firms use parentheses to signify expenses. Still other firms present expenses as positive numbers with the assumption that users know that expenses are subtracted in the income statement.*

The income statement also includes **gains and losses,** which result from incidental transactions outside the firm's primary business activities. For example, a firm might sell surplus equipment used in its manufacturing operation that is no longer needed. The difference between the sales price and book value is reported as a gain or loss on the income statement.

Presentation formats

A firm can present its income statement using a single-step or multi-step format. In a single-step statement, all revenues are grouped together and all expenses are grouped together. A multi-step format includes subtotals such as gross profit and operating profit.

Figure 1 is an example of a multi-step income statement format for the BHG Company.

Figure 1: Multi-step Income Statement

BHG Company Income Statement For the year ended December 31, 20X7	
Revenue	$579,312
Cost of goods sold	(362,520)
Gross profit	216,792
Selling, general, and administrative expense	(109,560)
Depreciation expense	(69,008)
Operating profit	38,224
Interest expense	(2,462)
Income before tax	35,762
Provision for income taxes	(14,305)
Income from continuing operations	21,457
Earnings (losses) from discontinued operations, net of tax	1,106
Net income	$22,563

Gross profit is the amount that remains after the direct costs of producing a product or service are subtracted from revenue. Subtracting operating expenses, such as selling, general, and administrative expenses, from gross profit results in another subtotal known as **operating profit** or operating income. For nonfinancial firms, operating profit is profit before financing costs and income taxes are considered and before non-operating items are considered. Subtracting interest expense and income taxes from operating profit results in the firm's net income, sometimes referred to as "earnings" or the "bottom line."

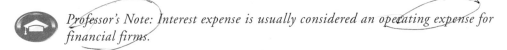 *Professor's Note: Interest expense is usually considered an operating expense for financial firms.*

If a firm has a controlling interest in a subsidiary, the pro-rata share of the subsidiary's income for the portion of the subsidiary that the firm does not own is reported in the parent's income statement as the **minority owners' interest**. This is subtracted since a controlling interest means the subsidiary's entire net income is included in the firm's income statement.

LOS 32.b: Explain the general principles of revenue recognition and accrual accounting, demonstrate specific revenue recognition applications (including accounting for long-term contracts, installment sales, barter transactions, and gross and net reporting of revenue), and discuss the implications of revenue recognition principles for financial analysis.

Under the accrual method of accounting, revenue is recognized when earned and expenses are recognized when incurred. The important point to remember is that accrual accounting does not necessarily coincide with the receipt or payment of cash. Consequently, firms can manipulate net income by recognizing revenue earlier or later or by delaying or accelerating the recognition of expenses.

According to the International Accounting Standards Board (IASB), the term "income" includes revenue and gains. Specifically, income is defined as increases in economic benefits during the accounting period in the form of inflows or enhancements of assets or decreases of liabilities that result in increases in equity, other than those relating to contributions from equity participants.[1]

According to the Financial Accounting Standards Board (FASB) revenue is recognized in the income statement when (a) realized or realizable and (b) earned. The Securities and Exchange Commission (SEC) provides additional guidance by listing four criteria to determine whether revenue should be recognized:[3]

1. There is evidence of an arrangement between the buyer and seller.

2. The product has been delivered or the service has been rendered.

---

1. IASB, *Framework for the Preparation and Presentation of Financial Statements,* paragraph 69.
2. Statement of Financial Accounting Concepts No. 5, paragraph 83(b).
3. SEC Staff Accounting Bulletin 101.

3. The price is determined or determinable.

4. The seller is reasonably sure of collecting money.

If a firm receives cash before revenue recognition is complete, the firm reports it as *unearned revenue*. Unearned revenue is reported on the balance sheet as a liability. The liability is reduced in the future as the revenue is earned. For example, a magazine publisher typically receives subscription payments in advance of delivery. When payments are received, both assets (cash) and liabilities (unearned revenue) increase. As the magazines are delivered, the publisher recognizes revenue on the income statement and the liability is reduced.

Specific Revenue Recognition Applications

Revenue is usually recognized at delivery using the revenue recognition criteria previously discussed. However, in some cases, revenue may be recognized before delivery occurs or even after delivery takes place.

Long-term Contracts

The percentage-of-completion method and the completed-contract method are used for contracts that extend beyond one accounting period, often contracts related to construction projects.

In certain cases involving service contracts or licensing agreements, the firm may simply recognize revenue equally over the term of the contract or agreement.

The **percentage-of-completion method** is appropriate when the project's cost and revenue can be reliably estimated. Accordingly, revenue, expense, and therefore profit, are recognized as the work is performed. The percentage of completion is measured by the total cost incurred to date divided by the total expected cost of the project.

The **completed-contract method** is used when the outcome of a project cannot be reliably measured or the project is short-term. Accordingly, revenue, expense, and profit are recognized only when the contract is complete. Under either method, if a loss is expected, the loss must be recognized immediately.

Under International Financial Reporting Standards (IFRS), if the firm cannot reliably measure the outcome of the project, revenue is recognized to the extent of contract costs, costs are expensed when incurred, and profit is recognized only at completion.

The effect of using these different revenue recognition methods for long-term contracts on the income statement is illustrated in the following example.

1. collect money

2. price deter

3. candelivered

4.

Example: Revenue recognition for long-term contracts

Assume that AAA Construction Corp. has a contract to build a ship for $1,000 and a reliable estimate of the contract's total cost is $800. Project costs incurred by AAA are as follows:

AAA Project Costs

Year	20X5	20X6	20X7	Total
Costs incurred	$400	$300	$100	$800

Determine AAA's net income from this project for each year using the percentage-of-completion and completed contract methods.

Answer:

Since one-half of the total contract cost [$400 / $800] was incurred during 20X5, the project was 50% complete at year-end. Under the *percentage-of-completion method,* 20X5 revenue is $500 [$1,000 × 50%]. Expenses (cost incurred) were $400; thus, net income for 20X5 was $100 [$500 revenue – $400 expense].

At the end of 20X6, the project is 87.5% complete [($400 + $300) / $800]. Revenue to date should total $875 [$1,000 × 87.5%]. Since AAA already recognized $500 of revenue in 20X5, 20X6 revenue is $375 [$875 – $500]. 20X6 expenses were $300 so 20X6 net income was $75 [$375 revenue – $300 expense].

At the end of 20X7, the project is 100% complete [($400 + $300 +$100) / $800]. Revenue to date should total $1,000 [$1,000 × 100%]. Since AAA already recognized $875 of revenue in 20X5 and 20X6, 20X7 revenue is $125 [$1,000 – $875]. 20X7 expenses were $100 so 20X7 net income was $25 [$125 revenue – $100 expense].

The table below summarizes the AAA's revenue, expense, and net income over the term of project under the percentage-of-completion method.

AAA Income Statements

	20X5	20X6	20X7	Total
Revenue	$500	$375	$125	$1,000
Expense	400	300	100	800
Net income	$100	$75	$25	$200

Under the *completed contract method,* revenue, expenses, and profit are not recognized until the contract is complete. Therefore, at the end of 20X7, AAA reports revenue of $1,000, expense of $800, and net income of $200.

As compared to the completed contract method, the percentage-of-completion method is more aggressive since revenue is reported sooner. Also, the percentage-of-completion method is more subjective because it involves cost estimates. However, the percentage-of-completion method provides smoother earnings and results in better matching of revenues and expenses over time. Cash flow is the same under both methods.

Installment Sales

An **installment sale** occurs when a firm finances a sale and payments are expected to be received over an extended period. If collectibility is certain, revenue is recognized at the time of sale using the normal revenue recognition criteria. If collectibility cannot be reasonably estimated, the installment method is used. If collectibility is highly uncertain, the cost recovery method is used.

Under the **installment method**, profit is recognized as cash is collected. Profit is equal to the cash collected during the period multiplied by the total expected profit as a percentage of sales. The installment method is used in limited circumstances, usually involving the sale of real estate or other firm assets.

Under the **cost recovery method**, profit is recognized only when cash collected exceeds costs incurred.

The effects of using the installment and the cost recovery methods are illustrated in the following example.

Example: Revenue recognition for installment sales

Assume that BBB Property Corp. sells a piece of land for $1,000. The original cost of the land was $800. Collections received by BBB for the sale are as follows:

BBB Installment Collections

Year	20X5	20X6	20X7	Total
Collections	$400	$400	$200	$1,000

Determine BBB's profit under the installment and cost recovery methods.

Answer:

Total expected profit as a percentage of sales is 20% [($1,000 – $800) / $1,000]. Under the installment method, BBB will report profit in 20X5 and 20X6 of $80 [$400 × 20%] each year. In 20X7, BBB will report profit of $40 [$200 × 20%].

Under the cost recovery method, the collections received during 20X5 and 20X6 are applied to the recovery of costs. In 20X7, BBB will report $200 of profit.

IFRS addresses when installment sale treatment is appropriate for certain real estate transactions. Specifically, the date when title to the property is transferred and the date when the buyer acquires a vested interest may differ. Also, installment sale treatment may be required when the risks and rewards of ownership are not transferred because the seller remains involved in the property. Finally, significant uncertainty that the buyer can complete the transaction may require installment sale treatment.

Barter Transactions

In a **barter transaction**, two parties exchange goods or services without cash payment. A **round-trip transaction** involves the sale of goods to one party with the simultaneous purchase of almost identical goods from the same party. The underlying issue with these transactions is whether revenue should be recognized. In the late 1990s several internet companies increased their revenue significantly by "buying" equal values of advertising space on each others' websites.

According to U.S. GAAP, revenue from a barter transaction can be recognized at fair value only if the firm has historically received cash payments for such goods and services and can use this historical experience to determine fair value.[4]

Under IFRS, revenue from barter transactions must be based on the fair value of revenue from similar nonbarter transactions with unrelated parties.[5]

Gross and Net Reporting of Revenue

Under **gross revenue reporting**, the selling firm reports sales revenue and cost of goods sold separately. Under **net revenue reporting**, only the difference in sales and cost is reported. While profit is the same, sales are higher using gross revenue reporting.

For example, consider a travel agent who arranges a first-class ticket for a customer flying to Singapore. The ticket price is $10,000 and the travel agent receives a $1,000 commission. Using gross reporting, the travel agent would report $10,000 of revenue, $9,000 of expense, and $1,000 of profit. Using net reporting, the travel agent would simply report $1,000 of revenue and no expense.

The following criteria must be met in order to use gross revenue reporting under U.S. GAAP. The firm must:

- Be the primary obligor under the contract.
- Bear the inventory risk and credit risk.
- Be able to choose its supplier.
- Have reasonable latitude to establish the price.

Implications for Financial Analysis

As noted previously, firms can recognize revenue before delivery, at the time of delivery, or after delivery takes place, as appropriate. Different revenue recognition methods can be used within the firm. Firms disclose their revenue recognition policies in the financial statement footnotes.

Users of financial information must consider two points when analyzing a firm's revenue: (1) how conservative are the firm's revenue recognition policies (recognizing revenue sooner rather than later is more aggressive), and (2) the extent to which the firm's policies rely on judgment and estimates.

---

4. Emerging Issues Task Force EITF 99-17, "Accounting for Advertising Barter Transactions."
5. IASB, SIC Interpretation 31, Revenue – Barter Transactions Involving Advertising Services, paragraph 5.

LOS 32.c: Discuss the general principles of expense recognition, such as the matching principle, specific expense recognition applications (including depreciation of long-term assets and inventory methods), and the implications of expense recognition principles for financial analysis.

Expenses are subtracted from revenue to calculate net income. According to the IASB, expenses are decreases in economic benefits during the accounting period in the form of outflows or depletions of assets or incurrence of liabilities that result in decreases in equity other than those relating to distributions to equity participants.[6]

If the financial statements were prepared on a cash basis, neither revenue recognition nor expense recognition would be an issue. The firm would simply recognize cash received as revenue and cash payments as expense.

Under the accrual method of accounting, expense recognition is based on the **matching principle** whereby expenses to generate revenue are recognized in the same period as the revenue. Inventory provides a good example. Assume inventory is purchased during the fourth quarter of one year and sold during the first quarter of the following year. Using the matching principle, both the revenue and the expense (cost of goods sold) are recognized in the first quarter, when the inventory is sold, not the period in which the inventory was purchased.

Not all expenses can be directly tied to revenue generation. These costs are known as **period costs**. Period costs, such as administrative costs, are expensed in the period incurred.

The cost of long-lived assets must also be matched with revenues. Long-lived assets are expected to provide economic benefits beyond one accounting period. The allocation of cost over an asset's useful life is known as depreciation, depletion, or amortization expense.

If a firm sells goods or services on credit or provides a warranty to the customer, the matching principle requires the firm to estimate bad debt expense and/or warranty expense. By doing so, the firm is recognizing the expense in the period of the sale, rather than a later period.

Implications for Financial Analysis

Like revenue recognition, expense recognition requires a number of estimates. Since estimates are involved, it is possible for firms to delay or accelerate the recognition of expenses. Delayed expense recognition increases current net income and is therefore more aggressive.

Analysts must consider the underlying reasons for a change in an expense estimate. If a firm's bad debt expense has recently decreased, did the firm lower its expense estimate because its collection experience improved, or was the expense decreased to manipulate net income?

---

6. IASB *Framework for the Preparation and Presentation of Financial Statements,* paragraph 70.

Analysts should also compare a firm's estimates to those of other firms within the firm's industry. If a firm's warranty expense is significantly less than that of a peer firm, is the lower warranty expense a result of higher quality products, or is the firm's expense recognition more aggressive than that of the peer firm?

Firms disclose their accounting policies and significant estimates in the financial statement footnotes and in the management discussion and analysis (MD&A) section of the annual report.

LOS 32.d: Determine which method of depreciation, accounting for inventory, or amortizing intangibles is appropriate, based on facts that might influence the decision.

Depreciation

Most firms use the *straight-line depreciation* method for financial reporting purposes. The straight-line method recognizes an equal amount of depreciation expense each period. However, most assets generate more benefits in the early years of their economic life and fewer benefits in the later years. In this case, an *accelerated depreciation method* is more appropriate for matching the expenses to revenues.

In the early years of an asset's life, the straight-line method will result in lower depreciation expense as compared to an accelerated method. Lower expense results in higher net income. In the later years of the asset's life, the effect is reversed, and straight-line depreciation results in higher expense and lower net income compared to accelerated methods.

Inventory

If a firm can identify exactly which items were sold and which items remain in inventory, it can use the *specific identification method*. For example, an auto dealer records each vehicle sold or in inventory by its identification number.

Under the *first-in, first-out* (FIFO) method, the first item purchased is assumed to be the first item sold. FIFO is appropriate for inventory that has a limited shelf life. For example, a food products company will sell its oldest inventory first to keep the inventory on hand fresh.

Under the *last-in, first-out* (LIFO) method, the last item purchased is assumed to be the first item sold. LIFO is appropriate for inventory that does not deteriorate with age. For example, a coal mining company will sell coal off the top of the pile.

In the United States, LIFO is popular because of its income tax benefits. In an inflationary environment, LIFO results in higher cost of goods sold. Higher cost of goods sold results in lower taxable income, and therefore lower income taxes.

The *weighted average cost* method is not affected by the physical flow of the inventory. It is popular because of its ease of use.

FIFO and average cost can be used under U.S. GAAP or IFRS. LIFO is allowed under U.S. GAAP, but is prohibited under IFRS.

Figure 2 summarizes the effects of the inventory methods.

Figure 2: Inventory Method Comparison

Method	Assumption	Cost of goods sold consists of...	Ending inventory consists of...
FIFO (U.S. and IFRS)	The items first purchased are the first to be sold.	first purchased	most recent purchases
LIFO (U.S. only)	The items last purchased are the first to be sold.	last purchased	earliest purchases
Weighted average cost (U.S. and IFRS)	Items sold are a mix of purchases.	average cost of all items	average cost of all items

Intangible assets

Amortization expense for intangible assets with limited lives is similar to depreciation. The expense should match the proportion of the asset's economic benefits used during the period. Most firms use the straight-line method for financial reporting. Goodwill and other intangible assets with indefinite lives are not amortized.

LOS 32.e: Demonstrate the depreciation of long-term assets using each approved method, accounting for inventory using each approved method, and amortization of intangibles.

Depreciation expense can be computed under a number of different methods.

Straight-line depreciation (SL) allocates an equal amount of depreciation each year over the asset's useful life as follows:

$$\text{SL Depreciation expense} = \frac{\text{Cost} - \text{Residual value}}{\text{Useful life}}$$

Example: Calculating straight-line depreciation expense

Littlefield Company recently purchased a machine at a cost of $12,000. The machine is expected to have a residual value of $2,000 at the end of its useful life in 5 years. Calculate depreciation expense using the straight-line method.

Answer:

The annual depreciation expense each year will be:

$$\frac{\text{Cost} - \text{Residual value}}{\text{Useful life}} = \frac{(\$12,000 - \$2,000)}{5} = \$2,000$$

Accelerated depreciation speeds up the recognition of depreciation expense in a systematic way to recognize more depreciation expense in the early years of the asset's useful life and less depreciation expense in the later years of its life. Total depreciation expense over the life of the asset will be the same as it would be if straight-line depreciation were used.

The **declining balance method (DB)** applies a constant rate of depreciation to a declining book value.

The most common form of the declining balance method is *double-declining balance* (DDB), which uses 200% of the straight-line rate as the percentage rate applied to the declining balance. If an asset's life is ten years, the straight-line rate is 1/10 or 10%. The DDB rate for this asset is 2/10 or 20%.

$$\text{DDB depreciation} = \left(\frac{2}{\text{useful life}} \right) \left(\cos t - \text{accumulated depreciation} \right)$$

DB does not explicitly use the asset's residual value in the calculations, but depreciation ends once the estimated residual value has been reached. If the asset is expected to have no residual value, the DB method will never fully depreciate it, so the method has to change (typically to straight-line) at some point in the asset's life.

Example: Calculating double-declining balance depreciation expense

Littlefield Company recently purchased a machine at a cost of $12,000. The machine is expected to have a residual value of $2,000 at the end of its useful life in five years. Calculate depreciation expense for all five years using the double-declining balance method.

Answer:

The depreciation expense using the double declining balance method is:

- Year 1: (2 / 5)($12,000) = $4,800
- Year 2: (2 / 5)($12,000 – $4,800) = $2,880
- Year 3: (2 / 5)($12,000 – $7,680) = $1,728

In years 1 through 3, the company has recognized cumulative depreciation expense of $9,408. Since the total depreciation expense is limited to $10,000 ($12,000 – $2,000 salvage value), the depreciation in year 4 is limited to $592, rather than the (2 / 5)($12,000 – $9,408) = $1,036.80 using the DDB formula.

Year 5: Depreciation expense is $0, since the asset is fully depreciated.

Note that the rate of depreciation is doubled (2/5) from straight-line, and the only thing that changes from year to year is the base amount (book value) used to calculate annual depreciation.

 Professor's Note: We've been discussing the "double" declining balance method, which uses a factor of two times the straight-line rate. You can compute declining balance depreciation based on any factor (e.g., 1.5, double, triple).

Inventory Accounting Methods

Three methods of inventory accounting are:

1. **First In, First Out** (FIFO)
   - The cost of inventory first acquired (beginning inventory and early purchases) is assigned to the cost of goods sold for the period.
   - The cost of the most recent purchases is assigned to ending inventory.

2. **Last In, First Out** (LIFO)
   - The cost of inventory most recently purchased is assigned to the cost of goods sold for the period.
   - The costs of beginning inventory and earlier purchases are assigned to ending inventory.

3. **Average cost**
   - The cost per unit is calculated by dividing cost of goods available by total units available.
   - This average cost is used to determine both cost of goods sold and ending inventory.
   - Average cost results in cost of goods sold and ending inventory values between LIFO and FIFO.

Example: Inventory costing

Use the inventory data in the table below to calculate the cost of goods sold and ending inventory under each of the three methods.

Inventory Data

January 1 (beginning inventory)	2 units @ $2 per unit =	$4
January 7 purchase	3 units @ $3 per unit =	$9
January 19 purchase	5 units @ $5 per unit =	$25
Cost of goods available	10 units	$38
Units sold during January	7 units	

Answer:

FIFO cost of goods sold: Value the seven units sold using the unit cost of first units purchased. Start with the beginning inventory and the earliest units purchased and work down, as illustrated in the following table.

FIFO COGS Calculation

From beginning inventory	2 units @ $2 per unit	$4
From first purchase	3 units @ $3 per unit	$9
From second purchase	2 units @ $5 per unit	$10
FIFO cost of goods sold	7 units	$23
Ending inventory	3 units @$5 per unit	$15

LIFO cost of goods sold: Value the seven units sold at unit cost of last units purchased. Start with the most recently purchased units and work up, as illustrated in the following table.

LIFO COGS Calculation

From second purchase	5 units @ $5 per unit	$25
From first purchase	2 units @ $3 per unit	$6
LIFO cost of goods sold	7 units	$31
Ending inventory	2 units @ $2 + 1 unit @ $3	$7

Average cost of goods sold: Value the seven units sold at the average unit cost of goods available:

Weighted Average COGS Calculation

Average unit cost	$38 / 10 units	$3.80 per unit
Weighted average cost of goods sold	7 units @ $3.80 per unit	$26.60
Ending inventory	3 units @ $3.80 per unit	$11.40

The table below summarizes the calculations of COGS and ending inventory for each method.

Summary:

Inventory system	COGS	Ending Inventory
FIFO	$23.00	$15.00
LIFO	$31.00	$7.00
Average Cost	$26.60	$11.40

Amortization of Intangible Assets

Amortization expense is the allocation of the cost of an intangible asset (such as a franchise agreement) over its useful life. Straight-line amortization is calculated exactly like straight-line depreciation.

Intangible assets with indefinite lives (e.g., goodwill) are not amortized. However, they must be tested for impairment at least annually. If the asset value is impaired, an expense equal to the impairment amount is recognized on the income statement.

LOS 32.f: Distinguish between the operating and nonoperating components of the income statement.

Operating and nonoperating transactions are usually reported separately in the income statement. For a nonfinancial firm, nonoperating transactions may result from investment income and financing expenses. For example, a nonfinancial firm may receive dividends and interest from investments in other firms. The investment income and any gains and losses from the sale of these securities are not a part of the firm's normal business operations. Interest expense is based on the firm's capital structure, which is also independent of the firm's operations.

LOS 32.g: Discuss the financial reporting treatment and analysis of nonrecurring items (including discontinued operations, extraordinary items, and unusual or infrequent items), and changes in accounting standards.

Discontinued operations. A *discontinued operation* is one that management has decided to dispose of, but either has not yet done so, or has disposed of in the current year after the operation had generated income or losses. To be accounted for as a discontinued operation, the business—in terms of assets, operations, and investing and financing activities—must be physically and operationally distinct from the rest of the firm.

The date when the company develops a formal plan for disposing of an operation is referred to as the *measurement date*, and the time between the measurement period and the actual disposal date is referred to as the *phaseout period*. Any income or loss from discontinued operations is reported separately in the income statement, net of tax, after income from continuing operations. Any past income statements presented must be restated, separating the income or loss from the discontinued operations. On the measurement date, the company will accrue any estimated loss during the phaseout period and any estimated loss on the sale of the business. Any expected gain on the disposal cannot be reported until after the sale is completed.

Analytical implications: The analysis is straightforward. Discontinued operations do not affect net income from continuing operations. The actual event of discontinuing a business segment or selling assets may provide information about the future cash flows of the firm, however.

Unusual or infrequent items. The definition of these items is obvious—these events are either unusual in nature *or* infrequent in occurrence, but *not* both. Examples of unusual or infrequent items include:

- Gains or losses from the sale of assets or part of a business.
- Impairments, write-offs, write-downs, and restructuring costs.

Unusual or infrequent items are included in income from continuing operations and are reported before tax.

Analytical implications: Even though unusual or infrequent items affect net income from continuing operations, an analyst may want to review them to determine whether they truly should be included when forecasting future firm earnings.

Extraordinary items. Under U.S. GAAP, an extraordinary item is a material transaction or event that is *both* unusual *and* infrequent in occurrence. Examples of these include:

- Losses from an expropriation of assets.
- Gains or losses from early retirement of debt (when it is judged to be both unusual and infrequent).
- Uninsured losses from natural disasters that are both unusual and infrequent.

Extraordinary items are reported separately in the income statement, net of tax, after income from continuing operations.

IFRS does not allow extraordinary items to be separated from operating results in the income statement.

Analytical implications: Judgment is required in determining whether a transaction or event is extraordinary. Although extraordinary items do not affect income from continuing operations, an analyst may want to review them to determine whether some portion should be included when forecasting future income. Some companies appear to be accident-prone and have "extraordinary" losses every year or every few years.

Changes in Accounting Standards

Accounting changes include changes in accounting principles, changes in accounting estimates, and prior-period adjustments.

A **change in accounting principle** refers to a change from one GAAP or IFRS method to another (e.g., a change in inventory accounting from LIFO to FIFO). A change in accounting principle requires *retrospective application*. Accordingly, all of the prior-period financial statements currently presented are restated to reflect the change.

©2008 Schweser

Retrospective application enhances the comparability of the financial statements over time.

Professor's Note: The treatment of a change in accounting principle for U.S. firms is now covered by SFAS No. 154, "Accounting Changes and Error Corrections." The old standard, APB No. 20, provided for the cumulative effect of the accounting change to be reported in the income statement, below the line, net of tax. For the exam, you are responsible for the new standard, which requires retrospective application.

Generally, a **change in accounting estimate** is the result of a change in management's judgment, usually due to new information. For example, management may change the estimated useful life of an asset because new information indicates the asset has a longer or shorter life than originally expected. A change in estimate is applied prospectively and does not require the restatement of prior financial statements.

Analytical implications: Accounting estimate changes typically do not affect cash flow. An analyst should review changes in accounting estimates to determine the impact on future operating results.

A change from an incorrect accounting method to one that is acceptable under GAAP or IFRS or the correction of an accounting error made in previous financial statements is reported as a **prior-period adjustment.** Prior-period adjustments are made by restating results for all prior periods presented in the current financial statements. Disclosure of the nature of the adjustment and its effect on net income is also required.

Analytical implications: Prior-period adjustments usually involve errors or new accounting standards and do not typically affect cash flow. Analysts should review adjustments carefully because errors may indicate weaknesses in the firm's internal controls.

LOS 32.h: Describe the components of earnings per share and calculate a company's earnings per share (both basic and diluted earnings per share) for both a simple and complex capital structure.

LOS 32.i: Distinguish between dilutive and antidilutive securities, and discuss the implications of each for the earnings per share calculation.

Earnings per share (EPS) is one of the most commonly used corporate profitability performance measures for publicly-traded firms (nonpublic companies are not required to report EPS data). EPS is reported only for shares of common stock.

A company may have either a simple or complex capital structure:

- A **simple capital structure** is one that contains *no* potentially dilutive securities. A simple capital structure contains only common stock, nonconvertible debt, and nonconvertible preferred stock.
- A **complex capital structure** contains *potentially dilutive securities* such as options, warrants, or convertible securities.

All firms with complex capital structures must report both *basic* and *diluted* EPS. Firms with simple capital structures report only basic EPS.

BASIC EPS

The basic EPS calculation does not consider the effects of any dilutive securities in the computation of EPS.

$$\text{basic EPS} = \frac{\text{net income} - \text{preferred dividends}}{\text{weighted average number of common shares outstanding}}$$

The current year's preferred dividends are subtracted from net income because EPS refers to the per-share earnings *available to common shareholders*. Net income minus preferred dividends is the income available to common stockholders. Common stock dividends are *not* subtracted from net income because they are a part of the net income available to common shareholders.

The **weighted average number of common shares** is the number of shares outstanding during the year, weighted by the portion of the year they were outstanding.

Example: Weighted average shares and basic EPS

Johnson Company has net income of $10,000 and paid $1,000 cash dividends to its preferred shareholders and $1,750 cash dividends to its common shareholders. At the beginning of the year, there were 10,000 shares of common stock outstanding. 2,000 new shares were issued on July 1. Assuming a simple capital structure, what is Johnson's basic EPS?

Answer:

Calculate Johnson's weighted average number of shares.

Shares outstanding all year = 10,000(12) = 120,000

Shares outstanding 1/2 year = 2,000(6) = 12,000

Weighted average shares = 132,000 / 12 = 11,000 shares

$$\text{Basic EPS} = \frac{\text{net income} - \text{pref. div.}}{\text{wt. avg. shares of common}} = \frac{\$10,000 - \$1,000}{11,000} = \$0.82$$

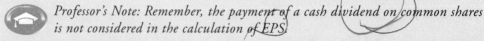 *Professor's Note: Remember, the payment of a cash dividend on common shares is not considered in the calculation of EPS.*

Effect of Stock Dividends and Stock Splits

A **stock dividend** is the distribution of additional shares to each shareholder in an amount proportional to their current number of shares. If a 10% stock dividend is paid, the holder of 100 shares of stock would receive 10 additional shares.

A **stock split** refers to the division of each "old" share into a specific number of "new" (post-split) shares. The holder of 100 shares will have 200 shares after a 2-for-1 split or 150 shares after a 3-for-2 split.

The important thing to remember is that each shareholder's proportional ownership in the company is unchanged by either of these events. Each shareholder has more shares but the same percentage of the total shares outstanding.

The effect of a stock dividend or a stock split on the weighted average number of common shares is illustrated in the following example.

Example: Effect of stock dividends

During the past year, R & J, Inc. had net income of $100,000, paid dividends of $50,000 to its preferred stockholders, and paid $30,000 in dividends to its common shareholders. R & J's common stock account showed the following:

January 1	Shares issued and outstanding at the beginning of the year	10,000
April 1	Shares issued	4,000
July 1	10% stock dividend	
September 1	Shares repurchased for the treasury	3,000

Compute the weighted average number of common shares outstanding during the year, and compute EPS.

Answer:

Step 1: Adjust the number of pre-stock-dividend shares to post-stock-dividend units (to reflect the 10% stock dividend) by multiplying all share numbers prior to the stock dividend by 1.1. Shares issued or retired after the stock dividend are not affected.

January 1	Initial shares adjusted for the 10% dividend	11,000
April 1	Shares issued adjusted for the 10% dividend	4,400
September 1	Shares of treasury stock repurchased (no adjustment)	−3,000

Step 2: Compute the weighted average number of post-stock dividend shares:

Initial shares	11,000 × 12 months outstanding	132,000
Issued shares	4,400 × 9 months outstanding	39,600
Retired treasury shares	−3,000 × 4 months retired	−12,000
Total share-month		159,600
Average shares	159,600 / 12	13,300

Step 3: Compute basic EPS:

$$\text{basic EPS} = \frac{\text{net income} - \text{pref. div.}}{\text{wt. avg. shares of common}} = \frac{\$100,000 - \$50,000}{13,300} = \$3.76$$

Things to know about the weighted average shares outstanding calculation:

- The weighting system is days outstanding divided by the number of days in a year, but on the exam, the monthly approximation method will probably be used.
- Shares issued enter into the computation from the date of issuance.
- Reacquired shares are excluded from the computation from the date of reacquisition.
- Shares sold or issued in a purchase of assets are included from the date of issuance.
- A stock split or stock dividend is applied to all shares outstanding prior to the split or dividend and to the beginning-of-period weighted average shares. A stock split or stock dividend adjustment is not applied to any shares issued or repurchased after the split or dividend date.

DILUTED EPS

Before calculating diluted EPS, it is necessary to understand the following terms:

- **Dilutive securities** are stock options, warrants, convertible debt, or convertible preferred stock that would *decrease EPS* if exercised or converted to common stock.
- **Antidilutive securities** are stock options, warrants, convertible debt, or convertible preferred stock that would *increase EPS* if exercised or converted to common stock.

The numerator of the basic EPS equation contains income available to common shareholders (net income less preferred dividends). In the case of diluted EPS, if there are dilutive securities, then the numerator must be adjusted as follows:

- If convertible preferred stock is dilutive (meaning EPS will fall if it is converted to common stock), the convertible preferred dividends must be added to earnings available to common shareholders.

- If convertible bonds are dilutive, then the bonds' after-tax interest expense is not considered an interest expense for diluted EPS. Hence, interest expense multiplied by (1 – the tax rate) must be added back to the numerator.

> *Professor's Note: Interest paid on bonds is typically tax deductible for the firm. If convertible bonds are converted to stock, the firm saves the interest cost but loses the tax deduction. Thus, only the after-tax interest savings are added back to income available to common shareholders.*

The basic EPS denominator is the weighted average number of shares. When the firm has dilutive securities outstanding, the denominator is the basic EPS denominator adjusted for the equivalent number of common shares that would be created by the conversion of all dilutive securities outstanding (convertible bonds, convertible preferred shares, warrants, and options), with each one considered separately to determine if it is dilutive.

If a dilutive security was issued during the year, the increase in the weighted average number of shares for diluted EPS is based on only the portion of the year the dilutive security was outstanding.

Dilutive stock options or warrants increase the number of common shares outstanding in the denominator for diluted EPS. There is no adjustment to the numerator.

Stock options and warrants are dilutive only when their exercise prices are less than the average market price of the stock over the year. If the options or warrants are dilutive, use the *treasury stock method* to calculate the number of shares used in the denominator.

The Treasury Stock Method

- The treasury stock method assumes that the hypothetical funds received by the company from the exercise of the options would be used to purchase shares of the company's common stock in the market at the average market price.
- The net increase in the number of shares outstanding (the adjustment to the denominator) is the number of shares created by exercising the options less the number of shares hypothetically repurchased with the proceeds of exercise.

Example: Treasury stock method

Baxter Company has 5,000 shares outstanding all year. Baxter had 2,000 outstanding warrants all year, convertible into one share each at $20 per share. The year-end price of Baxter stock was $40, and the average stock price was $30. What effect will these warrants have on the weighted average number of shares?

Answer:

If the warrants are exercised, the company will receive 2,000 × $20 = $40,000 and issue 2,000 new shares. The treasury stock method assumes the company uses these funds to repurchase shares at the average market price of $30. The company would repurchase $40,000 / $30 = 1,333 shares. Net shares issued would be 2,000 − 1,333 = 667 shares.

The **diluted EPS equation** is:

$$\text{diluted EPS} = \frac{\text{adjusted income available for common shares}}{\text{weighted-average common and potential common shares outstanding}}$$

where *adjusted income available for common shares* is:

Net income – preferred dividends
+ Dividends on convertible preferred stock
+ After-tax interest on convertible debt

Therefore, diluted EPS is:

$$\text{diluted EPS} = \frac{\left[\begin{array}{c}\text{net income} - \text{preferred} \\ \text{dividends}\end{array}\right] + \left[\begin{array}{c}\text{convertible} \\ \text{preferred} \\ \text{dividends}\end{array}\right] + \left[\begin{array}{c}\text{convertible} \\ \text{debt} \\ \text{interest}\end{array}\right](1-t)}{\left(\begin{array}{c}\text{weighted} \\ \text{average} \\ \text{shares}\end{array}\right) + \left(\begin{array}{c}\text{shares from} \\ \text{conversion of} \\ \text{conv. pfd. shares}\end{array}\right) + \left(\begin{array}{c}\text{shares from} \\ \text{conversion of} \\ \text{conv. debt}\end{array}\right) + \left(\begin{array}{c}\text{shares} \\ \text{issuable from} \\ \text{stock options}\end{array}\right)}$$

Remember, each potentially dilutive security must be examined separately to determine if it is actually dilutive (i.e., would reduce EPS if converted to common stock). The effect of conversion to common is included in the calculation of diluted EPS for a given security only if it is, in fact, dilutive.

Sometimes in an acquisition there will be a provision that the shareholders of the acquired company will receive additional shares of the acquiring firm's stock if certain performance targets are met. These *contingent shares* should be included in the calculation of diluted EPS if the target has been met as of the end of the reporting period.

Example 1: EPS with convertible debt

During 20X6, ZZZ Corp. reported net income of $115,600 and had 200,000 shares of common stock outstanding for the entire year. ZZZ also had 1,000 shares of 10%, $100 par, preferred stock outstanding during 20X6. During 20X5, ZZZ issued 600, $1,000 par, 7% bonds for $600,000 (issued at par). Each of these bonds is convertible to 100 shares of common stock. The tax rate is 40%. Compute the 20X6 basic and diluted EPS.

Answer:

Step 1:   Compute 20X6 basic EPS:

$$\text{basic EPS} = \frac{\$115,600 - \$10,000}{200,000} = \$0.53$$

Step 2:   Calculate diluted EPS:

- Compute the increase in common stock outstanding if the convertible debt is converted to common stock at the beginning of 20X6:

  shares issuable for debt conversion = (600)(100) = 60,000 shares

- If the convertible debt is considered converted to common stock at the beginning of 20X6, then there would be no interest expense related to the convertible debt. Therefore, it is necessary to increase ZZZ's after-tax net income for the after-tax effect of the decrease in interest expense:

  increase in income = [(600)($1,000)(0.07)] (1 − 0.40) = $25,200

- Compute diluted EPS as if the convertible debt were common stock:

$$\text{diluted EPS} = \frac{\text{net. inc.} - \text{pref. div.} + \text{convert. int. } (1-t)}{\text{wt. avg. shares} + \text{convertible debt shares}}$$

$$\text{diluted EPS} = \frac{\$115,600 - \$10,000 + \$25,200}{200,000 + 60,000} = \$0.50$$

- Check to make sure that *diluted EPS is less than basic EPS* [$0.50 < $0.53]. If diluted EPS is more than the basic EPS, the convertible bonds are *antidilutive* and should not be treated as common stock in computing diluted EPS.

A quick way to determine whether the convertible debt is antidilutive is to calculate its per share impact by:

$$\frac{\text{convertible debt interest } (1-t)}{\text{convertible debt shares}}$$

If this per share amount is greater than basic EPS, the convertible debt is antidilutive, and the effects of conversion should not be included when calculating diluted EPS.

If this per share amount is less than basic EPS, the convertible debt is dilutive, and the effects of conversion should be included in the calculation of diluted EPS.

For ZZZ:

$$\frac{\$25,200}{60,000} = \$0.42$$

The company's basic EPS is $0.53, so the convertible debt is dilutive, and the effects of conversion should be included in the calculation of diluted EPS.

Example 2: EPS with convertible preferred stock

During 20X6, ZZZ reported net income of $115,600 and had 200,000 shares of common stock and 1,000 shares of preferred stock outstanding for the entire year. ZZZ's 10%, $100 par value preferred shares are each convertible into 40 shares of common stock. The tax rate is 40%. Compute basic and diluted EPS.

Answer:

Step 1:   Calculate 20X6 basic EPS:

$$\text{basic EPS} = \frac{\$115,600 - \$10,000}{200,000} = \$0.53$$

Step 2:   Calculate diluted EPS:

- Compute the increase in common stock outstanding if the preferred stock is converted to common stock at the beginning of 20X6: (1,000)(40) = 40,000 shares.
- If the convertible preferred shares were converted to common stock, there would be no preferred dividends paid. Therefore, you should add back the convertible preferred dividends that had previously been subtracted from net income in the numerator.

- Compute diluted EPS as if the convertible preferred stock were converted into common stock:

$$\text{diluted EPS} = \frac{\text{net. inc.} - \text{pref. div.} + \text{convert. pref. dividends}}{\text{wt. avg. shares} + \text{convert. pref. common shares}}$$

$$\text{diluted EPS} = \frac{\$115,600 - \$10,000 + \$10,000}{200,000 + 40,000} = \$0.48$$

- Check to see if diluted EPS is less than basic EPS ($0.48 < $0.53). If the answer is yes, the preferred stock is dilutive and must be included in diluted EPS as computed above. If the answer is no, the preferred stock is antidilutive and conversion effects are not included in diluted EPS.

Example 3: EPS with stock options

During 20X6, ZZZ reported net income of $115,600 and had 200,000 shares of common stock outstanding for the entire year. ZZZ also had 1,000 shares of 10%, $100 par, preferred stock outstanding during 20X6. ZZZ has 10,000 stock options (or warrants) outstanding the entire year. Each option allows its holder to purchase one share of common stock at $15 per share. The average market price of ZZZ's common stock during 20X6 is $20 per share. Compute the diluted EPS.

Answer:

Number of common shares created if the options are exercised:	10,000 shares
Cash inflow if the options are exercised ($15/share)(10,000):	$150,000
Number of shares that can be purchased with these funds is: $150,000 / $20	7,500 shares
Net increase in common shares outstanding from the exercise of the stock options (10,000 – 7,500)	2,500 shares

$$\text{diluted EPS} = \frac{\$115,600 - \$10,000}{200,000 + 2,500} = \$0.52$$

A quick way to calculate the net increase in common shares from the potential exercise of stock options or warrants when the exercise price is less than the average market price is:

$$\left[\frac{AMP - EP}{AMP} \right] \times N$$

where :

AMP = average market price over the year

EP = exercise price of the options or warrants

N   = number of common shares that the options and warrants can be converted into

For ZZZ: $\dfrac{\$20 - \$15}{\$20} \times 10,000 \text{ shares} = 2,500 \text{ shares}$

Example 4: EPS with convertible bonds, convertible preferred, and options

During 20X6, ZZZ reported net income of $115,600 and had 200,000 shares of common stock outstanding for the entire year. ZZZ had 1,000 shares of 10%, $100 par convertible preferred stock, convertible into 40 shares each, outstanding for the entire year. ZZZ also had 600, 7%, $1,000 par value convertible bonds, convertible into 100 shares each, outstanding for the entire year. Finally, ZZZ had 10,000 stock options outstanding during the year. Each option is convertible into one share of stock at $15 per share. The average market price of the stock for the year was $20. What are ZZZ's basic and diluted EPS? (Assume a 40% tax rate.)

Answer:

Step 1: From Examples 1, 2, and 3, we know that the convertible preferred stock, convertible bonds, and stock options are all dilutive. Recall that basic EPS was calculated as:

$$\text{basic EPS} = \frac{\$115,600 - \$10,000}{200,000} = \$0.53$$

Step 2: Review the number of shares created by converting the convertible securities and options (the denominator):

Converting the convertible preferred shares	40,000 shares
Converting the convertible bonds	60,000 shares
Exercising the options	2,500 shares

©2008 Schweser

Step 3:   Review the adjustments to net income (the numerator):

Converting the convertible preferred shares	$10,000
Converting the convertible bonds	$25,200
Exercising the options	$0

Step 4:   Compute ZZZ's diluted EPS:

$$\text{diluted EPS} = \frac{115,600 - 10,000 + 10,000 + 25,200}{200,000 + 40,000 + 60,000 + 2,500} = \$0.47$$

LOS 32.j: Evaluate a company's financial performance using common-size income statements and financial ratios based on the income statement.

Common-size statements and ratios are tools used to facilitate analysis of the financial statements.

A **common-size income statement** expresses each income statement item as a percentage of sales. This format is known as *vertical common-size analysis* and allows the analyst to evaluate firm performance over time (time-series), as well as compare performance across firms, industries, or sectors (cross-sectional).

Example: Common-size income statements

The table below presents the income statements for Company A, Company B, and Company C. Also presented are the income statements in (vertical) common-size format. All three companies are involved in the same industry. Evaluate the financial performance of the three firms.

Income Statements – In Dollars and Common Size						
	Company A		Company B		Company C	
Revenue	$1,000	100%	$5,000	100%	$5,000	100%
COGS	400	40%	2,500	50%	2,000	40%
Gross profit	600	60%	2,500	50%	3,000	60%
SG&A	150	15%	750	15%	750	15%
Production R&D	100	10%	250	5%	500	10%
Operating profit	350	35%	1,500	30%	1,750	35%
Interest expense	50	5%	250	5%	250	5%
Pre-tax income	300	30%	1,250	25%	1,500	30%
Income taxes	120	12%	500	10%	600	12%
Net income	$180	18%	$750	15%	$900	18%

Answer:

As compared to Company B, Company A is smaller in terms of sales and net income when stated in dollars. However, in common-size terms, Company A's net income is higher than Company B's net income (18% versus 15%). By presenting the income statements in common-size format, the analyst is able to compare the firms without regard to size.

Common size analysis also provides information about a firm's business strategies. Revenues are the same at Company B and Company C. However, Company C reports higher gross profit, higher operating profit, and higher net income. The higher profit can be traced to lower cost of goods sold. Notice that Company C spends more on production research and development (R&D) than Company B. As a result, Company C has been able to lower its production costs.

Presenting income tax expense as an effective rate is usually more meaningful than the common-size percentage. The effective rate is equal to income tax expense divided by pre-tax income. In the above example, the effective tax rate for all three companies is 40%.

Financial Ratios Based on the Income Statement

Profitability ratios examine how good management is at turning their efforts into profits. Ratios such as gross profit margin, operating profit margin, and net profit margin compare the first value at the top of the income statement (sales) to various profit measures. The different ratios are designed to isolate specific costs and identify specific measures of performance. Generally, higher margin ratios are more desirable.

Gross profit margin is the ratio of gross profit (sales less cost of goods sold) to sales:

$$\text{Gross profit margin} = \frac{\text{Gross profit}}{\text{Revenue}}$$

Gross profit margin can be increased by raising sales prices or lowering per-unit cost.

Net profit margin is the ratio of net income to sales:

$$\text{Net profit margin} = \frac{\text{Net income}}{\text{Revenue}}$$

Any subtotal presented in the income statement can be expressed in terms of a margin ratio. For example, operating profit margin is equal to operating income divided by revenue. Pre-tax margin is equal to pre-tax earnings divided by revenue.

 Professor's Note: Ratios are discussed in detail in Study Session 10.

LOS 32.k: State the accounting classification for items that are excluded from the income statement but affect owners' equity, and list the major types of items receiving that treatment.

At the end of each accounting period, the net income of the firm is added to stockholders' equity through an account known as *retained earnings*. Therefore, any transaction that affects the income statement (net income) will also affect stockholders' equity. However, not all accounting transactions are reported in the income statement. For example, issuing stock and reacquiring stock are transactions that affect stockholders' equity but not net income. Dividends paid reduce stockholders' equity, but they do not reduce in net income. Finally, transactions included in *other comprehensive income* affect equity but not net income. Other comprehensive income includes:

1. Foreign currency translation gains and losses.

2. Adjustments for minimum pension liability.

3. Unrealized gains and losses from cash flow hedging derivatives.

4. Unrealized gains and losses from available-for-sale securities.

Available-for-sale securities are investment securities that are not expected to be held to maturity or sold in the near term. Available-for-sale securities are reported on the balance sheet at fair value. The unrealized gains and losses (the changes in fair value before the securities are sold) are not reported in the income statement but are reported directly in stockholders' equity as a component of other comprehensive income.

LOS 32.1: Describe and calculate comprehensive income.

Comprehensive income is a measure that includes all changes to equity other than owner contributions and distributions. That is, comprehensive income aggregates net income and other comprehensive income (foreign currency translation gains and losses, minimum pension liability adjustments, and unrealized gains and losses on cash flow hedging derivatives and available-for-sale securities).

Example: Calculating comprehensive income

Calculate comprehensive income for Triple C Corporation using the selected financial statement data found in the following table.

Triple C Corporation – Selected Financial Statement Data

Net income	$1,000
Dividends received from available-for-sale securities	60
Unrealized loss from foreign currency translation	(15)
Dividends paid	(110)
Reacquire common stock	(400)
Unrealized gain from cash flow hedge	30
Unrealized loss from available-for-sale securities	(10)
Realized gain on sale of land	65

Answer:

Net income	$1,000
Unrealized loss from foreign currency translation	(15)
Unrealized gain from cash flow hedge	30
Unrealized loss from available-for-sale securities	(10)
Comprehensive income	$1,005

The dividends received for available-for-sale securities and the realized gain on the sale of land are already included in net income. Dividends paid and the reacquisition of common stock are transactions with shareholders, so they are not included in comprehensive income.

KEY CONCEPTS

1. Revenue is recognized when realized and earned. Revenue is realized when payment is reasonably assured and revenue is earned when the seller has fulfilled all its obligations to provide goods or services.

2. There are five different revenue recognition methods:
   - At delivery – earnings process complete and payment is assured.
   - Percentage-of-completion – recognize revenue as work is performed.
   - Completed-contract – recognize revenue when contract is complete.
   - Installment method – recognize revenue as cash is collected.
   - Cost recovery method – recognize revenue once collections exceed cost.

3. There are three special income statement items:
   - Unusual or infrequent items – reported before tax and above income from continuing operations.
   - Extraordinary items – both unusual and infrequent. Reported below income from continuing operations, net of tax.
   - Discontinued operations – reported below income from continuing operations, net of tax.

4. A change in accounting principle requires retrospective restatement (of prior financial statements), while a change in an accounting estimate is applied prospectively (to subsequent periods).

5. The matching principle requires that firms match expenses incurred to generate revenues with the revenues. The matching principle also applies to inventory (cost of goods sold) and long-lived assets (depreciation).

6. Under FIFO, inventory purchased first is assumed to be sold first. Under LIFO, inventory purchased last is assumed to be sold first.

7. As compared to the straight-line method, accelerated depreciation methods will result in higher expenses in the early years and lower expenses in the later years of an asset's useful life.

8. A simple capital structure is one that contains no potentially dilutive securities, while a complex capital structure contains potentially dilutive securities such as options, warrants, or convertible securities.

9. The basic EPS calculation (the only EPS for firms with a simple capital structure) is:

$$\text{basic EPS} = \frac{\text{net income} - \text{preferred dividends}}{\text{weighted average number of common shares outstanding}}$$

10. Calculating the weighted average number of common shares outstanding:
    - Stock splits and dividends result in the additional shares being considered outstanding from the beginning of the year.
    - Shares issued enter into the computation from the date of issuance.
    - Reacquired shares are excluded from the computation from the date of reacquisition.

11. Dilutive securities are stock options, warrants, convertible debt, or convertible preferred stock that decrease EPS if exercised or converted to common stock.

12. Antidilutive securities are those that would increase EPS if exercised or converted to common stock.

13. Calculating diluted EPS with a complex capital structure:

$$\text{diluted EPS} = \frac{\left[\begin{array}{c}\text{net income} - \text{preferred} \\ \text{dividends}\end{array}\right] + \left[\begin{array}{c}\text{convertible} \\ \text{preferred} \\ \text{dividends}\end{array}\right] + \left[\begin{array}{c}\text{convertible} \\ \text{debt} \\ \text{interest}\end{array}\right](1-t)}{\left(\begin{array}{c}\text{weighted} \\ \text{average} \\ \text{shares}\end{array}\right) + \left(\begin{array}{c}\text{shares from} \\ \text{conversion of} \\ \text{conv. pfd. shares}\end{array}\right) + \left(\begin{array}{c}\text{shares from} \\ \text{conversion of} \\ \text{conv. debt}\end{array}\right) + \left(\begin{array}{c}\text{shares} \\ \text{issuable from} \\ \text{stock options}\end{array}\right)}$$

14. Warrants and options are potentially dilutive. In the diluted EPS calculation, if the average market price is greater than the exercise price, the number of shares is adjusted by adding:

$$\frac{\text{average market price} - \text{exercise price}}{\text{average market price}} \times \text{number of shares}$$

15. A company with a complex capital structure must report both basic and diluted EPS.

16. A common-size income statement expresses each line item as a percentage of sales.

17. Gross profit margin and net profit margin are profitability ratios.

18. Comprehensive income includes all changes in equity other than from transactions with shareholders, such as gains and losses from foreign currency translation, cash flow hedging derivatives, and available-for-sale securities. Pension obligation adjustments are also included.

CONCEPT CHECKERS

1. For a nonfinancial firm, are depreciation expense and interest expense included or excluded from operating expenses in the income statement?

	Depreciation expense	Interest expense
A.	Included	Included
B.	Included	Excluded
C.	Excluded	Included
D.	Excluded	Excluded

2. Are income taxes and cost of goods sold examples of expenses classified by nature or classified by function in the income statement?

	Income taxes	Cost of goods sold
A.	Nature	Nature
B.	Nature	Function
C.	Function	Nature
D.	Function	Function

3. Which of the following is *least likely* a condition necessary for revenue recognition?
    A. The price has been determined.
    B. The goods have been delivered.
    C. There is evidence of an arrangement between the buyer and seller.
    D. Cash has been collected.

4. AAA has a contract to build a building for $100,000 with an estimated time to completion of three years. A reliable cost estimate for the project is $60,000. In the first year of the project, AAA incurred costs totaling $24,000. How much profit should AAA report at the end of the first year under the percentage-of-completion method and the completed-contract method?

	Percentage-of-completion	Completed-contract
A.	$16,000	$0
B.	$16,000	$16,000
C.	$40,000	$0
D.	$40,000	$40,000

5. Which principle requires that cost of goods sold be recognized in the same period in which the sale of the related inventory is recorded?
    A. Going concern.
    B. Certainty.
    C. Matching.
    D. Economic.

6. Which of the following would *least likely* increase pretax income?
    A. Decreasing the bad debt expense estimate.
    B. Decreasing the residual value of a depreciable tangible asset.
    C. Decreasing the warranty expense estimate.
    D. Increasing the useful life of an intangible asset.

7. When accounting for inventory, are the first-in, first-out (FIFO) and last-in, first-out (LIFO) cost flow assumptions permitted under U.S. GAAP?

	FIFO	LIFO
A.	Yes	Yes
B.	Yes	No
C.	No	Yes
D.	No	No

    A

8. Which of the following *best* describes the impact of depreciating equipment with a useful life of 6 years using the declining balance method as compared to the straight-line method?
    A. Total depreciation expense will be higher over the life of the equipment.
    B. Depreciation expense will be higher in the first year.
    C. Scrapping the equipment after five years will result in a larger loss.
    D. Net income will be higher over the life of the equipment.

    B

9. CC Corporation reported the following inventory transactions (in chronological order) for the year:

    $13 \times 30 +$

Purchase	Sales
40 units at $30	13 units at $35
20 units at $40	35 units at $45
90 units at $50	60 units at $60

    6,500

    13

    42

    Assuming inventory at the beginning of the year was zero, calculate the year-end inventory using FIFO and LIFO.

	FIFO	LIFO
A.	$5,220	$1,280
B.	$5,220	$1,040
C.	$2,100	$1,280
D.	$2,100	$1,040

10. At the beginning of the year, Triple W Corporation purchased a new piece of equipment to be used in its manufacturing operation. The cost of the equipment was $25,000. The equipment is expected to be used for 4 years and then sold for $4,000. Depreciation expense to be reported for the second year using the double-declining-balance method is *closest to*:
    A. $0.
    B. $5,250.
    C. $6,250.
    D. $7,000.

11. Which of the following is *least likely* considered a nonoperating transaction from the perspective of a manufacturing firm?
    A. Dividends received from available-for-sale securities.
    B. Interest expense on subordinated debentures.
    C. Accruing bad debt expense for goods sold on credit.
    D. Recognizing an extraordinary loss from the destruction of a building.

12. Changing an accounting estimate:
    A. is reported prospectively.
    B. requires restatement of all prior-period statements presented in the current financial statements.
    C. is ignored for purposes of income statement analysis.
    D. is reported by adjusting the beginning balance of retained earnings for the cumulative effect of the change.

13. Which of the following transactions would *most likely* be reported below income from continuing operations, net of tax?
    A. Gain or loss from the sale of equipment used in a firm's manufacturing operation.
    B. A change from the accelerated method of depreciation to the straight-line method.
    C. Impairment charges and restructuring costs.
    D. The operating income of a physically and operationally distinct division that is currently for sale, but not yet sold.

14. Which of the following statements about nonrecurring items is *least accurate*?
    A. Gains from extraordinary items are reported net of taxes at the bottom of the income statement before net income.
    B. Unusual or infrequent items are reported before taxes above net income from continuing operations.
    C. A change in accounting principle is reported in the income statement net of taxes after extraordinary items and before net income.
    D. Losses from discontinued operations are reported net of taxes at the bottom of the income statement before net income.

15. The Hall Corporation had 100,000 shares of common stock outstanding at the beginning of the year. Hall issued 30,000 shares of common stock on May 1. On July 1, the company issued a 10% stock dividend. On September 1, Hall issued 1,000, 10% bonds, each convertible into 21 shares of common stock. What is the weighted average number of shares to be used in computing basic and diluted EPS, assuming the convertible bonds are dilutive?

	Average shares, basic	Average shares, dilutive
A.	130,000	132,000
B.	132,000	139,000
C.	132,000	146,000
D.	139,000	146,000

16. Given the following information, how many shares should be used in computing diluted EPS?
    - 300,000 shares outstanding.
    - 100,000 warrants exercisable at $50 per share.
    - Average share price is $55.
    - Year-end share price is $60.
    A. 9,091.
    B. 90,909.
    C. 309,091.
    D. 390,909.

17. An analyst gathered the following information about a company:
    - 100,000 common shares outstanding from the beginning of the year.
    - Earnings of $125,000.
    - 1,000, 7% $1,000 par bonds convertible into 25 shares each, outstanding as of the beginning of the year.
    - The tax rate is 40%.

    The company's diluted EPS is *closest* to:
    A. $1.22.
    B. $1.25.
    C. $1.34.
    D. $1.42.

18. An analyst has gathered the following information about a company:
    - 50,000 common shares outstanding from the beginning of the year.
    - Warrants outstanding all year on 50,000 shares, exercisable at $20 per share.
    - Stock is selling at year end for $25.
    - The average price of the company's stock for the year was $15.

    How many shares should be used in calculating the company's diluted EPS?
    A. 16,667.
    B. 33,333.
    C. 50,000.
    D. 66,667.

19. To study trends in a firm's cost of goods sold (COGS), the analyst should standardize cost of goods sold by dividing it by:
    A. sales.
    B. assets.
    C. net income.
    D. prior year COGS.

20. Which of the following ratios is a measure of profitability?
    A. Current ratio.
    B. Fixed asset turnover ratio.
    C. Long-term debt-to-total capital ratio.
    D. Pre-tax margin ratio.

21.   Which of the following transactions affects owners' equity but does not affect net income?
      A.   Realized loss on sale of investment securities.
      B.   Foreign currency translation gain.
      C.   Repaying the face amount on a bond issued at par.
      D.   Dividends received from available-for-sale securities.

22.   Which of the following is *least likely* to be included when calculating comprehensive income?
      A.   Unrealized loss from cash flow hedging derivatives.
      B.   Unrealized gain from available-for-sale securities.
      C.   Minimum pension liability.
      D.   Dividends paid to common shareholders.

ANSWERS – CONCEPT CHECKERS

1. **B**   Depreciation is included in the computation of operating expenses. Interest expense is a financing cost. Thus, it is excluded from operating expenses.

2. **B**   Income taxes are expenses grouped together by their nature. Cost of goods sold includes a number of expenses related to the same function, the production of inventory.

3. **D**   In order to recognize revenue, the seller must know the sales price and be reasonably sure of collection. Actual collection of cash is not required.

4. **A** $24,000/$60,000 = 40% of the project completed. 40% of $100,000 = $40,000 revenue. $40,000 revenue – $24,000 cost = $16,000 profit for the period. No profit would be reported in the first year using the completed contract method.

5. **C**   The matching principle requires that the expenses incurred to generate the revenue be recognized in the same accounting period as the revenue.

6. **B**   Decreasing the residual (salvage) value of a depreciable long-lived asset will result in higher depreciation expense and, thus, lower pretax income.

7. **A**   LIFO and FIFO are both permitted under U.S. GAAP. LIFO is prohibited under IFRS.

8. **B**   Accelerated depreciation will result in higher depreciation in the early years and lower depreciation in the later years compared to the straight-line method. Total depreciation expense will be the same under both methods. The book value would be higher in the later years using straight-line depreciation, so the loss from scrapping the equipment would be less compared to an accelerated method like declining balance. Net income over the life of the equipment is the same under either method.

9. **C**   108 units were sold (13 + 35 + 60) and 150 units were available for sale (beginning inventory of 0 plus purchases of 40 + 20 + 90), so there are 150 – 108 = 42 units in ending inventory. Under FIFO, units from the last batch purchased would remain in inventory: 42 × $50 = $2,100. Under LIFO, the first 42 units purchased would be in inventory: (40 × $30) + (2 × $40) = $1,280.

10. **C**   Year 1: (2/4) × 25,000 = $12,500. Year 2: (2/4) × (25,000 – 12,500) = $6,250.

11. **C**   Bad debt expense is an operating expense. All of the other choices are nonoperating from the perspective of a manufacturing firm.

12. **A**   A change in an accounting estimate is reported prospectively. No restatement of prior period statements is necessary.

13. **D**   A physically and operationally distinct division that is currently for sale is treated as a discontinued operation. The income from the division is reported net of tax below income from continuing operations. Changing a depreciation method is a change of accounting principle, which is applied retrospectively and will change operating income.

14. **C**   A change in accounting principle requires retrospective application; that is, all prior period financial statements currently presented are restated to reflect the change.

15. **B**   The new stock is weighted by 8 / 12. The bonds are weighted by 4 / 12 and are not affected by the stock dividend.

Basic shares = {[100,000 × (12 / 12)] + [30,000 × (8 / 12)]} × 1.10 = 132,000

Diluted shares = 132,000 + [21,000 × (4 / 12)] = 139,000

16. **C**   Since the exercise price of the warrants is less than the average share price, the warrants are dilutive. Using the treasury stock method to determine the denominator impact:

$$\frac{\$55 - \$50}{\$55} \times 100,000 \text{ shares} = 9,091 \text{ shares}$$

Thus, the denominator will increase by 9,091 shares to 309,091 shares. The question asks for the total, not just the impact of the warrants.

17. **B**   First, calculate basic EPS = $\frac{125,000}{100,000} = \$1.25$

Next, check if the convertible bonds are dilutive:

numerator impact = (1,000 × 1,000 × 0.07) × (1 − 0.4) = $42,000

denominator impact = (1,000 × 25) = 25,000 shares

$$\text{per share impact} = \frac{\$42,000}{25,000 \text{ shares}} = \$1.68$$

Since $1.68 is greater than the basic EPS of $1.25, the bonds are antidilutive. Thus, diluted EPS = basic EPS = $1.25.

18. **C**   The warrants in this case are antidilutive. The average price per share of $15 is less than the exercise price of $20. The year-end price per share is not relevant. The denominator consists of only the common stock for basic EPS.

19. **A**   In a common-size income statement, each income statement account is divided by sales. COGS is then production costs as a percentage of price.

20. **D**   Pre-tax margin (pre-tax earnings / revenue) measures profitability.

21. **B**   A foreign currency translation gain is not included in net income but the gain increases owners' equity. Dividends received are reported in the income statement. The repayment of principal does not affect owners' equity.

22. **D**   Comprehensive income includes all changes in equity except transactions with shareholders. Therefore, dividends paid to common shareholders are not included in comprehensive income.

The following is a review of the Financial Statement Analysis principles designed to address the learning outcome statements set forth by CFA Institute®. This topic is also covered in:

UNDERSTANDING THE BALANCE SHEET

EXAM FOCUS

While the income statement presents a picture of a firm's economic activities over a period of time, its balance sheet is a snapshot of its financial and physical assets and its liabilities at a point in time. Just as with the income statement, understanding balance sheet accounts, how they are valued, and what they represent, is also crucial to the financial analysis of a firm. Again, different choices of accounting methods and different accounting estimates will affect a firm's financial ratios, and an analyst must be careful to make the necessary adjustments in order to compare two or more firms. Special attention should be paid to the method by which each balance sheet item is calculated and how changes in balance sheet values relate to the income statement, to the statement of other comprehensive income, and to shareholders' equity. Study Session 9 includes more detailed information on several balance sheet accounts, including inventories, long-term assets, deferred taxes, debt liabilities, and off-balance-sheet financing.

LOS 33.a: Illustrate and interpret the components of the assets, liabilities, and equity sections of the balance sheet, and discuss the uses of the balance sheet in financial analysis.

Assets provide probable future economic benefits controlled by an entity as a result of previous transactions.

Assets can be created by operating activities (e.g., generating net income), investing activities (e.g., purchasing manufacturing equipment), and financing activities (e.g., issuing debt). Figure 1 lists some of the more common asset accounts found on the balance sheet.

Figure 1: Common Balance Sheet Asset Accounts

Cash and equivalents

Accounts receivable (trade receivables)

Inventory

Prepaid expenses

Investments

Property, plant, and equipment

Intangible assets

Deferred tax assets

Pension assets

Liabilities are obligations owed by an entity from previous transactions that are expected to result in an outflow of economic benefits in the future.

Liabilities are created by financing activities (e.g., issuing debt) and operating activities (e.g., recognizing expense before payment is made). Figure 2 lists some of the more common liability accounts found in the balance sheet.

Figure 2: Common Balance Sheet Liability Accounts

Accounts payable (trade payables)

Accrued expenses

Unearned revenue

Notes payable

Bonds payable

Capital (financial) lease obligations

Pension liabilities

Deferred tax liabilities

Inherent in the definition of both assets and liabilities is that a future economic impact is probable and can be reliably measured.

Stockholders' equity is the residual interest in assets that remains after subtracting a firm's liabilities. Stockholders' equity is also referred to as "shareholders' equity" and "owners' equity," or sometimes just "equity" or "net assets."

Equity is created by financing activities (e.g., issuing capital stock) and by operating activities (e.g., generating net income). Figure 3 lists some of the more common equity accounts found in the balance sheet.

Figure 3: Common Balance Sheet Equity Accounts

Capital stock

Additional paid-in-capital (capital in excess of par)

Treasury stock

Retained earnings

Accumulated other comprehensive income

The balance sheet is important to investors and lenders alike. However, the analyst must understand its limitations. Not all assets and liabilities are reported on the balance sheet, and those that are not necessarily reported at fair value.

LOS 33.b: Describe the various formats of balance sheet presentation.

There is no standardized balance sheet format. However, two common formats are the account format and the report format.

Just like the balance sheet equation, an **account format** is a layout in which assets are presented on the left hand side of the page and liabilities and equity are presented on the right hand side. In a **report format**, the assets, liabilities, and equity are presented in one column.

A **classified balance sheet** groups together similar items to arrive at significant subtotals. For example, current assets are grouped together and current liabilities are grouped together. Similarly, noncurrent assets are grouped together, as are noncurrent liabilities.

LOS 33.c: Explain how assets and liabilities arise from the accrual process.

Assets and liabilities are created by business transactions. For example, if a firm issues bonds in exchange for cash, assets (cash) increase and liabilities (bonds payable) increase by the same amount.

The accrual method of accounting also creates assets and liabilities. Under accrual accounting, revenue recognition and expense recognition do not necessarily coincide with cash receipts and cash payments. In particular:

- Cash received in advance of recognizing revenue results in an increase in assets (cash) and an increase in liabilities (unearned revenue). Once the revenue is earned, liabilities (unearned revenue) decrease and equity (retained earnings) increases.
- Recognizing revenue before cash is received results in an increase in assets (accounts receivable) and an increase in equity (retained earnings). Once the cash is collected, an asset (cash) increases and another asset (accounts receivable) decreases by the same amount.
- Cash paid in advance of recognizing an expense results in a decrease in one asset (cash) and an increase in another asset (prepaid expenses) by the same amount. Once the expense is recognized, assets (prepaid expenses) decrease and equity (retained earnings) decreases by an equal amount.
- Recognizing an expense before cash is paid results in an increase in liabilities (accrued expenses) and a decrease in equity (retained earnings). Once the expense is paid, assets (cash) decrease and liabilities (accrued expenses) decrease by an equal amount.

LOS 33.d: Compare and contrast current and noncurrent assets and liabilities.

Current assets include cash and other assets that will likely be converted into cash or used up within one year or one operating cycle, whichever is greater. The **operating cycle** is the time it takes to produce or purchase inventory, sell the product, and collect the cash. Current assets are usually presented in the order of their liquidity, with cash being the most liquid. Current assets reveal information about the operating activities of the firm.

Current liabilities are obligations that will be satisfied within one year or one operating cycle, whichever is greater. More specifically, a liability that meets any of the following criteria is considered current:

- Settlement is expected during the normal operating cycle.
- Settlement is expected within one year.
- There is not an unconditional right to defer settlement for more than one year.

Current assets minus current liabilities equals **working capital**. Not enough working capital may indicate liquidity problems. Too much working capital may be an indication of inefficient use of assets.

Noncurrent assets do not meet the definition of current assets because they will not be converted into cash or used up within one year or operating cycle. Noncurrent assets provide information about the firm's investing activities, which form the foundation upon which the firm operates.

Noncurrent liabilities do not meet the criteria of current liabilities. Noncurrent liabilities provide information about the firm's long-term financing activities.

International Financial Reporting Standards (IFRS) requires the current/noncurrent format unless a **liquidity-based presentation** is more relevant, as in the banking industry.

If a firm has a controlling interest in a subsidiary that is not 100% owned, the parent reports a minority (noncontrolling) interest in its consolidated balance sheet. The **minority interest** is the pro-rata share of the subsidiary's net assets (equity) not owned by the parent company.

Under IFRS, the minority interest is reported in the equity section of the consolidated balance sheet. Under U.S. GAAP, the minority interest can be reported in the liabilities section, the equity section, or the "mezzanine section" of the balance sheet. The mezzanine section is located between liabilities and equity.

LOS 33.e: Explain the measurement bases (e.g., historical cost and fair value) of assets and liabilities, including current assets, current liabilities, tangible assets, and intangible assets.

Under current accounting standards, the balance sheet contains a mixture of historical costs and fair values. In addition, sometimes replacement cost and the present value of future cash flows are used to measure assets and liabilities.

Historical cost is the value that was exchanged at the acquisition date. Historical cost is verifiable and objective; however, its relevance to investment analysis declines over time as prices change.

Fair value is the amount at which an asset can be bought or sold, or a liability can be incurred or settled, between knowledgeable, willing parties in an arm's-length transaction. Fair value is subjective to a significant extent.

Because of this mixture of measurement bases, the balance sheet value of total assets should not be interpreted as the value of the firm. Analysts must adjust the balance sheet to better assess a firm's investment potential or creditworthiness.

Specific assets and their related liabilities are not usually offset (netted) on the balance sheet. For example, if a firm purchases manufacturing equipment for $3 million that is subject to a loan of $2 million, the asset and liability are shown separately on the balance sheet rather than reporting a net asset value of $1 million.

The financial statement footnotes should include the following information about the measurement of the firm's assets and liabilities:

- Basis for measurement.
- Carrying value of inventory by category.
- Amount of inventory carried at fair value less costs to sell.
- Write-downs and reversals, with a discussion of the circumstances that led to them.
- Inventories pledged as collateral for liabilities.
- Inventories recognized as an expense.

Current Assets

Current assets include cash and other assets that will be converted into cash or used up within one year or the firm's operating cycle, whichever is greater. Some of the more common current assets include the following:

- Cash and cash equivalents (liquid low-risk securities with maturities less than 90 days).
- Accounts receivable (trade receivables)—amounts expected to be collected from the sale of goods and services. Receivables are typically reported net of an allowance for bad debt (net receivables). This is not considered offsetting because of the nature of the allowance.
- Inventories—items held for sale or used in the manufacturing of goods to be sold. Manufacturing firms separately report inventories of raw materials, work-in-process, and finished goods.

- Marketable securities—debt or equity securities that are traded in a public market (e.g., Treasury securities, certain equity securities, and mutual funds).
- Other current assets including prepaid expenses.

Inventory is reported at the lower of cost or net realizable value. **Net realizable value** is the selling price of the inventory less the estimated cost of completion and disposal costs. For a manufacturer, inventory cost includes direct materials, direct labor, and overhead. Inventory cost excludes the following:

- Abnormal amounts of wasted materials, labor, and overhead.
- Storage costs beyond the production process.
- Administrative overhead.
- Disposal (selling) costs.

As discussed in the topic review on understanding the income statement, the cost flow assumption (i.e., FIFO, LIFO, average cost, or specific identification) affects the carrying (book) value of the inventory.

Standard costing and the retail method are used by some firms to measure inventory. **Standard costing**, often used by manufacturing firms, involves assigning predetermined costs to goods produced. Firms that use the **retail method** measure inventory at retail prices and then subtract gross profit in order to reflect cost.

Prepaid expenses are operating costs that have been paid in advance. As the costs are actually incurred, an expense is recognized in the income statement and prepaid expenses (an asset) decrease. For example, if a firm makes an annual rent payment of $400,000 at the beginning of the year, an asset (cash) decreases and another asset (prepaid rent) increases by the amount of the payment. At the end of three months, one-quarter of the prepaid rent has been used. At this point, the firm may recognize $100,000 of rent expense in its income statement and reduce assets (prepaid rent) by $100,000 to $300,000.

Current Liabilities

Current liabilities are obligations that will be satisfied within one year or operating cycle, whichever is greater.

Accounts payable (trade payables) are amounts owed to suppliers for goods or services purchased on credit.

Notes payable are obligations in the form of promissory notes owed to creditors. Notes payable can also be included in noncurrent liabilities, if their maturities are greater than one year.

The **current portion of long-term debt** is the principal portion of debt due within one year or the firm's operating cycle, whichever is greater.

Taxes payable are current taxes that have been recognized in the income statement but have not yet been paid.

Accrued liabilities (accrued expenses) are expenses that have been recognized in the income statement but are not yet contractually due. Accrued expenses result from the accrual method of accounting, under which expenses are recognized as incurred. For example, consider a firm that is required to make annual year-end interest payments of $100,000 on an outstanding bank loan. At the end of March, the firm would recognize one-quarter ($25,000) of the total interest expense in its income statement and an accrued liability would be increased by the same amount, even though the liability is not actually due until the end of the year.

Unearned revenue (unearned income) is cash collected in advance of providing goods and services. For example, a magazine publisher receives subscription payments in advance of delivery. When payment is received, both assets (cash) and liabilities (unearned revenue) increase by the same amount. As the magazines are delivered, the publisher recognizes revenue in the income statement and the liability is reduced.

Tangible Assets

Long-term assets with physical substance are known as **tangible assets.** Tangible assets, such as plant, equipment, and natural resources, are reported on the balance sheet at historical cost less accumulated depreciation or depletion. Historical cost includes the original cost of the asset plus all costs necessary to get the asset ready for use (e.g., freight and installation).

Land is also a tangible asset that is reported at historical cost. However, land is not depreciated.

Tangible assets not used in the operations of the firm should be classified as investment assets.

Intangible Assets

Intangible assets are long-term assets that lack physical substance. Financial securities are not considered intangible assets. The value of an *identifiable intangible asset* is based on the rights or privileges conveyed to its owner over a finite period. Accordingly, the cost of an identifiable intangible asset is amortized over its useful life. Examples of identifiable intangibles include patents, trademarks, and copyrights. Note, however, that the value of internally produced intangible assets may not be recorded on the balance sheet.

An intangible asset that is *unidentifiable* cannot be purchased separately and may have an infinite life. Intangible assets with infinite lives are not amortized, but are tested for impairment at least annually. The best example of an unidentifiable intangible asset is goodwill.

Intangible assets that are purchased are reported on the balance sheet at historical cost less accumulated amortization. Except for certain legal costs, intangible assets that are created internally, including research and development costs, are expensed as incurred under U.S. GAAP. Under IFRS, a firm must identify the research stage and the development stage. Accordingly, the firm must expense costs during the research stage but can capitalize costs during the development stage.

All of the following should be expensed as incurred:

- Start-up and training costs.
- Administrative overhead.
- Advertising and promotion.
- Relocation and reorganization costs.
- Termination costs.

Some analysts completely eliminate intangible assets, particularly unidentifiable intangibles, for analytical purposes. Analysts should, however, consider the value to the firm of each intangible asset before making any adjustments.

Goodwill is the excess of purchase price over the fair value of the identifiable assets and liabilities acquired in a business acquisition. Let's look at an example of calculating goodwill.

Example: Goodwill

Wood Corporation paid $600 million for the outstanding stock of Pine Corporation. At the acquisition date, Pine reported the following condensed balance sheet:

Pine Corporation – Condensed Balance Sheet

	Book value (millions)
Current assets	$80
Plant and equipment, net	760
Goodwill	30
Liabilities	400
Stockholders' equity	470

The fair value of the plant and equipment was $120 million more than its recorded book value. The fair values of all other identifiable assets and liabilities were equal to their recorded book values. Calculate the amount of goodwill Wood should report in its consolidated balance sheet.

Answer:

	Book value (millions)
Current assets	$80
Plant and equipment, net	880
Liabilities	(400)
Fair value of net assets	560
Purchase price	600
Less: Fair value of net assets	(560)
Acquisition goodwill	40

Goodwill is equal to the excess of purchase price over the fair value of identifiable assets and liabilities acquired. The plant and equipment was "written-up" by $120 million to reflect fair value. The goodwill reported on Pine's balance sheet is an unidentifiable asset and is thus ignored in the calculation of Wood's goodwill.

Accounting goodwill should not be confused with economic goodwill. Economic goodwill derives from the expected future performance of the firm, while accounting goodwill is the result of past acquisitions.

Goodwill is created in a purchase acquisition. Internally generated goodwill is expensed as incurred. Goodwill is not amortized but must be tested for impairment at least annually. If impaired, goodwill is reduced and a loss is recognized in the income statement. The impairment loss does not affect cash flow. As long as goodwill is not impaired, it can remain on the balance sheet indefinitely.

Since goodwill is not amortized, firms can manipulate net income upward by allocating more of the acquisition price to goodwill and less to the identifiable assets. The result is less depreciation and amortization expense, resulting in higher net income.

When computing ratios, analysts should eliminate goodwill from the balance sheet and goodwill impairment charges from the income statement for comparability. Also, analysts should evaluate future acquisitions in terms of the price paid relative to the earning power of the acquired assets.

LOS 33.f: Discuss off-balance-sheet disclosures.

The financial statement footnotes should disclose information about the firm's:

- Accounting policies, including revenue recognition, other accounting methods, and judgments used.
- Estimation of uncertainty, including key assumptions that pose a significant risk.
- Debt agreement terms.
- Leases and off-balance-sheet financing.
- Business segments.
- Contingent assets and liabilities.
- Pension plans.

The footnotes should include a description of the firm and its legal identification details.

LOS 33.g: Demonstrate the appropriate classifications and related accounting treatments for marketable and non-marketable financial instruments held as assets or owed by the company as liabilities.

Financial instruments can be found on both the asset side and liability side of the balance sheet. Financial assets include investment securities (stocks and bonds), derivatives, loans, and receivables. Financial liabilities include derivatives, notes payable, and bonds payable.

Some financial assets and liabilities are reported on the balance sheet at fair value, while others are reported at cost or present value. Reporting assets and liabilities at fair value is known as **marking-to-market**. Certain marketable investment securities and derivatives (both assets and liabilities) are subject to mark-to-market adjustments.

 Professor's Note: The Financial Accounting Standards Board recently issued SFAS No. 159, "The Fair Value Option for Financial Assets and Financial Liabilities." This new standard extends the ability to report almost all financial assets and liabilities at fair value if a firm chooses to do so. SFAS No. 159 is not part of the assigned curriculum.

Marketable investment securities are classified as either held-to-maturity, trading, or available-for-sale.

Held-to-maturity securities are debt securities acquired with the intent that they will be held to maturity. Held-to-maturity securities are reported on the balance sheet at amortized cost. Amortized cost is equal to the face (par) value less any unamortized discount or plus any unamortized premium. Subsequent changes in market value are ignored.

Trading securities are debt and equity securities acquired with the intent to profit over the near term. Trading securities are reported on the balance sheet at fair value. Unrealized gains and losses, that is, changes in market value before the securities are sold, are reported in the income statement.

Available-for-sale securities are debt and equity securities that are not expected to be held to maturity or traded in the near term. Like trading securities, available-for-sale securities are reported on the balance sheet at fair value. However, any unrealized gains and losses are not recognized in the income statement, but are reported in other comprehensive income as a part of stockholders' equity.

Dividend and interest income, and realized gains and losses (actual gains or losses when the securities are sold) are recognized in the income statement for all three classifications of securities.

Figure 4 summarizes the different classifications of investment securities.

Figure 4: Summary of Investment Security Classifications

	Trading	*Available-for-sale*	*Held-to-maturity*
Balance sheet	Fair value	Fair value	Amortized cost
Income statement	Dividends Interest Realized gains/losses Unrealized gains/losses	Dividends Interest Realized gains/losses	Interest Realized gains/losses

Example: Classification of investment securities

Triple D Corporation purchased a 6% bond, at par, for $1,000,000 at the beginning of the year. Interest rates have recently increased and the market value of the bond declined $20,000. Determine the bond's effect on Triple D's financial statements under each classification of securities.

Answer:

If the bond is classified as a *held-to-maturity* security, the bond is reported on the balance sheet at $1,000,000. Interest income of $60,000 [$1,000,000 × 6%] is reported in the income statement.

If the bond is classified as a *trading* security, the bond is reported on the balance sheet at $980,000. The $20,000 unrealized loss and $60,000 of interest income are both recognized in the income statement.

If the bond is classified as an *available-for-sale* security, the bond is reported on the balance sheet at $980,000. Interest income of $60,000 is recognized in the income statement. The $20,000 unrealized loss is not recognized in the income statement. Rather, it is reported as a change in stockholders' equity.

LOS 33.h: List and explain the components of owners' equity.

Owners' equity is the residual interest in assets that remains after subtracting an entity's liabilities. The owners' equity section of the balance sheet includes contributed capital, any minority (noncontrolling) interest, retained earnings, treasury stock, and accumulated other comprehensive income.

Contributed capital is the total amount paid in by the common and preferred shareholders. Preferred shareholders have certain rights and privileges not possessed by the common shareholders. For example, preferred shareholders are paid dividends at a specified rate, usually expressed as a percentage of their par values, and have priority over the claims of the common shareholders in the event of liquidation.

The par value of common stock and preferred stock is a "stated" or "legal" value. Par value has no relationship to fair value. Some common shares are even issued without a par value. When par value exists, it is reported separately in stockholders' equity.

Also disclosed is the number of common shares that are authorized, issued, and outstanding. **Authorized shares** are the number of shares that may be sold under the firm's articles of incorporation. **Issued shares** are the number of shares that have actually been sold to shareholders. The number of **outstanding shares** is equal to the issued shares less shares that have been reacquired by the firm (i.e., treasury stock).

Minority interest (noncontrolling interest) is the minority shareholders' pro-rata share of the net assets (equity) of a subsidiary that is not wholly owned by the parent.

Retained earnings are the undistributed earnings (net income) of the firm since inception, the cumulative earnings that have not been paid out to shareholders as dividends.

Treasury stock is stock that has been reacquired by the issuing firm but not yet retired. Treasury stock reduces stockholders' equity. It does not represent an investment in the firm. Treasury stock has no voting rights and does not receive dividends.

Accumulated other comprehensive income includes all changes in stockholders' equity except for transactions recognized in the income statement (net income) and transactions with shareholders, such as issuing stock, reacquiring stock, and paying dividends.

As discussed in the topic review on understanding the income statement, comprehensive income aggregates net income and certain special transactions that are not reported in the income statement but that affect stockholders' equity. These special transactions comprise what is known as "other comprehensive income." Comprehensive income is equal to net income plus other comprehensive income.

Professor's Note: It is easy to confuse the two terms "comprehensive income" and "accumulated other comprehensive income." Comprehensive income is an income measure over a period of time. It includes net income and other comprehensive income for the period. Accumulated other comprehensive income does not include net income but is a component of stockholders' equity at a point in time.

Under U.S. GAAP, the firm can report comprehensive income in the income statement (below net income), in a separate statement of comprehensive income, or in the statement of changes in stockholders' equity. Firms are not required to report comprehensive income under IFRS.

LOS 33.i: Interpret balance sheets, common-size balance sheets, the statement of changes in equity, and commonly used balance sheet ratios.

The statement of changes in stockholders' equity summarizes all transactions that increase or decrease the equity accounts for the period. The statement includes transactions with shareholders, and a reconciliation of the beginning and ending balance of each equity account, including capital stock, additional paid-in-capital, retained earnings, and accumulated other comprehensive income. In addition, the components of accumulated other comprehensive income are disclosed (i.e., unrealized gains and losses from available-for-sale securities, cash flow hedging derivatives, foreign currency translation, and adjustments for minimum pension liability).

A statement of changes in stockholders' equity is illustrated in Figure 5.

Figure 5: Sample Statement of Changes in Stockholders' Equity

	Common Stock	Retained Earnings (in thousands)	Accumulated Other Comprehensive Income (loss)	Total
Beginning balance	$49,234	$26,664	($406)	$75,492
Net income		6,994		6,994
Net unrealized loss on available-for-sale securities			(40)	(40)
Net unrealized loss on cash flow hedges			(56)	(56)
Minimum pension liability			(26)	(26)
Cumulative translation adjustment			42	42
Comprehensive income				6,914
Issuance of common stock	1,282			1,282
Repurchases of common stock	(6,200)			(6,200)
Dividends		(2,360)		(2,360)
Ending balance	$44,316	$31,298	($486)	$75,128

Common-Size Balance Sheets

As with the income statement, common-size balance sheets and ratios can facilitate analysis of a firm.

A **common-size balance sheet** expresses each balance sheet account as a percentage of total assets. This format is known as *vertical common-size analysis* and allows the analyst to evaluate the balance sheet items over time (time-series analysis), as well as to compare a firm's balance sheet items to those of other firms, industry averages, and sector data (cross-sectional analysis). Several commercial services provide data for comparison.

Commonly Used Balance Sheet Ratios

Liquidity ratios and solvency ratios are considered pure balance sheet ratios since both the numerator and denominator are from the balance sheet. **Liquidity ratios** measure the firm's ability to satisfy short-term obligations when due. **Solvency ratios** measure the firm's ability to satisfy long-term obligations.

Liquidity ratios

The **current ratio** is the best known measure of liquidity.

$$\text{current ratio} = \frac{\text{current assets}}{\text{current liabilities}}$$

A current ratio of less than one means that the firm has negative working capital and may be facing a liquidity crisis. Working capital is equal to current assets minus current liabilities.

The **quick ratio** (acid test ratio) is a more conservative measure of liquidity because it excludes inventories and less liquid current assets from the numerator.

$$\text{quick ratio} = \frac{\text{cash} + \text{marketable securities} + \text{receivables}}{\text{current liabilities}}$$

The **cash ratio** is the most conservative measure of liquidity.

$$\text{cash ratio} = \frac{\text{cash} + \text{marketable securities}}{\text{current liabilities}}$$

The higher the liquidity ratios, the more likely the firm will be able to pay its short-term bills when they are due. The ratios differ only in the assumed liquidity of the current assets.

Solvency ratios

The following ratios measure financial risk and leverage. With all four ratios, the higher the ratio, the greater the leverage and the greater the risk.

The **long-term debt-to-equity ratio** measures long-term financing sources relative to the equity base.

$$\text{long-term debt-to-equity} = \frac{\text{total long-term debt}}{\text{total equity}}$$

The **debt-to-equity ratio** measures total debt relative to the equity base.

$$\text{debt-to-equity} = \frac{\text{total debt}}{\text{total equity}}$$

The **total debt ratio** measures the extent to which assets are financed by creditors.

$$\text{total debt ratio} = \frac{\text{total debt}}{\text{total assets}}$$

The **financial leverage ratio** is a variation of the debt-to-equity ratio that is used as a component of the DuPont model.

$$\text{financial leverage} = \frac{\text{total assets}}{\text{total equity}}$$

 Professor's Note: More detail on the precise definitions and calculation of commonly used financial ratios is presented in a subsequent topic review.

Usefulness and limitations of ratio analysis

Even in forward-looking "efficient markets" (where securities prices reflect all available information), financial ratios based on backward-looking data provide useful information to analysts. Specifically, ratios provide the following:

- Insights into the financial relationships that are useful in forecasting future earnings and cash flows.
- Information about the financial flexibility of the firm.
- A means of evaluating management's performance.

Financial ratios are not without limitations:

- Ratios are not useful when viewed in isolation.
- Comparisons with other companies are made more difficult because of different accounting methods. Some of the more common differences include inventory methods (FIFO and LIFO), depreciation methods (accelerated and straight-line), and lease accounting (capital and operating).
- There may be difficulty in locating comparable ratios when analyzing companies that operate in multiple industries.
- Conclusions cannot be made from viewing one set of ratios. Ratios must be viewed relative to one another over time, between companies or relative to benchmark values.
- Judgment is required. Determining the target or comparison value for a ratio is difficult and may actually be some range of acceptable values rather than a single target value.

KEY CONCEPTS

1. Assets are probable future economic benefits owned or controlled by an entity as a result of previous transactions.

2. Liabilities are obligations owed by an entity from previous transactions that are expected to result in an outflow of economic benefits in the future.

3. Stockholders' equity is the residual interest in assets that remains after subtracting an entity's liabilities. Equity = assets – liabilities.

4. Assets and liabilities are created from business transactions and because of the accrual method of accounting.

5. Current and noncurrent classifications are based on a 1-year period or the firm's operating cycle, whichever is greater.

6. The balance sheet is a mixture of historical costs and fair values.

7. Accounts receivable are reported at net realizable value (based on management's estimates of collectibility).

8. Inventory is reported at the lower of cost or net realizable value.

9. Noncurrent assets are reported at their historical costs less accumulated depreciation.

10. Accounting goodwill is equal to the excess of purchase price minus the fair value of the net assets acquired in a business acquisition. Goodwill is not amortized but is tested for impairment at least annually.

11. Held-to-maturity securities are reported at amortized cost.

12. Trading securities are reported at fair value, and any unrealized gains and losses are reported in net income.

13. Available-for-sale securities are reported at fair value, and the unrealized gains and losses are reported as a component of stockholders' equity.

14. Retained earnings are the cumulative undistributed earnings of the firm since inception.

15. Accumulated other comprehensive income includes all changes to equity from sources other than net income and transactions with shareholders.

16. A common-size balance sheet expresses each balance sheet item as a percentage of total assets.

17. Liquidity ratios include the current ratio, the quick ratio, and the cash ratio.

18. Solvency ratios include the long-term debt-to-equity ratio, the debt-to-equity ratio, the debt ratio, and the financial leverage ratio.

19. Comparisons of ratios among firms may be difficult because of different accounting methods and the judgment and estimates that are involved.

CONCEPT CHECKERS

1. Which of the following is *most likely* an essential characteristic of an asset?
    A. An asset is tangible.
    B. An asset is obtained at a cost.
    C. The claims to an asset's benefits are legally enforceable.
    D. An asset provides future benefits.

2. Which of the following is *least likely* a satisfactory statement of the balance sheet equation?
    A. stockholders' equity = assets – liabilities.
    B. assets = liabilities + stockholders' equity.
    C. liabilities = assets – stockholders' equity.
    D. assets = liabilities – stockholders' equity.

3. Century Company's balance sheet follows:

    Century Company
    Balance Sheet
    (in millions)

	20X7	20X6
Current assets	$340	$280
Noncurrent assets	660	630
Total assets	$1,000	$910
Current liabilities	$170	$110
Noncurrent liabilities	50	50
Total liabilities	$220	$160
Equity	$780	$750
Total liabilities and equity	$1,000	$910

    Is Century's balance sheet presentation an example of a report format and is the balance sheet a classified presentation?

	Report format	Classified
A.	Yes	No
B.	Yes	Yes
C.	No	No
D.	No	Yes

4. At the beginning of the year, Tenant Company paid its annual operating lease obligation in advance. What is the immediate impact of this transaction on Tenants' total assets and total liabilities?

	Assets	Liabilities
A.	No effect	No effect
B.	No effect	Decrease
C.	Increase	No effect
D.	Increase	Decrease

5. How should the proceeds received from the advance sale of tickets to a sporting event be treated by the seller, assuming the tickets are nonrefundable?
   A. Unearned revenue is recognized to the extent that costs have been incurred.
   B. Revenue is recognized to the extent that costs have been incurred.
   C. Revenue is deferred until the sporting event is held.
   D. Revenue is recognized as the tickets are sold.

6. Which of the following would *most likely* result in a current liability?
   A. Probable bankruptcy of an important customer whose account is already delinquent.
   B. Estimated income taxes for the current year.
   C. Possible warranty claims.
   D. Future operating lease payments.

7. Which of the following inventory valuation methods is required according to the Financial Accounting Standards Board?
   A. Lower-of-cost-or-net-realizable-value.
   B. Weighted average cost.
   C. Last-in, First-out.
   D. First-in, First-out.

8. SF Corporation has created employee goodwill by reorganizing its retirement benefit package. An independent management consultant estimated the value of the goodwill at $2 million. In addition, SF recently purchased a patent that was developed by a competitor. The patent has an estimated useful life of five years. Should SF report the goodwill and patent on its balance sheet?

	Goodwill	Patent
A.	Yes	Yes
B.	Yes	No
C.	No	Yes
D.	No	No

9. At the beginning of the year, Parent Company purchased all 500,000 shares of Sub Incorporated for $15 per share. Just before the acquisition date, Sub's balance sheet reported net assets of $6 million. Parent determined the fair value of Sub's property and equipment was $1 million higher than reported by Sub. What amount of goodwill should Parent report as a result of its acquisition of Sub?
   A. $0.
   B. $500,000.
   C. $750,000.
   D. $1,500,000.

10.   Which of the following is *least likely* to be disclosed in the financial statement footnotes?
       A. Revenue recognition policies and other accounting methods.
       B. Fair value of noncurrent assets used in the production of income.
       C. Contingencies and commitments.
       D. Off-balance-sheet financing.

Use the following information to answer Questions 11 and 12.

At the beginning of the year, Company P purchased 1,000 shares of Company S for $80 per share. During the year, Company S paid a dividend of $4 per share. At the end of the year, Company S's share price was $75.

11.   What amount should Company P report on its balance sheet at year-end if the investment in Company S is considered a trading security, and what amount should be reported if the investment is considered an available-for-sale security?

	Trading	Available-for-sale
A.	$75,000	$75,000
B.	$75,000	$80,000
C.	$80,000	$75,000
D.	$80,000	$80,000

12.   What amount of investment income should Company P recognize in its income statement if the investment in Company S is considered trading and what amount should be recognized if the investment is considered available-for-sale?

	Trading	Available-for-sale
A.	($1,000)	($1,000)
B.	($1,000)	$4,000
C.	($5,000)	($1,000)
D.	($5,000)	$4,000

13.   Miller Corporation has 160,000 shares of common stock authorized. There are 92,000 shares issued and 84,000 shares outstanding. How many shares of treasury stock does Miller own?
       A. 0.
       B. 8,000.
       C. 68,000
       D. 76,000.

14.   Selected data from Alpha Company's balance sheet at the end of the year
       follows:

Investment in Beta Company, at fair value	$150,000
Deferred taxes	$86,000
Common stock, $1 par value	$550,000
Preferred stock, $100 par value	$175,000
Retained earnings	$893,000
Accumulated other comprehensive income	$46,000

The investment in Beta Company had an original cost of $120,000. Assuming
the investment in Beta is classified as available-for-sale, Alpha's total owners'
equity at year-end is *closest* to:
A. $1,568,000.
B. $1,618,000.
C. $1,664,000.
D. $1,714,000.

15.   How would the collection of accounts receivable *most likely* affect the current
       and cash ratios?

	Current ratio	Cash ratio
A.	Increase	Increase
B.	Increase	No effect
C.	No effect	Increase
D.	No effect	No effect

16.   Comparing a company's ratios with those of its competitors is known as:
A. Longitudinal analysis.
B. Common-size analysis.
C. Time-series analysis.
D. Cross-sectional analysis.

ANSWERS – CONCEPT CHECKERS

1. **D** An asset is a future economic benefit obtained or controlled as a result of past transactions. Some assets are intangible (e.g., goodwill) and others may be donated.

2. **D** Assets must equal liabilities plus stockholders' equity. Otherwise, the balance sheet would not balance.

3. **B** In a report format, the assets, liabilities, and equity are presented in one column. A classified balance sheet groups together similar items (e.g., current and noncurrent assets and liabilities) to arrive at significant subtotals.

4. **A** Tenant has simply prepaid its annual payment; rent expense has not yet been incurred. When cash is paid in advance of recognizing an expense, one asset (cash) decreases and another asset (prepaid expenses) increases by the same amount. Liabilities are not affected.

5. **C** The ticket revenue should not be recognized until it is earned. Even though the tickets are nonrefundable, the seller is still obligated to hold the event.

6. **B** Estimated income taxes for the current year are likely reported as a current liability. To recognize the warranty expense, it must be probable, not just possible. Future operating lease payments are not reported on the balance sheet. The bankruptcy of a customer would affect assets (receivables), not liabilities.

7. **A** The lower-of-cost-or-net-realizable-value is the inventory valuation method required under U.S. GAAP. LIFO, FIFO, and average cost are the inventory cost flow assumptions among which a firm has a choice.

8. **C** Goodwill developed internally is expensed as incurred. The purchased patent is reported on the balance sheet.

9. **B** Purchase price of $7,500,000 [$15 per share × 500,000 shares] – Fair value of net assets of $7,000,000 [$6,000,000 book value + $1,000,000 increase in property and equipment] = Goodwill of $500,000.

10. **B** Property and equipment (i.e., noncurrent assets used in the production of income) is reported at original cost less accumulated depreciation. There is no requirement to disclose the fair value in the footnotes.

11. **A** Both trading securities and available-for-sale securities are reported on the balance sheet at their fair values. At year-end, the fair value is $75,000 [$75 per share × 1,000 shares].

12. **B** A loss of $1,000 is recognized if the securities are considered trading securities [$4 dividend × $1,000 shares) – ($5 unrealized loss × 1,000 shares)]. Income is $4,000 if the investment in Company S is considered available-for-sale [$4 dividend × $1,000].

13. **B** The difference between the issued shares and the outstanding shares is the treasury shares.

14. **C** Total stockholders' equity consists of common stock of $550,000, preferred stock of $175,000, retained earnings of $893,000, and accumulated other comprehensive

income of $46,000, for a total of $1,644,000. The $30,000 unrealized gain from the investment in Beta is already included in accumulated other comprehensive income.

15. **C** The collection of accounts receivable would increase cash and decrease accounts receivable. Thus, current assets would not change and the current ratio would remain the same. Since the numerator of the cash ratio only includes cash and marketable securities, the collection of receivables would increase the cash ratio.

16. **D** Comparing ratios of a firm to those of its competitors is known as cross-sectional analysis.

The following is a review of the Financial Statement Analysis principles designed to address the learning outcome statements set forth by CFA Institute®. This topic is also covered in:

UNDERSTANDING THE CASH FLOW STATEMENT

EXAM FOCUS

This topic review covers the third important required financial statement, the statement of cash flows. Since the income statement is based on the accrual method, net income may not represent cash generated from operations. A company may be generating positive and growing net income, but may be headed for insolvency because insufficient cash is being generated from operating activities. Constructing a statement of cash flows, by either the direct or indirect method, is therefore very important in an analysis of a firm's activities and prospects. Make sure you understand the preparation of a statement of cash flows by either method, the classification of various cash flows as operating, financing, or investing cash flows, and the key differences in these classifications between U.S. GAAP and international accounting standards. This is very testable material, and you should expect several questions based on it.

THE CASH FLOW STATEMENT

The **cash flow statement** provides information beyond that available from the income statement, which is based on accrual, rather than cash, accounting. The cash flow statement provides the following:

- Information about a company's cash receipts and cash payments during an accounting period.
- Information about a company's operating, investing, and financing activities.
- An understanding of the impact of accrual accounting events on cash flows.

The cash flow statement provides information to assess the firm's liquidity, solvency, and financial flexibility. An analyst can use the statement of cash flows to determine whether:

- Regular operations generate enough cash to sustain the business.
- Enough cash is generated to pay off existing debts as they mature.
- The firm is likely to need additional financing.
- Unexpected obligations can be met.
- The firm can take advantage of new business opportunities as they arise.

LOS 34.a: Compare and contrast cash flows from operating, investing, and financing activities, and classify cash flow items as relating to one of these three categories, given a description of the items.

Items on the cash flow statement come from two sources: (1) income statement items and (2) changes in balance sheet accounts. A firm's cash receipts and payments are classified on the cash flow statement as either operating, investing, or financing activities.

Cash flow from operating activities (CFO), sometimes referred to as "cash flow from operations" or "operating cash flow," consists of the inflows and outflows of cash resulting from transactions that affect a firm's net income.

Cash flow from investing activities (CFI) consists of the inflows and outflows of cash resulting from the acquisition or disposal of long-term assets and certain investments.

Cash flow from financing activities (CFF) consists of the inflows and outflows of cash resulting from transactions affecting a firm's capital structure.

Examples of each cash flow classification, in accordance with U.S. GAAP, are presented in Figure 1.

Figure 1: U.S. GAAP Cash Flow Classifications

Operating Activities

Inflows	*Outflows*
Cash collected from customers	Cash paid to employees and suppliers
Interest and dividends received	Cash paid for other expenses
Sale proceeds from trading securities	Acquisition of trading securities
	Interest paid
	Taxes paid

Investing Activities

Inflows	*Outflows*
Sale proceeds from fixed assets	Acquisition of fixed assets
Sale proceeds from debt & equity investments	Acquisition of debt & equity investments
Principal received from loans made to others	Loans made to others

Financing Activities

Inflows	*Outflows*
Principal amounts of debt issued	Principal paid on debt
Proceeds from issuing stock	Payments to reacquire stock
	Dividends paid to shareholders

Note that the acquisition of debt and equity investments (other than trading securities) and loans made to others are reported as investing activities; however, the income from these investments (interest and dividends received) is reported as an operating activity. Also, note that principal amounts borrowed from others are reported as financing activities; however, the interest paid is reported as an operating activity. Finally, note that dividends paid to the firm's shareholders are financing activities.

 Professor's Note: Don't confuse dividends received and dividends paid. Under U.S. GAAP, dividends received are operating activities and dividends paid are financing activities.

LOS 34.b: Describe how noncash investing and financing activities are reported.

Noncash investing and financing activities are not reported in the cash flow statement since they do not result in inflows or outflows of cash.

For example, if a firm acquires real estate with financing provided by the seller, the firm has made an investing and financing decision. This transaction is the equivalent of borrowing the purchase price. However, since no cash is involved in the transaction, it is not reported as an investing and financing activity in the cash flow statement.

Another example of a noncash transaction is an exchange of debt for equity. Such an exchange results in a reduction of debt and an increase in equity. However, since no cash is involved in the transaction, it is not reported as a financing activity in the cash flow statement.

Noncash transactions must be disclosed in either a footnote or supplemental schedule to the cash flow statement. Analysts should be aware of the firm's noncash transactions, incorporate them into analysis of past and current performance, and include their effects in estimating future cash flows.

LOS 34.c: Compare and contrast the key differences in cash flow statements prepared under international financial reporting standards and U.S. generally accepted accounting principles.

Recall from Figure 1 that under U.S. GAAP, dividends paid to the firm's shareholders are reported as financing activities while interest paid is reported in operating activities. Interest received and dividends received from investments are also reported as operating activities.

International Financial Reporting Standards (IFRS) allow more flexibility in the classification of cash flows. Under IFRS, interest and dividends received may be classified as either operating *or* investing activities. Dividends paid to the company's shareholders and interest paid on the company's debt may be classified as either operating *or* financing activities.

Another important difference relates to income taxes paid. Under U.S. GAAP, all taxes paid are reported as operating activities, even taxes related to investing and financing transactions. Under IFRS, income taxes are also reported as operating activities unless the expense is associated with an investing or financing transaction.

For example, consider a company that sells land that was held for investment for $1 million. Income taxes on the sale total $160,000. Under U.S. GAAP, the firm reports an inflow of cash from investing activities of $1 million and an outflow of cash from operating activities of $160,000. Under IFRS, the firm can report a net inflow of $840,000 from investing activities.

LOS 34.d: Demonstrate the difference between the direct and indirect methods of presenting cash from operating activities and explain the arguments in favor of each.

There are two methods of presenting the cash flow statement: the direct method and the indirect method. Both methods are permitted under U.S. GAAP and IFRS. The use of the direct method, however, is encouraged by both standard setters. The difference in the two methods relates to the presentation of cash flow from operating activities. The presentation of cash flows from investing activities and financing activities is exactly the same under both methods.

Direct Method

Under the direct method, each line item of the accrual-based income statement is converted into cash receipts or cash payments. Recall that under the accrual method of accounting, the timing of revenue and expense recognition may differ from the timing of the related cash flows. Under cash-basis accounting, revenue and expense recognition occur when cash is received or paid. Simply stated, the direct method converts an accrual-basis income statement into a cash-basis income statement.

Figure 2 contains an example of a presentation of operating cash flow for Seagraves Supply Company using the direct method.

Figure 2: Direct Method of Presenting Operating Cash Flow

Seagraves Supply Company Operating Cash Flow – Direct Method For the year ended December 31, 20X7	
Cash collections from customers	$429,980
Cash paid to suppliers	(265,866)
Cash paid for operating expenses	(124,784)
Cash paid for interest	(4,326)
Cash paid for taxes	(14,956)
Operating cash flow	$20,048

Notice the similarities of the direct method cash flow presentation and an income statement. The direct method begins with cash inflows from customers and then deducts cash outflows for purchases, operating expenses, interest, and taxes.

Indirect Method

Under the **indirect method**, net income is converted to operating cash flow by making adjustments for transactions that affect net income but are not cash transactions. These adjustments include eliminating noncash expenses (e.g., depreciation and amortization), nonoperating items (e.g., gains and losses), and changes in balance sheet accounts resulting from accrual accounting events.

Figure 3 contains an example of a presentation of operating cash flow for Seagraves Supply Company under the indirect method.

Figure 3: Indirect Method of Presenting Operating Cash Flow

Seagraves Supply Company *Operating Cash Flow – Indirect Method* *For the year ended December 31, 20X7*	
Net income	$18,788
Adjustments to reconcile net income to cash flow provided by operating activities:	
Depreciation and amortization	7,996
Deferred income taxes	416
Increase in accounts receivable	(1,220)
Increase in inventory	(20,544)
Decrease in prepaid expenses	494
Increase in accounts payable	13,406
Increase in accrued liabilities	712
Operating cash flow	$20,048

Notice that under the indirect method, the starting point is net income, the "bottom line" of the income statement. Under the direct method the starting point is the top of the income statement, revenues, adjusted to show cash received from customers. Total cash flow from operating activities is exactly the same under both methods, only the presentation methods differ.

Arguments in Favor of Each Method

The primary advantage of the direct method is that it presents the firm's operating cash receipts and payments, while the indirect method only presents the net result of these receipts and payments. Therefore, the direct method provides more information than the indirect method. This knowledge of past receipts and payments is useful in estimating future operating cash flows.

The main advantage of the indirect method is that it focuses on the differences in net income and operating cash flow. This provides a useful link to the income statement when forecasting future operating cash flow. Analysts forecast net income and then derive operating cash flow by adjusting net income for the differences between accrual accounting and the cash basis of accounting.

Disclosure requirements

Under U.S. GAAP, a direct method presentation must also disclose the adjustments necessary to reconcile net income to cash flow from operating activities. This disclosure is the same information that is presented in an indirect method cash flow statement. This reconciliation is not required under IFRS.

Under IFRS, payments for interest and taxes must be disclosed separately in the cash flow statement under either method (direct or indirect). Under U.S. GAAP, payments for interest and taxes can be reported in the cash flow statement or disclosed in the footnotes.

LOS 34.e: Demonstrate how the cash flow statement is linked to the income statement and balance sheet.

The cash flow statement reconciles the beginning and ending balances of cash over an accounting period. The change in cash is a result of the firm's operating, investing, and financing activities as follows:

$$
\begin{array}{cl}
 & \text{Operating cash flow} \\
+ & \text{Investing cash flow} \\
+ & \underline{\text{Financing cash flow}} \\
= & \text{Change in cash balance} \\
+ & \underline{\text{Beginning cash balance}} \\
= & \text{Ending cash balance}
\end{array}
$$

It is important to understand that net income, based on accrual accounting, is not the same thing as cash earnings. When the timing of revenue or expense recognition differs from the receipt or payment of cash, it is reflected in changes in balance sheet accounts.

For example, when revenues (sales) exceed cash collections, accounts receivable increase. The opposite occurs when cash collections exceed revenues; accounts receivable (an asset) decrease. When purchases from suppliers exceed cash payments, accounts payable (a liability) increase. When cash payments exceed purchases, payables decrease.

Investing activities typically relate to the firm's noncurrent assets, while financing activities typically relate to the firm's noncurrent liabilities and equity.

Each balance sheet account can be analyzed in terms of the transactions that increase or decrease the account over a period of time. For example, the following is a reconciliation of inventory:

$$
\begin{array}{cl}
 & \text{Beginning inventory balance} \\
+ & \text{Inventory purchases} \\
- & \underline{\text{Cost of goods sold}} \\
= & \text{Ending inventory balance}
\end{array}
$$

Professor's Note: Given three of the four variables in the above reconciliation, it is easy to solve for the fourth. This type of analysis can be applied to any balance sheet account as long as you know which transactions increase and which transactions decrease the account.

The firm's balance sheet, income statement, and cash flow statement are all related. Understanding these relationships is important for analytical purposes, as well as for detecting possible aggressive accounting practices.

LOS 34.f: Demonstrate the steps in the preparation of direct and indirect cash flow statements, including how cash flows can be computed using income statement and balance sheet data.

Professor's Note: Throughout the discussion of the direct and indirect methods, remember the following points:

- *CFO is calculated differently, but the result is the same under both methods.*
- *The calculation of CFI and CFF is identical under both methods.*
- *There is an inverse relationship between changes in assets and changes in cash flows. In other words, an increase in an asset account is a use of cash, and a decrease in an asset account is a source of cash.*
- *There is a direct relationship between changes in liabilities and changes in cash flow. In other words, an increase in a liability account is a source of cash, and a decrease in a liability is a use of cash.*
- *Sources of cash are positive numbers (cash inflows) and uses of cash are negative numbers (cash outflows).*

Direct Method

The direct method presents operating cash flow by taking each item from the income statement and converting it to its cash equivalent by adding or subtracting the changes in the associated balance sheet accounts. Footnotes are often helpful in learning how inflows and outflows have affected the balance sheet accounts. The following are common examples of operating cash flow components:

- Cash collected from customers is typically the main component of CFO. Cash collections are calculated by adjusting sales revenues for changes in accounts receivable and changes in unearned (deferred) revenue.
- Cash used in the production of goods and services (cash inputs) is calculated by adjusting cost of goods sold (COGS) for any change in inventory and any change in accounts payable.
- Cash operating expenses are calculated by adjusting selling, general, and administrative (SG&A) expenses for the changes in any related accrued liabilities and/or prepaid expenses.
- Cash paid for interest is calculated by adjusting interest expense for any change in interest payable.
- Cash paid for taxes is calculated by adjusting income tax expense for any change in taxes payable and/or deferred taxes.

Professor's Note: A common "trick" in direct method questions is to provide information on depreciation expense along with other operating cash flow components. When using the direct method, ignore depreciation expense—it's a noncash charge. We'll see later that we do consider depreciation expense in indirect method computations, but we do this solely because depreciation expense and other noncash expenses have been subtracted in calculating net income (our starting point) and need to be added back to get cash flow.

Investing cash flows (CFI) are calculated by examining the change in the gross asset accounts that result from investing activities, such as property, plant, and equipment, intangible assets, and investment securities. Related accumulated depreciation or amortization accounts are ignored since they do not represent cash expenses.

Professor's Note: In this context, "gross" simply means an amount that is presented on the balance sheet before deducting any accumulated depreciation or amortization.//

When calculating cash paid for a new asset, it is necessary to determine whether old assets were sold. If assets were sold during the period, you must use the following formula:

cash paid for new asset = ending gross assets + gross cost of old assets sold – beginning gross assets

Professor's Note: It may be easier to think in terms of the account reconciliation format discussed earlier. That is, beginning gross assets + cash paid for new assets – gross cost of assets sold = ending gross assets. Given three of the variables, simply solve for the fourth.

When calculating the cash flow from an asset that has been sold, it is necessary to consider any gain or loss from the sale using the following formula:

cash from asset sold = book value of the asset + gain (or – loss) on sale

Financing cash flows (CFF) are determined by measuring the cash flows occurring between the firm and its suppliers of capital. Cash flows between the firm and its creditors result from new borrowings (positive CFF) and debt principal repayments (negative CFF). Note that interest paid is technically a cash flow to creditors, but it is included in CFO under U.S. GAAP. Cash flows between the firm and its shareholders occur when equity is issued, shares are repurchased, or dividends are paid. CFF is the sum of these two measures:

net cash flows from creditors = new borrowings – principal amounts repaid

net cash flows from shareholders = new equity issued – share repurchases – cash dividends paid

Cash dividends paid can be calculated from dividends declared and any changes in dividends payable.

Finally, total cash flow is equal to the sum of CFO, CFI, and CFF. If calculated correctly, the total cash flow will equal the change in cash from one balance sheet to the next.

Example: Direct method for computing CFO

Prepare a cash flow statement using the direct method for a company with the following income statement and balance sheets.

Income Statement for 20X7

Sales	$100,000
Expenses	
Cost of goods sold	$40,000
Wages	5,000
Depreciation	7,000
Interest	500
Total expenses	$52,500
Income from continuing operations	$47,500
Gain from sale of land	10,000
Pretax income	57,500
Provision for taxes	20,000
Net income	$37,500
Common dividends declared	$8,500

Balance Sheets for 20X7 and 20X6

	20X7	20X6
Assets		
Current assets		
Cash	$33,000	$9,000
Accounts receivable	10,000	9,000
Inventory	5,000	7,000
Noncurrent assets		
Land	$35,000	$40,000
Gross plant and equipment	85,000	60,000
less: Accumulated depreciation	(16,000)	(9,000)
Net plant and equipment	$69,000	$51,000
Goodwill	10,000	10,000
Total assets	$162,000	$126,000
Liabilities		
Current liabilities		
Accounts payable	$9,000	$5,000
Wages payable	4,500	8,000
Interest payable	3,500	3,000
Taxes payable	5,000	4,000

Dividends payable	6,000	1,000
Total current liabilities	28,000	21,000
Noncurrent liabilities		
Bonds	$15,000	$10,000
Deferred tax liability	20,000	15,000
Total liabilities	$63,000	$46,000
Stockholders' equity		
Common stock	$40,000	$50,000
Retained earnings	59,000	30,000
Total equity	$99,000	$80,000
Total liabilities & stockholders' equity	$162,000	$126,000

Answer:

Professor's Note: There are many ways to think about these calculations and lots of sources and uses and pluses and minuses to keep track of. It's easier if you use a "+" sign for net sales and a "−" sign for cost of goods sold and other cash expenses used as the starting points. Doing so will allow you to consistently follow the rule that an increase in assets or decrease in liabilities is a use of cash and a decrease in assets or an increase in liabilities is a source. We'll use this approach in the answer to the example. Remember, sources are always + and uses are always −.

The calculations that follow include a reconciliation of each account, analyzing the transactions that increase and decrease the account for the period. As previously discussed, this reconciliation is useful in understanding the interrelationships between the balance sheet, income statement, and cash flow statement.

Cash from operations:

Keep track of the balance sheet items used to calculate CFO by marking them off the balance sheet. They will not be needed again when determining CFI and CFF.

cash collections = sales − increase in accounts receivable = $100,000 − $1,000 = $99,000

beginning receivables + sales − cash collections = ending receivables = $9,000 + $100,000 − $99,000 = $10,000

cash paid to suppliers = – COGS + decrease in inventory + increase in accounts payable = –$40,000 + $2,000 + $4,000 = –$34,000

beginning inventory + purchases – COGS = ending inventory = $7,000 + $38,000 (not provided) – $40,000 = $5,000

beginning accounts payable + purchases – cash paid to suppliers = ending accounts payable = $5,000 + $38,000 (not provided) – $34,000 = $9,000

cash wages = – wages – decrease in wages payable = –$5,000 – $3,500 = –$8,500

beginning wages payable + wages expense – wages paid = ending wages payable = $8,000 + $5,000 – $8,500 = $4,500

cash interest = – interest expense + increase in interest payable = –$500 + $500 = 0

beginning interest payable + interest expense – interest paid = ending interest payable = $3,000 + $500 – $0 = $3,500

cash taxes = – tax expense + increase in taxes payable + increase in deferred tax liability

= –$20,000 + $1,000 + $5,000 = –$14,000

beginning taxes payable + beginning deferred tax liability + tax expense – taxes paid = ending taxes payable + ending deferred tax liability = $4,000 + $15,000 + $20,000 – $14,000 = $5,000 + $20,000

Cash collections	$99,000
Cash to suppliers	(34,000)
Cash wages	(8,500)
Cash interest	0
Cash taxes	(14,000)
Cash flow from operations	$42,500

Investing cash flow:

In this example, we have two components of investing cash flow: the sale of land and the change in gross plant and equipment (P&E).

cash from sale of land = decrease in asset + gain on sale = $5,000 + $10,000 = $15,000 (source)

    beginning land + land purchased – gross cost of land sold = ending land = $40,000 + $0 – $5,000 = $35,000

Note: If the land had been sold at a loss, we would have subtracted the loss amount from the decrease in land.

P&E purchased = ending gross P&E + gross cost of P&E sold – beginning gross P&E
        = $85,000 + $0 – $60,000 = $25,000 (use)

    beginning gross P&E + P&E purchased – gross cost of P&E sold = ending P&E
    = $60,000 + $25,000 – $0 = $85,000

Cash from sale of land	$15,000
Purchase of plant and equipment	(25,000)
Cash flow from investments	($10,000)

Financing cash flow:

cash from bond issue = ending bonds payable + bonds repaid – beginning bonds payable = $15,000 + $0 – $10,000 = $5,000 (source)

    beginning bonds payable + bonds issued – bonds repaid = ending bonds payable
    = $10,000 + $5,000 – $0 = $15,000

cash to reacquire stock = beginning common stock + stock issued – ending common stock = $50,000 + $0 – $40,000 = $10,000 (use, or a net share repurchase of $10,000)

    beginning common stock + stock issued – stock reacquired = ending common stock = $50,000 + $0 – $10,000 = $40,000

cash dividends = – dividend declared + increase in dividends payable
        = –$8,500* + $5,000 = –$3,500 (use)

    beginning dividends payable + dividends declared – dividends paid = ending dividends payable = $1,000 + $8,500 – $3,500 = $6,000

*Note: If the dividend declared amount is not provided, you can calculate the amount as follows: dividends declared = beginning retained earnings + net income – ending retained earnings. Here, $30,000 + $37,500 – $59,000 = $8,500.

Sale of bonds	$5,000
Repurchase of stock	(10,000)
Cash dividends	(3,500)
Cash flow from financing	($8,500)

Total cash flow:

Cash flow from operations	$42,500
Cash flow from investments	(10,000)
Cash flow from financing	(8,500)
Total cash flow	$24,000

The total cash flow of $24,000 is equal to the increase in the cash account. The difference between beginning cash and ending cash should be used as a check figure to ensure that the total cash flow calculation is correct.

Indirect Method

The three components of cash flow under the indirect method are equal to the three components of cash flow as under the direct method. The only difference in presentation is that cash flow from operations is calculated in a different manner.

Using the indirect method, operating cash flow is calculated in four steps:

Step 1: Begin with net income.

Step 2: Subtract gains or add losses that resulted from financing or investing cash flows (such as gains from sale of land).

Step 3: Add back all noncash charges to income (such as depreciation and amortization) and subtract all noncash components of revenue.

Step 4: Add or subtract changes to balance sheet operating accounts as follows:

- Increases in the operating asset accounts (uses of cash) are subtracted, while decreases (sources of cash) are added.
- Increases in the operating liability accounts (sources of cash) are added, while decreases (uses of cash) are subtracted.

Cash flow from investing activities and cash flow from financing activities are calculated the same way as under the direct method. As was true for the direct method, total cash flow is equal to the sum of cash flow from operating activities, investing activities, and financing activities. If calculated correctly, the total cash flow will be equal to the change in the cash balance over the period.

Discrepancies between the changes in accounts reported on the balance sheet and those reported in the statement of cash flows are typically due to business combinations and changes in exchange rates.

Example: Indirect method for computing CFO

Calculate cash flow from operations using the indirect method for the same company in the previous example.

Answer:

Step 1: Start with net income of $37,500.

Step 2: Subtract gain from sale of land of $10,000.

Step 3: Add back noncash charges of depreciation of $7,000.

Step 4: Subtract increases in receivables and inventories and add increases of payables and deferred taxes.

Net income	$37,500
Gain from sale of land	(10,000)
Depreciation	7,000
Subtotal	$34,500
Changes in operating accounts	
Increase in receivables	($1,000)
Decrease in inventories	2,000
Increase in accounts payable	4,000
Decrease in wages payable	(3,500)
Increase in interest payable	500
Increase in taxes payable	1,000
Increase in deferred taxes	5,000
Cash flow from operations	$42,500

LOS 34.g: Describe the process of converting a statement of cash flows from the indirect to the direct method of presentation.

Most firms present the cash flow statement using the indirect method. For analysis, it may be beneficial to convert an indirect cash flow statement to a direct cash flow statement.

The only difference between the indirect and direct methods of presentation is in the cash flow from operations (CFO) section. CFO under the direct method can be computed using a combination of the income statement and a statement of cash flows prepared under the indirect method.

There are two major sections in CFO under the direct method: cash inflows (receipts) and cash outflows (payments). We will illustrate the conversion process using some frequently used accounts. Please note that the list below is for illustrative purposes only and is far from all-inclusive of what may be encountered in practice. The general principle here is to adjust each income statement item for its corresponding balance sheet accounts and to eliminate noncash and nonoperating transactions.

Cash collections from customers:

1. Begin with net sales from the income statement.

2. Subtract (add) any increase (decrease) in the accounts receivable balance as reported in the indirect method. If the company has sold more on credit than has been collected from customers, accounts receivable will increase and cash collections will be less than net sales.

3. Add (subtract) an increase (decrease) in unearned revenue. Unearned revenue includes cash advances from customers. Cash received from customers when the goods or services have yet to be delivered is not included in net sales, so the advances must be added to net sales in order to calculate cash collections.

Cash payments to suppliers:

1. Begin with cost of goods sold (COGS) as reported in the income statement.

2. If depreciation and/or amortization have been included in COGS (they increase COGS), these items must be added back to COGS when computing the cash paid to suppliers.

3. Reduce (increase) COGS by any increase (decrease) in the accounts payable balance as reported in the indirect method. If payables have increased, then more was spent on credit purchases during the period than was paid on existing payables, so cash payments are reduced by the amount of the increase in payables.

4. Add (subtract) any increase (decrease) in the inventory balance as disclosed in the indirect method. Increases in inventory are not included in COGS for the period but still represent the purchase of inputs, so they increase cash paid to suppliers.

5. Subtract an inventory write-off that occurred during the period. An inventory write-off, as a result of applying the lower of cost or market rule, will reduce ending inventory and increase COGS for the period. However, no cash flow is associated with the write-off.

Other items in a direct method cash flow statement follow the same principles. Cash taxes paid, for example, can be derived by starting with income tax expense on the income statement. Adjustment must be made for changes in related balance sheet accounts (deferred tax assets and liabilities, and income taxes payable).

Cash operating expense is equal to selling, general, and administrative expense (SG&A) from the income statement, increased (decreased) for any increase (decrease) in prepaid expenses. Any increase in prepaid expenses is a cash outflow that is not included in SG&A for the current period.

Professor's Note: Converting an indirect statement of cash flows to a direct statement of cash flows involves the same steps as constructing a direct statement from the income statement and balance sheets.

LOS 34.h: Analyze and interpret a cash flow statement using both total currency amounts and common-size cash flow statements.

Major Sources and Uses of Cash

Cash flow analysis begins with an evaluation of the firm's sources and uses of cash from operating, investing, and financing activities. Sources and uses of cash change as the firm moves through its life cycle. For example, when a firm is in the early stages of growth, it may experience negative operating cash flow as it uses cash to finance increases in inventory and receivables. This negative operating cash flow is usually financed externally by issuing debt or equity securities. These sources of financing are not sustainable. Eventually, the firm must begin generating positive operating cash flow or the sources of external capital may no longer be available. Over the long term, successful firms must be able to generate operating cash flows that exceed capital expenditures and provide a return to debt and equity holders.

Operating Cash Flow

An analyst should identify the major determinants of operating cash flow. Positive operating cash flow can be generated by the firm's earning-related activities. However, positive operating cash flow can also be generated by decreasing noncash working capital, such as liquidating inventory and receivables or increasing payables. Decreasing noncash working capital is not sustainable, since inventories and receivables cannot fall below zero and creditors will not extend credit indefinitely unless payments are made when due.

Operating cash flow also provides a check of the quality of a firm's earnings. A stable relationship of operating cash flow and net income is an indication of quality earnings. (This relationship can also be affected by the business cycle and the firm's life cycle.) Earnings that significantly exceed operating cash flow may be an indication of aggressive (or even improper) accounting choices such as recognizing revenues too soon or delaying the recognition of expenses. The variability of net income and operating cash flow should also be considered.

Investing Cash Flow

The sources and uses of cash from investing activities should be examined. Increasing capital expenditures, a use of cash, is usually an indication of growth. Conversely, a firm may reduce capital expenditures or even sell capital assets in order to save or generate cash. This may result in higher cash outflows in the future as older assets are replaced or growth resumes. As mentioned above, generating operating cash flow that exceeds capital expenditures is a desirable trait.

Financing Cash Flow

The financing activities section of the cash flow statement reveals information about whether the firm is generating cash flow by issuing debt or equity. It also provides information about whether the firm is using cash to repay debt, reacquire stock, or pay dividends. For example, an analyst would certainly want to know if a firm issued debt and used the proceeds to reacquire stock or pay dividends to shareholders.

Common-Size Cash Flow Statement

Like the income statement and balance sheet, common-size analysis can be used to analyze the cash flow statement.

The cash flow statement can be converted to common-size format by expressing each line item as a percentage of revenue. Alternatively, each inflow of cash can be expressed as a percentage of total cash inflows and each outflow of cash can be expressed as a percentage of total cash outflows.

Example: Common-size cash flow statement analysis

Triple Y Corporation's common-size cash flow statement is shown in the table below. Explain the decrease in Triple Y's total cash flow as a percentage of revenues.

Triple Y Corporation

Cash Flow Statement (Percent of Revenues)

Year	20X9	20X8	20X7
Net income	13.4%	13.4%	13.5%
Depreciation	4.0%	3.9%	3.9%
Accounts receivable	–0.6%	–0.6%	–0.5%
Inventory	–10.3%	–9.2%	–8.8%
Prepaid expenses	0.2%	–0.2%	0.1%
Accrued liabilities	5.5%	5.5%	5.6%
Operating cash flow	12.2%	12.8%	13.8%
Cash from sale of fixed assets	0.7%	0.7%	0.7%
Purchase of plant and equipment	–12.3%	–12.0%	–11.7%
Investing cash flow	–11.6%	–11.3%	–11.0%
Sale of bonds	2.6%	2.5%	2.6%
Cash dividends	–2.1%	–2.1%	–2.1%
Financing cash flow	0.5%	0.4%	0.5%
Total cash flow	1.1%	1.9%	3.3%

Answer:

Operating cash flow has decreased as a percentage of revenues. This appears to be due largely to accumulating inventories. Investing activities, specifically purchases of plant and equipment, have also required an increasing percentage of the firm's cash flow.

LOS 34.i: Explain and calculate free cash flow to the firm, free cash flow to equity, and other cash flow ratios.

Free cash flow is a measure of cash that is available for discretionary purposes. This is the cash flow that is available once the firm has covered its capital expenditures. This is a fundamental cash flow measure and is often used for valuation. There are measures of free cash flow. Two of the more common measures are free cash flow to the firm and free cash flow to equity.

Free Cash Flow to the Firm

Free cash flow to the firm (FCFF) is the cash available to all investors, both equity owners and debt holders. FCFF can be calculated by starting with either net income or operating cash flow.

FCFF is calculated from net income as:

$$FCFF = NI + NCC + [Int \times (1 - tax\ rate)] - FCInv - WCInv$$

where:
NI = net income
NCC = noncash charges (depreciation and amortization)
Int = interest expense
FCInv = fixed capital investment (net capital expenditures)
WCInv = working capital investment

Note that interest expense, net of tax, is added back to net income. This is because FCFF is the cash flow available to stockholders and debt holders. Since interest is paid to (and therefore "available to") the debt holders, it must be included in FCFF.

FCFF can also be calculated from operating cash flow as:

$$FCFF = CFO + [Int \times (1 - tax\ rate)] - FCInv$$

where:
CFO = cash flow from operations
Int = interest expense
FCInv = fixed capital investment (net capital expenditures)

It is not necessary to adjust for noncash charges and changes in working capital when starting with CFO, since they are already reflected in the calculation of CFO. For firms that follow IFRS, it is not necessary to adjust for interest expense that is included as a part of financing activities. Additionally, firms that follow IFRS can report dividends paid as operating activities. In this case, the dividends paid would be added back to CFO. Again, the goal is to calculate the cash flow that is available to the shareholders and debt holders. It is not necessary to adjust dividends for taxes since dividends paid are not tax deductible.

Free Cash Flow to Equity

Free cash flow to equity (FCFE) is the cash flow that would be available for distribution to common shareholders. FCFE can be calculated as follows:

$$FCFE = CFO - FCInv + Net\ borrowing$$

where:
CFO   = cash flow from operations
FCInv   = fixed capital investment (net capital expenditures)
Net borrowing = debt issued – debt repaid

If firms that follow IFRS have subtracted dividends paid in calculating CFO, dividends must be added back when calculating FCFE.

Other Cash Flow Ratios

Just as with the income statement and balance sheet, the cash flow statement can be analyzed by comparing the cash flows either over time or to those of other firms. Cash flow ratios can be categorized as performance ratios and coverage ratios.

Performance Ratios

The **cash flow-to-revenue ratio** measures the amount of operating cash flow generated for each dollar of revenue.

$$Cash\ flow\text{-}to\text{-}revenue = \frac{CFO}{net\ revenue}$$

The **cash return-on-assets ratio** measures the return of operating cash flow attributed to all providers of capital.

$$Cash\ return\text{-}on\text{-}assets = \frac{CFO}{average\ total\ assets}$$

The **cash return-on-equity ratio** measures the return of operating cash flow attributed to shareholders.

$$Cash\ return\text{-}on\text{-}equity = \frac{CFO}{average\ total\ equity}$$

The **cash-to-income ratio** measures the ability to generate cash from firm operations.

$$\text{Cash-to-income} = \frac{\text{CFO}}{\text{operating income}}$$

Cash flow per share is a variation of basic earnings per share measured by using CFO instead of net income.

$$\text{Cash flow per share} = \frac{\text{CFO} - \text{preferred dividends}}{\text{weighted average number of common shares}}$$

Coverage Ratios

The **debt coverage ratio** measures financial risk and leverage.

$$\text{Debt coverage} = \frac{\text{CFO}}{\text{total debt}}$$

The **interest coverage ratio** measures the firm's ability to meet its interest obligations.

$$\text{Interest coverage} = \frac{\text{CFO} + \text{interest paid} + \text{taxes paid}}{\text{interest paid}}$$

The **reinvestment ratio** measures the firm's ability to acquire long-term assets with operating cash flow.

$$\text{Reinvestment} = \frac{\text{CFO}}{\text{cash paid for long-term assets}}$$

The **debt payment ratio** measures the firm's ability to satisfy long-term debt with operating cash flow.

$$\text{Debt payment} = \frac{\text{CFO}}{\text{cash long-term debt repayment}}$$

The **dividend payment ratio** measures the firm's ability to make dividend payments from operating cash flow.

$$\text{Dividend payment} = \frac{\text{CFO}}{\text{dividends paid}}$$

The **investing and financing ratio** measures the firm's ability to purchase assets, satisfy debts, and pay dividends.

$$\text{Investing and financing} = \frac{\text{CFO}}{\text{cash outflows from investing and financing activities}}$$

KEY CONCEPTS

1. A firm's cash receipts and payments are classified on the cash flow statement as either operating, investing, or financing activities.
   - Cash flow from operating activities (CFO) consists of the inflows and outflows of cash resulting from transactions that affect a firm's net income.
   - Cash flow from investing activities (CFI) consists of the inflows and outflows of cash resulting from the acquisition or disposal of long-term assets and certain investments.
   - Cash flow from financing activities (CFF) consists of the inflows and outflows of cash resulting from transactions affecting a firm's capital structure.
2. Noncash investing and financing activities are not reported in the cash flow statement but must be disclosed in the footnotes or a supplemental schedule.
3. Under U.S. GAAP, dividends paid are financing activities. Interest paid, interest received, and dividends received are operating activities.
4. Under IFRS, dividends paid and interest paid can be reported as either operating activities or financing activities. Interest received and dividends received can be reported as either operating activities or investing activities.
5. Under the direct method of presenting CFO, each line item of the accrual-based income statement is adjusted to get cash receipts or cash payments.
6. Under the indirect method of presenting CFO, net income is adjusted for transactions that affect net income but do not affect cash flow to get CFO.
7. An indirect cash flow statement can be converted to a direct cash flow statement by adjusting each income statement account for changes in associated balance sheet accounts and by eliminating noncash and nonoperating items.
8. Free cash flow to the firm (FCFF) is the cash available to all investors, both equity owners and debt holders.

   $$FCFF = NI + NCC + [Int \times (1 - tax\ rate)] - FCInv - WCInv$$
   $$FCFF = CFO + [Int \times (1 - tax\ rate)] - FCInv$$

9. Free cash flow to equity (FCFE) is the cash flow that is available for distribution to the common shareholders after all obligations have been paid.

   $$FCFE = CFO - FCInv + Net\ borrowing$$

10. Cash flow performance and coverage ratios assess the (cash) profitability and the solvency of the firm.

CONCEPT CHECKERS

1. Using the following information, what is the firm's cash flow from operations?

Net income	$120
Decrease in accounts receivable receivable	20
Depreciation	25
Increase in inventory	10
Increase in accounts payable	7
Decrease in wages payable	5
Increase in deferred taxes	15
Profit from the sale of land	2

    A. $142.
    B. $158.
    C. $170.
    D. $174.

    $-10 + 35 - 30 + 50 - 15$

Use the following data to answer Questions 2 through 4.

Net income	$45
Depreciation	75
Taxes paid	25
Interest paid	5
Dividends paid	10
Cash received from sale of company building	40
Sale of preferred stock	35
Repurchase of common stock	30
Purchase of machinery	20
Issuance of bonds	50
Debt retired through issuance of common stock	45
Paid off long-term bank borrowings	15
Profit on sale of building	20

$40 - 20$

2. The cash flow from *operations* is:
    A. $70.
    B. $100.
    C. $120.
    D. $185.

3. The cash flow from *investing activities* is:
   A. –$30.
   B. $20.
   C. $70.
   D. $50.

4. The cash flow from *financing activities* is:
   A. $30.
   B. $55.
   C. $75.
   D. $85.

5. Given the following:

Sales	$1,500
Increase in inventory	100
Depreciation	150
Increase in accounts receivable	50
Decrease in accounts payable	70
After-tax profit margin	25%
Gain on sale of machinery	$30

   The cash flow from *operations* is:
   A. $25.
   B. $115.
   C. $275.
   D. $375.

6. Which of the following items is *least likely* considered a cash flow from financing activity under U.S. GAAP?
   A. Receipt of cash from the sale of capital stock.
   B. Receipt of cash from the sale of bonds.
   C. Payment of cash for dividends.
   D. Payment of interest on debt.

7. Which of the following would be *least likely* to cause a change in investing cash flow?
   A. The sale of a division of the company.
   B. The purchase of new machinery.
   C. An increase in depreciation expense.
   D. The sale of obsolete equipment with no remaining book value.

8. Which of the following is *least likely* a change in cash flow from operations under U.S. GAAP?
   A. A decrease in notes payable.
   B. An increase in interest expense.
   C. An increase in accounts payable.
   D. An increase in cost of goods sold.

9.   Where are dividends paid to shareholders reported in the cash flow statement
      under U.S. GAAP and IFRS?

      U.S. GAAP   IFRS
      A. Operating or financing activities   Financing activities
      B. Operating or financing activities   Operating or financing activities
      C. Financing activities   Operating or financing activities
      D. Operating activities   Financing activities

10.   Sales of inventory would be classified as:
      A. operating cash flow.
      B. investing cash flow.
      C. financing cash flow.
      D. no cash flow impact.

11.   Issuing bonds would be classified as:
      A. operating cash flow.
      B. investing cash flow.
      C. financing cash flow.
      D. no cash flow impact.

12.   Sale of land would be classified as:
      A. operating cash flow.
      B. investing cash flow.
      C. financing cash flow.
      D. no cash flow impact.

13.   An increase in taxes payable would be classified as:
      A. operating cash flow.
      B. investing cash flow.
      C. financing cash flow.
      D. no cash flow impact.

14.   An increase in notes payable would be classified as:
      A. operating cash flow.
      B. investing cash flow.
      C. financing cash flow.
      D. no cash flow impact.

15.   Under U.S. GAAP, an increase in interest payable would be classified as:
      A. operating cash flow.
      B. investing cash flow.
      C. financing cash flow.
      D. no cash flow impact.

16.   Under U.S. GAAP, an increase in dividends payable would be classified as:
      A. operating cash flow.
      B. investing cash flow.
      C. financing cash flow.
      D. no cash flow impact.

17. The write-off of obsolete equipment would be classified as:
    A. operating cash flow.
    B. investing cash flow.
    C. financing cash flow.
    D. no cash flow impact.

18. Sale of obsolete equipment would be classified as:
    A. operating cash flow.
    B. investing cash flow.
    C. financing cash flow.
    D. no cash flow impact.

19. Under IFRS, interest expense would be classified as:
    A. either operating cash flow or financing cash flow.
    B. operating cash flow only.
    C. financing cash flow only.
    D. no cash flow impact.

20. Depreciation expense would be classified as:
    A. operating cash flow.
    B. investing cash flow.
    C. financing cash flow.
    D. no cash flow impact.

21. Under U.S. GAAP, dividends received from investments would be classified as:
    A. operating cash flow.
    B. investing cash flow.
    C. financing cash flow.
    D. no cash flow impact.

22. Torval Inc. retires debt securities by issuing equity securities. This is considered a:
    A. cash flow from operations.
    B. cash flow from investing.
    C. cash flow from financing.
    D. noncash transaction.

23. Net income for Monique Inc. for the year ended December 31, 20X7 was $78,000. Its accounts receivable balance at December 31, 20X7 was $121,000 and this balance was $69,000 at December 31, 20X6. The accounts payable balance at December 31, 20X7 was $72,000 and was $43,000 at December 31, 20X6. Depreciation for 20X7 was $12,000 and there was an unrealized gain of $15,000 included in 20X7 income from the change in value of trading securities. Which of the following amounts represents Monique's cash flow from operations for 20X7?
    A. $52,000.
    B. $67,000.
    C. $82,000.
    D. $98,000.

24.   Martin Inc. had the following transactions during 20X7:
   • Purchased new fixed assets for $75,000.
   • Converted $70,000 worth of preferred shares to common shares.
   • Received cash dividends of $12,000. Paid cash dividends of $21,000.
   • Repaid mortgage principal of $17,000.

   Assuming Martin follows U.S. GAAP, which of the following amounts
   represents Martin's cash flows from investing and cash flows from financing in
   20X7, respectively?

Cash flows from investing	Cash flows from financing
A. ($5,000)	($21,000)
B. ($75,000)	($21,000)
C. ($5,000)	($38,000)
D. ($75,000)	($38,000)

25.   In preparing a common-size cash flow statement, each cash flow is expressed as
   a percentage of:
   A. total assets.
   B. operating cash flow.
   C. total revenues.
   D. the change in cash.

COMPREHENSIVE PROBLEMS

Use the following data to answer Questions A through F.

Balance Sheet Data	20X7	20X6
Assets		
Cash	$290	$100
Accounts receivable	250	200
Inventory	740	800
Property, plant, & equipment	920	900
Accumulated depreciation	(290)	(250)
Total Assets	$1,910	$1,750
Liabilities and Equity		
Accounts payable	$470	$450
Interest payable	15	10
Dividends payable	10	5
Mortgage	535	585
Bank note	100	0
Common stock	430	400
Retained earnings	350	300
Total Liabilities and Equity	$1,910	$1,750

Income Statement for the Year 20X7	20X7
Sales	$1,425
Cost of goods sold	1,200
Depreciation	100
Interest Expense	30
Gain on sale of old machine	10
Taxes	45
Net income	$60

Notes:

- Dividends declared to shareholders were $10.
- New common shares were sold at par for $30.
- Fixed assets were sold for $30. Original cost of these assets was $80, and $60 of accumulated depreciation has been charged to their original cost.
- The firm borrowed $100 on a 10-year bank note—the proceeds of the loan were used to pay for new fixed assets.
- Depreciation for the year was $100 (accumulated depreciation up $40 and depreciation on sold assets $60).

A. Calculate cash flow from operations, using the *indirect* method.

B. Calculate total cash collections, cash paid to suppliers, and other cash expenses.

C. Calculate cash flow from operations using the *direct* method.

D. Calculate cash flow from financing, cash flow from investing, and total cash flow.

E. Calculate free cash flow to equity owners.

F. What would the impact on investing cash flow and financing cash flow have been if the company leased the new fixed assets instead of borrowing the money and purchasing the equipment?

ANSWERS – CONCEPT CHECKERS

1. **C** Net income – profits from sale of land + depreciation + decrease in receivables – increase in inventories + increase in accounts payable – decrease in wages payable + increase in deferred taxes = 120 – 2 + 25 + 20 – 10 + 7 – 5 + 15 = $170. Note that the profit on the sale of land should be subtracted from net income to avoid double counting the gain in net income and investing activities.

2. **B** Net income – profit on sale of building + depreciation = 45 – 20 + 75 = $100. Note that taxes and interest are already deducted in calculating net income, and that the profit on the sale of the building should be subtracted from net income.

3. **B** Cash from sale of building – purchase of machinery = 40 – 20 = $20

4. **A** Sale of preferred stock + issuance of bonds – principal payments on bank borrowings – repurchase of common stock – dividends paid = 35 + 50 – 15 – 30 – 10 = $30. Note that we did not include $45 of debt retired through issuance of common stock since this was a noncash transaction. Knowing how to handle noncash transactions is important.

5. **C** Net income = $1,500 × 0.25 = $375, and cash flow from operations = net income – gain on sale of machinery + depreciation – increase in accounts receivable – increase in inventory – decrease in accounts payable = 375 – 30 + 150 – 50 – 100 – 70 = $275.

6. **D** The payment of interest on debt is an *operating* cash flow under U.S. GAAP.

7. **C** Depreciation does not represent a cash flow. To the extent that it affects the firm's taxes, an increase in depreciation changes operating cash flows, but not investing cash flows.

8. **A** A change in notes payable is a financing cash flow.

9. **C** Under U.S. GAAP, dividends paid are reported as financing activities. Under IFRS, dividends paid can be reported as either operating or financing activities.

10. **A** Sales of inventory would be classified as operating cash flow.

11. **C** Issuing bonds would be classified as financing cash flow.

12. **B** Sale of land would be classified as investing cash flow.

13. **A** Increase in taxes payable would be classified as operating cash flow.

14. **C** Increase in notes payable would be classified as financing cash flow.

15. **A** Increase in interest payable would be classified as operating cash flow under U.S. GAAP.

16. **C** Increase in dividends payable would be classified as financing cash flow under U.S. GAAP.

17. **D** Write-off of obsolete equipment has no cash flow impact.

18. **B** Sale of obsolete equipment would be classified as investing cash flow.

19. **A**   Under IFRS, interest expense can be classified as either an operating cash flow or financing cash flow.

20. **D**   Depreciation expense would be classified as no cash flow impact.

21. **A**   Dividends received from investments would be classified as operating cash flow under U.S. GAAP.

22. **D**   The exchange of debt securities for equity securities is a noncash transaction.

23. **A**

Net income	$78,000
Depreciation	12,000
Unrealized gain	(15,000)
Increase in accounts receivable	(52,000)
Increase in accounts payable	29,000
Cash flow from operations	$52,000

24. **D**   Purchased new fixed assets for $75,000 – cash <u>outflow</u> from investing
Converted $70,000 of preferred shares to common shares – noncash transaction
Received dividends of $12,000 – cash <u>inflow</u> from operations
Paid dividends of $21,000 – cash <u>outflow</u> from financing
Mortgage repayment of $17,000 – cash <u>outflow</u> from financing
CFI = –75,000
CFF = –21,000 – 17,000 = –$38,000

25. **C**   The cash flow statement can be converted to common-size format by expressing each line item as a percentage of revenue.

ANSWERS – COMPREHENSIVE PROBLEMS

A.   Net income – gain on sale of machinery + depreciation – increase in receivables + decrease in inventories + increase in accounts payable + increase in interest payable = 60 – 10 + 100 – 50 + 60 + 20 + 5 = $185.

B.   Cash collections = sales – increase in receivables = 1,425 – 50 = $1,375.

Cash paid to suppliers = –cost of goods sold + decrease in inventory + increase in accounts payable = –1,200 + 60 + 20 = –$1,120. (Note that the question asks for cash paid to suppliers, so no negative sign is needed in the answer.)

Other cash expenses = –interest expense + increase in interest payable – tax expense = –30 + 5 – 45 = –$70. (Note that the question asks for cash expenses so no negative sign is needed in the answer.)

C.   CFO cash collections – cash to suppliers – other cash expenses = 1,375 – 1,120 – 70 = $185. This must match the answer to Question A, because CFO using the direct method will be the same as CFO under the indirect method.

D.   CFF = sale of stock + new bank note – payment of mortgage – dividends + increase in dividends payable = 30 + 100 – 50 – 10 + 5 = $75.

CFI = sale of fixed assets – new fixed assets = 30 – 100 = –$70. Don't make this difficult. We sold assets for 30 and bought assets for 100. Assets sold had an original cost of 80, so (gross) PP&E only went up by 20.

The easiest way to determine total cash flow is to simply take the change in cash from the balance sheet. However, adding the three components of cash flow will yield 185 – 70 + 75 = $190.

E.   FCFE = cash flow from operations – capital spending + sale of fixed assets + debt issued – debt repaid = $185 + 100 + 30 + 100 – 50 = $165. No adjustment is necessary for interest since FCFE includes debt service.

F.   Investing cash flow would be higher and financing cash flow would be lower. The company would spend less on investments but would not have inflows from the borrowing.

ANALYSIS OF INVENTORIES

EXAM FOCUS

This topic review discusses specific analytical processes for inventory. The complication in analyzing inventory is that firms can use three different methods to account for inventory—FIFO, LIFO, and average cost. You should memorize the basic inventory relationship, EI = BI + P – COGS, and be able to algebraically convert this equation to solve for its other components (i.e., solve for COGS given the other three). You should also know how to calculate inventory balances and COGS using all three methods and how to convert inventory or COGS data derived from FIFO into LIFO and from LIFO into FIFO. Finally, you should know and be able to explain why LIFO accounting produces a better measure of COGS and why FIFO accounting produces a better measure of inventory value.

INVENTORY ACCOUNTING

The choice of accounting method used to account for inventory affects the firm's income statement, balance sheet, and related financial ratios. More importantly, the choice of inventory accounting method affects cash flow because taxes paid by the firm are affected by the choice of inventory method. Unlike depreciation methods, inventory accounting methods must be the same for taxes as for financial reporting.

U.S. Generally Accepted Accounting Principles (GAAP) require inventory valuation on the basis of *lower of cost or market* (LCM). If replacement cost is rising, the gains in the value of inventory are ignored, and the inventory is valued at cost. However, losses in the value of inventory due to obsolescence, deterioration, etc., are recognized, and inventory is written down to its new market value. Remember, LCM is applied regardless of the inventory costing method used.

In general, *cost* represents reasonable and necessary costs to get the asset in place and ready to use.

- Merchandise inventories include costs of purchasing, transportation, receiving, inspecting, etc.
- Manufactured inventories include costs of direct materials, direct labor, and manufacturing overhead (i.e., all other indirect costs).

A basic inventory formula relates the beginning balance, purchases, and cost of goods sold (COGS) to the ending balance. Memorize and understand the relationships in the following equation:

$$\text{ending inventory} = \text{beginning inventory} + \text{purchases} - \text{COGS}$$

This equation is rearranged for several purposes, such as:

purchases = ending inventory – beginning inventory + COGS

or COGS = purchases + beginning inventory – ending inventory

or COGS + ending inventory = beginning inventory + purchases

LOS 35.a: Compute ending inventory balances and cost of goods sold using the LIFO, FIFO, and average cost methods to account for product inventory.

Three methods of inventory accounting are:

1. **First In, First Out (FIFO):**
   - The cost of inventory first acquired (beginning inventory and early purchases) is assigned to the cost of goods sold for the period.
   - The cost of the most recent purchases is assigned to ending inventory.

2. **Last In, First Out (LIFO):**
   - The cost of inventory most recently purchased is assigned to the cost of goods sold for the period.
   - The costs of beginning inventory and earlier purchases go to ending inventory.
   - Note that in the United States, companies using LIFO for tax purposes must also use LIFO in their financial statements.

3. **Average cost:**
   - Under the average cost (weighted average) method, cost per unit is calculated by dividing cost of goods available by total units available. This average cost is used to determine both cost of goods sold and ending inventory.

Figure 1: Inventory Method Comparison

Method	Assumption	Cost of goods sold consists of...	Ending inventory consists of...
FIFO	The items first purchased are the first to be sold.	first purchased	most recent purchases
LIFO	The items last purchased are the first to be sold.	last purchased	earliest purchases
Weighted average cost	Items sold are a mix of purchases.	average cost of all items	average cost of all items

Example: Inventory costing

Use the inventory data in the following figure to calculate the cost of goods sold and ending inventory under each of the three methods.

Inventory Data

January 1 (beginning inventory)	2 units @ $2 per unit =	$4
January 7 purchase	3 units @ $3 per unit =	$9
January 19 purchase	5 units @ $5 per unit =	$25
Cost of goods available	10 units	$38
Units sold during January		7 units

Answer:

FIFO cost of goods sold. Value the seven units sold at unit cost of first units purchased. Start with the earliest units purchased and work down as illustrated in the following figure.

FIFO COGS Calculation

From beginning inventory	2 units @ $2 per unit =	$4
From first purchase	3 units @ $3 per unit =	$9
From second purchase	2 units @ $5 per unit =	$10
FIFO cost of goods sold	7 units	$23
Ending inventory	3 units @$5 =	$15

LIFO cost of goods sold. Value the seven units sold at unit cost of last units purchased. Start with the most recently purchased units and work up as illustrated in the following figure.

LIFO COGS Calculation

From second purchase	5 units @ $5 per unit =	$25
From first purchase	2 units @ $3 per unit =	$6
LIFO cost of goods sold	7 units	$31
Ending inventory	2@$2 + 1@$3 =	$7

Average cost of goods sold. Value the seven units sold at the average unit cost of goods available.

Weighted Average COGS Calculation

Average unit cost	$38 / 10 =	$3.80 per unit
Weighted average cost of goods sold	7 units @ $3.80 per unit =	$26.60
Ending inventory	3 units @ $3.80 per unit =	$11.40

Summary

Inventory system	COGS	Ending Inventory
FIFO	$23.00	$15.00
LIFO	$31.00	$7.00
Average Cost	$26.60	$11.40

Note that prices and inventory levels were rising over the period and that the costs of purchases during the period are the same for all costing methods.

LOS 35.b: Explain the relationship among and the usefulness of inventory and cost of goods sold data provided by the LIFO, FIFO, and average cost methods when prices are (1) stable or (2) changing.

During periods of rising prices, LIFO cost of goods sold is greater than FIFO cost of goods sold. Therefore, LIFO net income will be less than FIFO net income. Consistently, LIFO inventory is less than FIFO inventory because items remaining in inventory are taken to be those acquired earlier at lower prices. Average cost methods yield COGS, net income, and balance sheet inventory values between the other two.

This should make intuitive sense because during periods of rising prices, the last units purchased are more expensive. Under LIFO, the last in (more costly) is the first out (to cost of goods sold). This results in LIFO profitability ratios being smaller than under FIFO. When prices are rising, LIFO inventory is smaller than under FIFO, the firm's current ratio will be lower, and inventory turnover will be higher.

If financial statements are compared for firms using different cost flow assumptions, then adjustments have to be made to achieve comparability. Consider the following diagram in Figure 2 to help you visualize the FIFO-LIFO difference during periods of *rising prices* and growing inventory levels. Remember, it's not that older or newer inventory items are being sold. The difference is only in the costs we assign to the units sold and those remaining in inventory.

Figure 2: LIFO and FIFO Diagram—Rising Prices and Growing Inventory Balances

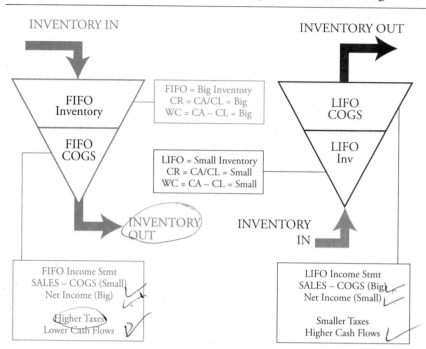

During periods of rising prices, LIFO results in higher COGS, lower net income, and lower inventory levels. This decreases the current ratio (CA / CL) and increases inventory turnover (COGS / average inventory). If prices do not change, then the different inventory valuation methods do not affect the financial statements.

> *Professor's Note: For the exam, you should understand that if prices are decreasing (deflation), then the opposite relationships between FIFO and LIFO hold. Also, when you are finished with this review, please take the time to look at these graphs and relationships again to solidify the concepts in your mind.*

By decreasing inventory to levels below normal levels, thus dipping into the old "cheap" inventory, a firm's management can increase profits for the period under LIFO. When this strategy is employed, COGS under LIFO will be lower and profits will be higher than if more inventory were purchased and inventory levels not drawn down. This is called a **LIFO liquidation**.

If there is LIFO liquidation (e.g., the firm sells more items than it purchased during the period), LIFO, COGS and, hence, income are distorted. COGS does not reflect current costs.

Most U.S. firms use LIFO on their statements because the Internal Revenue Code states that if firms use LIFO on their tax returns, they must use LIFO on their general-purpose statements. (This is an exception to the general rule that firms can use different methods in computing tax and financial income.) During the last 40 years of rising prices, firms have saved money by using LIFO on their tax returns, since their reported net income is lower than if they had used FIFO. This results in the peculiar situation where *lower income is associated with a higher cash flow from operations.*

Usefulness of Inventory and Cost-of-Goods-Sold Data Provided by the LIFO, FIFO, and Average Cost Methods

 Professor's Note: The presumption in this section is that inventory quantities are stable or increasing.

During periods of stable prices, all three inventory valuation processes will yield the same results for inventory, COGS, and earnings. During periods of changing prices, the key point to remember is that *FIFO will provide the most useful estimate of the inventory value and LIFO will provide the most useful estimate of the cost of goods sold.* This is a crucial point.

Inventory Value

When prices are changing, FIFO inventory costing provides the best balance sheet information on the value of inventory. If prices are steadily rising, FIFO inventory is valued at the more recent purchase prices, which are higher and provide a better estimate of the replacement value of the inventory. If prices are steadily falling, FIFO inventory valuation is still preferred from a balance sheet perspective, since the value of existing inventory is based on the new, lower replacement cost.

U.S. GAAP require that inventory be valued at the lower of cost or market (LCM), where "market" is usually taken to mean replacement cost. If replacement cost is falling, the usefulness of LIFO-based carrying values for inventory is improved by applying LCM. Without LCM and with price declines, LIFO inventory values will be high compared to economic value or replacement cost. When the LCM method is also applied, units of inventory acquired earlier, at higher cost, are revalued downward, reducing the overstatement in LIFO inventory carrying values. Since inventory carrying values are not revalued upward for changes in replacement cost, the usefulness of LIFO-based inventory values is not improved by the LCM adjustment during periods of rising prices. LCM cannot be used for tax purposes if the firm is using LIFO.

Cost of Goods Sold

By the same logic applied in the previous section, LIFO provides the better measure of the cost of goods sold when prices are either rising or falling. Viewing the firm as an ongoing concern, the economic profit is best approximated by using the replacement cost of inventory items. While LIFO inventory costing may fall short of this goal, it provides a better estimate of the replacement cost of goods sold than does FIFO. If prices are falling, inventory replacement cost is falling, and the most recently acquired inventory items will be closer to replacement cost than items purchased earlier. For calculating earnings, the FIFO cost of goods sold will overstate replacement cost. The same logic holds if prices are rising. LIFO costing will produce a cost of goods sold much closer to replacement cost than FIFO costing, which will understate the replacement cost and overstate income.

FIFO, LIFO, and average cost inventory accounting will all produce the same inventory value and COGS when prices are stable. When prices are changing, the average cost method will produce values of COGS and ending inventory between those of FIFO and LIFO.

The previous discussion assumes the value for purchases is known, but this too may be affected by management choice. For example, in a manufacturing business with raw materials, work in process, and finished goods inventories, the allocation of overhead such as rent, depreciation, supervisor salaries, maintenance expenses, and utilities to various classes of inventory is subject to management discretion.

At higher production levels, less of a particular fixed cost (such as factory rent) is allocated to each unit produced. However, if more units are produced than sold, then some of the allocated overhead ends up in ending inventory. If all the units produced were sold, then all of the fixed costs would be in COGS and expensed in the current period.

Firms may choose different inventory methods for different product lines, business segments, or geographical locations. FIFO inventory accounting is the primary method outside the United States. Information about inventory accounting methods should be available in the footnotes to financial statements and information is available that allows the analyst to restate financial statements using an alternative inventory accounting method.

LOS 35.c: Compare and contrast the effect of the different methods on cost of goods sold and inventory balances and discuss how a company's choice of inventory accounting method affects other financial items such as income, cash flow, and working capital.

Often, an analyst wants to compare a company to other companies in the same industry. When two companies use different methods of accounting for inventory, one of the firms' inventories must be adjusted in order to make the comparison relevant. There are two types of conversion: LIFO to FIFO and FIFO to LIFO.

The LIFO to FIFO conversion is relatively simple because U.S. GAAP require all companies that use LIFO to also report a **LIFO reserve**, which is the difference between what ending inventory would have been under FIFO accounting and its value under LIFO.

Figure 3: LIFO Reserve

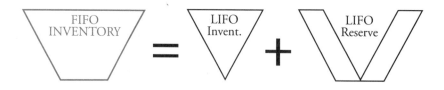

current cost of inventory (FIFO) = LIFO inventory + LIFO reserve

If you add the LIFO reserve to the LIFO inventory, you will get the FIFO inventory. An alternative expression is:

LIFO reserve = FIFO inventory – LIFO inventory

The LIFO reserve is typically shown in the footnotes to the financial statements.

To convert LIFO inventory balances to a FIFO basis, simply add the LIFO reserve to the LIFO inventory:

$$Inv_F = Inv_L + \text{LIFO reserve}$$

To convert COGS from LIFO to FIFO use the formula:

$$COGS_{FIFO} = COGS_{LIFO} - \text{change in the LIFO reserve}$$

$$= COGS_{LIFO} - (\text{LIFO reserve}_{ENDING} - \text{LIFO reserve}_{BEGINNING})$$

Remember that during a period of rising prices $COGS_{FIFO}$ is too low (below replacement costs). Also, the LIFO reserve is increasing when prices are rising. This increase in the LIFO reserve is exactly the difference between $COGS_{LIFO}$ and $COGS_{FIFO}$. During a period of falling prices we would still subtract the change in the LIFO reserve from $COGS_{LIFO}$ to get $COGS_{FIFO}$, but the change is a negative number and $COGS_{FIFO}$ will be the larger of the two measures.

We can derive the above relation by using the basic inventory equation:

$$COGS_{FIFO} = \text{purchases} + BEG\ INV_{FIFO} - END\ INV_{FIFO}$$

We know the relation between FIFO and LIFO inventory balances is:

$$BEG\ INV_{FIFO} = BEG\ INV_{LIFO} + \text{LIFO Reserve}_{BEG}$$

$$END\ INV_{FIFO} = END\ INV_{LIFO} + \text{LIFO Reserve}_{END}$$

Substituting we get:

$$COGS_{FIFO} = [\text{purchases} + BEG\ INV_{LIFO} - END\ INV_{LIFO}] - [\text{LIFO Reserve}_{END} - \text{LIFO Reserve}_{BEG}]$$

Which is:

$$COGS_{FIFO} = [COGS_{LIFO}] - [\text{change in LIFO reserve}], \text{ as previously shown}$$

Example: Converting from LIFO to FIFO

Sipowitz Company, which uses LIFO, reported end-of-year inventory balances of $500 in 2005 and $700 in 2006. The LIFO reserve was $200 for 2005 and $300 for 2006. COGS during 2006 was $3,000. Convert 2006 ending inventory and COGS to a FIFO basis.

Answer:

Inventory:

$$\text{Inv}_F = \text{Inv}_L + \text{LIFO reserve} = \$700 + \$300 = \$1,000$$

COGS:

$$\text{COGS}_F = \text{COGS}_L - (\text{LIFO reserve}_E - \text{LIFO reserve}_B)$$

$$= \$3,000 - (\$300 - \$200) = \$2,900$$

FIFO to LIFO conversions are typically not done for inventory, since inventory under LIFO is not a reflection of current value. However, it may be useful to consider what COGS would be under LIFO. The adjustment process is completely different than the process of converting COGS from LIFO to FIFO. There is no precise calculation; an analyst must estimate what the costs would have been under LIFO.

The estimate of COGS is equal to:

$$\text{COGS}_L = \text{COGS}_F + (\text{BI}_F \times \text{inflation rate})$$

The inflation rate should not be a general inflation rate for the economy but should be an inflation rate appropriate for the firm or industry. It can be determined two ways:

1. Industry statistics.

2. The increase in the LIFO reserve for another company in the same industry divided by that company's beginning inventory level converted to FIFO accounting.

An analyst can also estimate what the COGS would have been under the LIFO method for a company that uses the average cost method. The logic is that because the average cost method always reports inventory values and costs of goods sold *between* values reported under LIFO and FIFO, the adjustment for the COGS estimate should be half of the adjustment used for FIFO accounting:

$$\text{COGS}_L = \text{COGS}_W + 1/2 \times (\text{BI}_W \times \text{inflation rate})$$

where:
COGS_W = the COGS under the average cost method
BI_W = the beginning inventory under the average cost method

Example: FIFO to LIFO conversion

Logan Company is in the same industry as Sipowitz Company from the previous example. Logan uses FIFO accounting and has COGS of $2,000, ending inventory of $500, and beginning inventory of $350. Estimate Logan's COGS under LIFO accounting.

Answer:

First estimate the inflation rate using data from Sipowitz. The increase in the LIFO reserve for Sipowitz is $300 – $200 = $100. The beginning inventory converted to FIFO is $500 + $200 = $700. That means the inflation rate is $100 / $700 = 14.3%.

Now the estimate of COGS can be calculated as:

$$COGS_L = COGS_F + (BI_F \times \text{inflation rate}) = \$2,000 + (\$350 \times 14.3\%) = \$2,050]$$

How a Company's Choice of Inventory Accounting Method Affects Other Financial Items

Professor's Note: The presumption in this section is that prices are rising and inventory quantities are stable or increasing. The implications when inventories or prices decline will be discussed later.

In the absence of taxes, there would be no difference in cash flow between LIFO and FIFO. With taxes, however, the higher LIFO COGS causes reported income to be lower, also causing taxes (a cash cost) to be lower. This causes cash flow to be higher. The U.S. tax code requires the same method of inventory accounting to be used in both GAAP and tax accounting. The results in periods of rising prices and stable or increasing inventory quantities are shown in Figure 4.

Figure 4: LIFO and FIFO Comparison—Rising Prices and Stable or Increasing Inventories

LIFO results in...	FIFO results in...
higher COGS	lower COGS
lower taxes	higher taxes
lower net income (EBT and EAT)	higher net income (EBT and EAT)
lower inventory balances	higher inventory balances
lower working capital (CA – CL)	higher working capital (CA – CL)
higher cash flows (less taxes paid out)	lower cash flows (more taxes paid out)

- With rising prices, LIFO is the best choice because it increases after-tax cash flow.
- LIFO firm liquidity measures are misleading because of the understatement of working capital (inventory too low).
- The analyst must be aware that FIFO firms will show higher net income (all else the same).

The effect of taxes is a real effect so that, during a period of rising prices, the choice of LIFO can increase firm value, although lower net income will be reported. In general, when prices are changing, an analyst should use *LIFO-based values for income statement items* and ratios, and *FIFO-based values for balance sheet items* and ratios because of the distortions described in the previous LOS.

The following example illustrates the difference between net income under the FIFO and LIFO methods.

Example: FIFO vs. LIFO and net income

Consider the assumptions in the following figure.

Assumption

Beginning inventory	50 units @ $1.00	= $50
Purchases	100 purchased @ $2.00 150 purchased @ $3.00	= $200 + 450 = $650
Ending inventory	200 units	
Sales	100 units @$7	

Suggestion: Keep track of the number of units

Beginning	50
Purchased	+100
Purchased	+150
Sold	−100
Ending	200

The COGS and inventory balances under FIFO and LIFO are shown in the following figure.

COGS and Inventory

	Cost of goods sold	Inventory
FIFO	50 units @ $1 + 50 @ $2 = $150	50 @ $2 + 150 @ $3 = $550
LIFO	100 @ $3 = $300	50 @ $1 + 100 @ $2 + 50 @ $3 = $400

Net income is calculated as shown in the following figure.

Net Income Under FIFO and LIFO

	FIFO	LIFO	LIFO lower by ...
Sales	$700	$700	$0
Cost of goods sold	$150	$300	$(150)
Income before tax	$550	$400	$150
Tax @ 40%	$220	$160	$60
Net income	$330	$240	$90 ⇦LIFO produces lower income

With taxes $60 higher under FIFO, cash flow will be $60 lower.

LOS 35.d: Compare and contrast the effects of the choice of inventory method on profitability, liquidity, activity, and solvency ratios.

Professor's Note: The presumption in this section is that prices are rising and inventory quantities are stable or increasing.

Since the choice of inventory accounting method has an impact on income statement and balance sheet items, it will have an impact on ratios as well. In general, *an analyst should use LIFO values when examining profitability or cost ratios and FIFO values when examining asset or equity ratios.*

Profitability

Compared to FIFO, LIFO produces COGS balances that are higher and are a better measure of true economic cost. Consequently, we have seen that LIFO produces income values that are lower than FIFO, and LIFO figures are a better measure of future profitability. Profitability ratios, such as gross margin and net profit margin, are lower under LIFO than under FIFO, and ratios calculated using LIFO figures are better for comparison purposes. For firms that use FIFO, income ratios should be recalculated using estimates of what COGS would be under LIFO.

Liquidity

Compared to LIFO, FIFO produces inventory figures that are higher and are a better measure of economic value. LIFO inventory figures use prices that are outdated and have less relevance to the economic value of inventory. Liquidity ratios, such as the current ratio, are higher under FIFO than under LIFO, and ratios calculated using FIFO figures are better for comparison purposes. For firms that use LIFO, liquidity ratios should be recalculated using inventory balances that have been restated using the LIFO reserve.

Activity

Inventory turnover makes little sense for firms using LIFO due to the mismatching of costs (the numerator is largely influenced by current or recent past prices, while the denominator is largely influenced by historical prices). Using LIFO when prices are rising causes the inventory turnover ratio to trend higher even if physical turnover does not change. FIFO-based inventory ratios are relatively unaffected by price changes and are a better approximation of actual turnover. However, the ratio itself can still be misleading because the numerator does not reflect COGS as well as LIFO accounting does. The preferred method of analysis is to use LIFO COGS and FIFO average inventory. In this way, current costs are matched in the numerator and denominator. This method is called the *current cost method*.

Some firms use an economic order quantity (EOQ) model to determine optimal inventory ordering policies. For these firms, the level of sales will greatly influence inventory turnover; the lower the sales, the lower the turnover will be. Some firms are adopting just-in-time inventory policies and keep no inventory (at most, very little) on hand. This results in very large inventory turnover ratios. For these firms, there would be virtually no differences due to the choice between the LIFO and FIFO methods.

LIFO firms tend to carry larger quantities of inventory than comparable FIFO firms. This can most likely be explained by the tax advantages (i.e., lower taxes due to higher COGS) of LIFO.

Solvency

FIFO produces higher inventory values that are more relevant than LIFO inventory values. To reconcile the balance sheet, stockholders' equity must also be adjusted by adding the LIFO reserve. Solvency ratios such as the debt ratio and debt-to-equity ratio will be lower under FIFO because the denominators are larger. For firms that use LIFO, equity, and therefore assets, should be increased by adding the LIFO reserve.

Professor's Note: It may seem inconsistent to use LIFO figures for net income and FIFO figures for stockholders' equity. Nonetheless, that is exactly what an analyst should do.

Example: Converting LIFO to FIFO

A balance sheet for a company for 2005 and 2006, along with its income statement for 2006, are shown below.

Part A: Convert inventory for 2005 and 2006 and COGS for 2006 into FIFO.

Part B: Calculate the net profit margin, current ratio, inventory turnover, and long-term debt-to-equity ratio using the accounting figures that are most appropriate to compare to industry norms.

Sample Balance Sheet

Year	2006	2005
Assets		
Cash	$105	$95
Receivables	205	195
Inventories	310	290
Total current assets	620	580
Gross property, plant, and equipment	$1,800	$1,700
Accumulated depreciation	360	340
Net property, plant, and equipment	1,440	1,360
Total assets	$2,060	$1,940
Liabilities		
Payables	$110	$90
Short-term debt	160	140
Current portion of long-term debt	55	45
Current liabilities	$325	$275
Long-term debt	$610	$690
Deferred taxes	105	95
Common stock	300	300
Additional paid in capital	400	400
Retained earnings	320	180
Common shareholders equity	1,020	880
Total liabilities and equity	$2,060	$1,940

Year	2006
Sales	$4,000
Cost of goods sold	3,000
Gross profit	$1,000
Operating expenses	650
Operating profit	350
Interest expense	50
Earnings before taxes	300
Taxes	100
Net income	200
Common dividends	$60

* **Footnote:** The company uses the LIFO inventory
cost-flow assumption to account for inventories. As
compared to FIFO, inventories would have been
$100 higher in 2006 and $90 higher in 2005.

Answer:

Part A:

2005: $Inv_F = Inv_L + \text{LIFO reserve} = 290 + 90 = 380$

2006: $Inv_F = Inv_L + \text{LIFO reserve} = 310 + 100 = 410$

$$COGS_F = COGS_L - (\text{LIFO reserve}_E - \text{LIFO reserve}_B) = 3,000 - (100 - 90) = 2,990$$

Part B:

$$\text{net profit margin} = \frac{\text{net income under LIFO}}{\text{sales}}$$
$$= \frac{200}{4,000} = 5.0\%$$

$$\text{current ratio} = \frac{\text{current assets under FIFO}}{\text{current liabilities}}$$
$$= \frac{\text{current assets under LIFO + LIFO reserve}}{\text{current liabilities}}$$
$$= \frac{620 + 100}{325} = 2.2$$

$$\text{inventory turnover} = \frac{\text{COGS under LIFO}}{\text{average inventory under FIFO}}$$
$$= \frac{3,000}{(380 + 410)\big/2} = 7.6$$

$$\text{debt-to-equity} = \frac{\text{long-term debt}}{\text{equity under FIFO}}$$
$$= \frac{\text{long-term debt}}{\text{equity under LIFO + LIFO reserve}}$$
$$= \frac{610}{1,020 + 100} = 54.5\%$$

When calculating FIFO equity, we have added the entire LIFO reserve without any adjustment for taxes. Note the difference between the questions: What would retained earnings (COGS, net income) have been if the company had used FIFO instead of LIFO? and, How should an analyst adjust retained earnings (assets, equity) for a firm using LIFO to get more meaningful ratios for analysis? In the first case (assuming rising prices), if the firm had used FIFO, then earnings before tax, taxes, net income and retained earnings would all have been higher. In the second case, we are not asking the effects of a different inventory accounting method, but are adjusting ratios to make them more meaningful. The fact that the LIFO firm has an artificially low inventory value is corrected by adding the LIFO reserve to both inventory and retained earnings (equity). Unless there is a reason to believe the firm will actually have a LIFO liquidation, there is no reason to subtract taxes that have been avoided in adjusting the inventory value, retained earnings, and stockholders' equity of LIFO firms.

LOS 35.e: Indicate the reasons that a LIFO reserve might decline during a given period and evaluate the implications of such a decline for financial analysis.

The analysis above assumed that prices and inventory were stable or rising. Stable or rising prices and stable or increasing inventory quantities are a typical situation for a business. In these cases, the LIFO reserve will not decline. However, the *LIFO reserve will decline if*:

- Inventory quantity is falling.
- Prices are falling.

A **LIFO liquidation** refers to a declining inventory balance for a company using LIFO (i.e., units available for sale are declining). In this case, the prices for goods being sold are no longer recent prices and can be many years out of date. This would make COGS appear to be very low and gross and net profits to be artificially high. An analyst must adjust COGS for the decline in the LIFO reserve that is caused by the decline in inventory quantity. This amount is typically listed in the footnotes of the financial statements.

If *prices decline*, the differences in the values of inventory and COGS under LIFO and FIFO are the opposite of what was stated before. Specifically:

- If prices are declining, the value of inventory under FIFO will be lower than the value of inventory under LIFO (more recently purchased goods have a lower value relative to goods purchased earlier).
- If prices are declining, the COGS under LIFO will be lower than the COGS under FIFO.

However, even when prices decline, FIFO still provides a more accurate estimate of the economic value of inventory, and LIFO still provides a more accurate estimate of the economic COGS. The decline in the LIFO reserve does *not* mean COGS has to be adjusted if it occurs because of a price decline.

LOS 35.f: Illustrate how inventories are reported in the financial statements and how the lower-of-cost-or-market principle is used and applied.

U.S. GAAP requires that inventories be reported on the financial statements using the lower of historical cost or market (LCM) principle. This is consistent with the broader accounting concept of conservatism as it will prevent the overstatement of inventories on the balance sheet (and the related income statement effects). Under normal circumstances, inventories are reported at historical cost, and even if market value is higher than historical cost, inventory is not written up above the historical cost.

However, if the realizable market value or cost to replace inventory is less than historical cost, a writedown is required.

Inventory gains are not realized until items are sold, but losses prior to sale may be realized on the financial statements as they occur.

Cost is calculated using the actual purchase prices of the items, and the calculation follows one of the three cost-flow assumptions (FIFO, LIFO, or weighted-average) that were discussed earlier.

Market is calculated using the replacement cost of the inventory at a particular point in time. However, the replacement cost must fall within a range of values. The higher end of the range is the **net realizable value (NRV)**. NRV is generally equal to the selling price of the inventories less the selling costs. The lower end is NRV less normal profit margin.

So if replacement cost is greater than NRV, then market equals net realizable value. If replacement cost is less than NRV less a normal profit margin, then market equals net realizable value minus normal profit margin.

Professor's Note: Think of lower of cost or "market" where market cannot be outside a range of values. That range is from net realizable value less a normal profit margin to net realizable value. So the size of this range is normal profit margin in dollars. "Net" means net of the selling costs.

KEY CONCEPTS

1. The three methods of accounting for inventory are FIFO, LIFO, and average cost, and the basic formula for inventory calculations is:

   ending inventory = beginning inventory + purchases – COGS.

2. When prices are changing, FIFO provides the more useful estimate of inventory and balance sheet information, while LIFO provides the more useful estimate of COGS and operating income.

3. Adjusting LIFO inventory balances to FIFO balances requires adding the LIFO reserve to inventory; adjusting LIFO COGS to FIFO requires subtracting the difference between the ending and beginning LIFO reserve.

4. Adjusting FIFO COGS to LIFO requires estimating the inflation rate for the firm and adding the product of the inflation rate and the beginning inventory to the reported FIFO COGS.

5. In periods of rising prices and stable or increasing inventory quantities, LIFO and FIFO result in the following:

LIFO results in:	FIFO results in:
higher COGS	lower COGS
lower taxes	higher taxes
lower net income (EBT and EAT)	higher net income (EBT and EAT)
lower inventory balances	higher inventory balances
lower working capital	higher working capital
higher cash flows (less taxes paid out)	lower cash flows (more taxes paid out)
lower net and gross margins	higher net and gross margins
lower current ratio	higher current ratio
higher inventory turnover	lower inventory turnover
D/A and D/E higher	D/A and D/E lower

6. The LIFO reserve may decline because:
   - Inventory is falling (a LIFO liquidation)—adjust COGS for decrease in LIFO reserve.
   - Prices are declining—no need to adjust COGS for LIFO firms—FIFO still provides a better estimate of inventory value.

7. Under U.S. GAAP, inventory values are written down to replacement cost when that is lower than historical cost, or to NRV if that is lower than replacement cost, but not to less than NRV minus a normal profit margin in any case.

CONCEPT CHECKERS

1. The choice of inventory accounting method has cash flow effects because it affects:
    A. purchases.
    B. sales.
    C. taxes.
    D. the turnover ratio.

2. An analyst gathered the following information about a company:
    *   Beginning inventory $40,000
    *   Purchases over the accounting period $55,000
    *   COGS $60,000

    Ending inventory will be:
    A. $35,000.
    B. $45,000.
    C. $50,000.
    D. Cannot determine without knowing inventory method.

3. An analyst gathered the following information about a company:
    *   Beginning inventory $2.8 million
    *   Purchases $11.2 million
    *   Ending inventory $3.0 million

    COGS is:
    A. $5.4 million.
    B. $5.8 million.
    C. $11 million.
    D. $14 million.

4. If COGS is overstated by $2,000, and purchases and beginning inventory are correct, ending inventory will be:
    A. unaffected.
    B. understated by $2,000.
    C. overstated by $2,000.
    D. cannot determine without knowing inventory method.

5. If beginning inventory is overstated by $2,000 and ending inventory is understated by $3,000, the firm's before tax income will be:
    A. overstated by $1,000.
    B. overstated by $5,000.
    C. understated by $1,000.
    D. understated by $5,000.

6.   An analyst gathered the following information about a firm:
        • Beginning inventory $15,000
        • Net purchases $25,000
        • Ending inventory $17,000

        COGS is:
        A. $15,000.
        B. $23,000.
        C. $25,000.
        D. $27,000.

7.   When a firm uses first-in, first-out (FIFO) accounting, COGS reflects the cost
        of items purchased:
        A. first and ending inventory reflects the value of the items purchased first.
        B. first and ending inventory reflects the cost of the most recent purchases.
        C. most recently and ending inventory reflects the cost of items purchased
            most recently.
        D. most recently and ending inventory reflects the cost of items purchased
            first.

Use the following data to answer Questions 8 through 13.

Purchase	Sales
40 units at $30	13 units at $35
20 units at $40	35 units at $45
90 units at $50	60 units at $60

Assume beginning inventory was zero.

8.   Inventory value at the end of the period using FIFO is:
        A. $1,200.
        B. $2,100.
        C. $2,400.
        D. $6,000.

9.   Inventory value at the end of the period using LIFO is:
        A. $1,200.
        B. $1,280.
        C. $2,100.
        D. $2,400.

10.   Using LIFO and information for the entire period, gross profit at the end of
        the period is:
        A. $360.
        B. $410.
        C. $990.
        D. $1,230.

11. Using FIFO and information for the entire period, gross profit is:
    A. $360.
    B. $410.
    C. $990.
    D. $1,230.

12. Inventory value at the end of the period using the weighted average method is:
    A. $1,540.
    B. $1,820.
    C. $2,100.
    D. $4,680.

13. Using the weighted average cost method for the entire period, gross profit at the end of period is:
    A. $950.
    B. $1,230.
    C. $2,100.
    D. $3,810.

14. During periods of rising prices and stable or increasing inventory levels:
    A. LIFO COGS > weighted average COGS > FIFO COGS.
    B. LIFO COGS < weighted average COGS < FIFO COGS.
    C. LIFO COGS = weighted average COGS = FIFO COGS.
    D. weighted average COGS > LIFO COGS > FIFO COGS.

15. During periods of falling prices:
    A. LIFO income > weighted average income > FIFO income.
    B. LIFO income < weighted average income < FIFO income.
    C. LIFO income = weighted average income = FIFO income.
    D. LIFO COGS < weighted average COGS > FIFO COGS.

16. From an analyst's perspective, inventories based on:
    A. LIFO are preferable since they reflect historical cost.
    B. FIFO are preferable since they reflect current cost.
    C. weighted averages are preferable since they reflect normal results.
    D. All three methods are equivalent because the equity account is unaffected by the accounting method.

17. From an analyst's perspective:
    A. LIFO provides a better measure of current income because it allocates recent costs to COGS.
    B. FIFO provides a better measure of current income because it allocates historical costs to COGS.
    C. weighted average is best because it allocates average costs to COGS and requires no flow assumptions.
    D. Any method provides the same value because the equity account is unaffected by the accounting method.

©2008 Schweser

18. In periods of rising prices and stable or increasing inventory quantities, LIFO (as compared to FIFO) results in:
    A. lower COGS, higher taxes, lower net income, and lower cash flows.
    B. lower COGS, higher taxes, lower inventory, and higher COGS.
    C. higher COGS, lower taxes, lower inventory, and lower cash flows.
    D. higher COGS, lower taxes, lower inventory, and higher cash flows.

19. If prices are rising and two firms are identical except for inventory methods, the firm using FIFO will have:
    A. higher net income.
    B. lower inventory.
    C. lower net income.
    D. higher total cash flow.

20. Which of the following is the *most likely* result of a LIFO liquidation?
    A. An increase in the gross profit margin.
    B. A sharp increase in inventory.
    C. A sharp increase in accounts receivable.
    D. All of the above.

21. In periods of falling prices, firms using FIFO will:
    A. report higher earnings than equivalent firms using LIFO.
    B. report lower earnings than equivalent firms using LIFO.
    C. report identical earnings as equivalent firms using LIFO.
    D. Cannot tell without knowing the timing of the price decline.

22. Which of the following statements about inventory accounting is *least accurate*?
    A. If a U.S. firm uses LIFO for tax reporting, it must use LIFO for financial reporting.
    B. During periods of rising prices, LIFO income will be lower than FIFO income.
    C. During periods of rising prices, LIFO cash flows will be higher than FIFO cash flows.
    D. During periods of rising prices, FIFO-based current ratios will be smaller than LIFO-based current ratios.

23. An analyst is evaluating a company after a period of time when prices have fallen. The company uses LIFO accounting. Which of the following is *most likely* correct?
    A. The analyst must restate COGS because it is lower than what it would be under FIFO accounting.
    B. Income will be lower than it would have been under FIFO accounting.
    C. Inventory need not be restated because the LIFO reserve will have decreased.
    D. COGS need not be restated because LIFO COGS is always an accurate measure of current cost as long as inventory quantity does not decline.

24. Assuming no LIFO layer liquidation, a LIFO firm reports higher net income than an otherwise identical FIFO firm. Prices must be:
    A. steady.
    B. rising.
    C. falling.
    D. falling first and then rising.

25. In periods of rising prices and stable or increasing inventory levels, compared to FIFO accounting for inventories, LIFO accounting will give:
    A. lower profitability ratios.
    B. lower inventory levels.
    C. a lower current ratio.
    D. All of the above.

26. If all else holds constant in periods of rising prices and inventory levels, which of the following statements is *most likely* correct?
    A. FIFO firms have higher debt-to-equity ratios than LIFO firms.
    B. LIFO firms have higher gross profit margins than FIFO firms.
    C. FIFO firms will have greater stockholder's equity than LIFO firms.
    D. LIFO firms will have greater current asset balances than FIFO firms.

27. A firm uses LIFO for inventory accounting and reports the following:
    - COGS $125,000
    - Beginning inventory $25,000
    - Ending inventory $27,000
    - Footnotes to the financial statements reveal a beginning LIFO reserve of $12,000 and an ending LIFO reserve of $15,000.

    The COGS on a FIFO basis is:
    A. $122,000.
    B. $125,000.
    C. $128,000.
    D. $140,000.

Use the following data to answer Questions 28 through 32.

The beginning of period LIFO reserve is $50,000, and the ending period LIFO reserve is $60,000. The firm's tax rate is 40%.

28. To adjust end-of-period LIFO inventory to FIFO inventory:
    A. add $10,000.
    B. subtract $10,000.
    C. add $60,000.
    D. subtract $60,000.

29. To adjust end-of-period owner's equity in order to calculate the debt-to-equity ratio, an analyst should:
    A. make no adjustment.
    B. add $10,000.
    C. add $36,000.
    D. add $60,000.

30. To adjust end-of-period accounts payable from LIFO based to FIFO based:
    A. make no adjustment.
    B. add $24,000.
    C. add $36,000.
    D. subtract $36,000.

31. To adjust COGS from LIFO to FIFO, an analyst should adjust the LIFO
    COGS by:
    A. increasing it by $60,000.
    B. decreasing it by $60,000.
    C. increasing it by $10,000.
    D. decreasing it by $10,000.

32. The effect on after-tax income of using FIFO instead of LIFO would be to:
    A. increase it by $6,000.
    B. decrease it by $6,000.
    C. increase it by $10,000.
    D. decrease it by $10,000.

33. Which of the following statements concerning a firm using FIFO is *least likely*
    correct?
    A. There is no reason to convert inventory to LIFO because LIFO inventory is
       less reflective of current value.
    B. It is impossible to estimate COGS on a LIFO basis.
    C. If prices are rising and inventory levels are stable, the firm will have higher
       inventory than a firm using LIFO.
    D. If prices have been rising and the firm is located in the United States, taxes
       would be lower under LIFO than under FIFO.

34. A firm's financial statements were prepared using LIFO. What accounts should
    be adjusted when the financial statements are restated for the purpose of
    comparing ratios to industry averages?
    A. Net income.
    B. Accounts receivable.
    C. Long-term debt.
    D. Stockholders' equity.

35. Three analysts are debating about the inflation rate that should be used to
    adjust a firm's COGS, which was reported using FIFO, to a LIFO basis. The
    first states that they should use the inflation rate for the economy. The second
    states that they should use an inflation rate derived from a competitor's LIFO
    reserve calculations. The third states that they should use figures derived for
    the industry by a trade association. Which of the three are valid?
    A. First only.
    B. Third only.
    C. First and the third.
    D. Second and the third.

36. Kamp, Inc. sells specialized bicycle shoes. At year-end, due to a sudden increase in manufacturing costs, the replacement cost per pair of shoes is $55. The historical cost is $43, and the current selling price is $50. The normal profit margin is 10% of the selling price, and the selling costs are $3 per pair.

At which of the following amounts should each pair of shoes be recorded on Kamp's year-end balance sheet?
   A. $42.
   B. $43.
   C. $47.
   D. $55.

[handwritten: 43]

[handwritten: NRV = 50-3 = 47]

[handwritten: 4]

[handwritten: Replacement]

[handwritten: = NRV]

[handwritten: NRV − Profit]

[handwritten: = 47−5 = 42]

[handwritten: (42, 47)]

ANSWERS – CONCEPT CHECKERS

1. **C** The choice of inventory accounting method flows through the income statement to ultimately affect taxes.

2. **A** Beginning inventory + purchases – COGS = $40,000 + $55,000 – $60,000 = $35,000.

3. **C** Purchases + beginning inventory – ending inventory = $11.2 + $2.8 – $3 = $11.

4. **B** If COGS is overstated, ending inventory must be understated.

5. **D** Overstated beginning inventory coupled with understated ending inventory implies that COGS is overstated by $5,000. If COGS is overstated, income will be understated.

6. **B** Purchases + beginning inventory – ending inventory = $25,000 + $15,000 – $17,000 = $23,000.

7. **B** COGS reflects the items purchased first-in FIFO accounting. Remember, first in, first out.

8. **B** 108 units were sold (13 + 35 + 60), and 150 units were available for sale (beginning inventory of 0 plus purchases of 40 + 20 + 90), so there are 150 – 108 = 42 units in ending inventory. Under FIFO, units from the last batch purchased would remain: 42 × $50 = $2,100.

9. **B** Under LIFO, the first 42 units purchased would be in inventory: (40 × $30) + (2 × $40) = $1,280.

10. **B** Revenue = (13 × $35) + (35 × $45) + (60 × $60) = $5,630.
    Purchases = (40 × $30) + (20 × $40) + (90 × $50) = $6,500.
    COGS = purchases + beginning inventory – ending inventory = 6,500 + 0 – 1,280 = $5,220.
    Gross profit = $5,630 – $5,220 = $410.

11. **D** COGS = purchases + beginning inventory – ending inventory = 6,500 + 0 – 2,100 = $4,400.
    Gross profit = $5,630 – $4,400 = $1,230.

12. **B** The average cost of inventory is [(40 × $30) + (20 × $40) + (90 × $50)] / (40 + 20 + 90) = $43.33.
    Inventory value = $43.33 × 42 units = $1,820.

13. **A** COGS = 43.33 × 108 = 4,680.
    Gross profit = $5,630 – $4,680 = $950.

14. **A** Weighted average COGS will always be in the middle of FIFO and LIFO whether prices are rising or falling. If prices are rising, LIFO COGS will be the highest because the most recent goods produced go to COGS.

15. **A** LIFO COGS will be the lowest of the three methods when prices are falling. That means LIFO income will be the highest.

16. **B** With FIFO, older inventory is sold first, so current inventory is a better reflection of the current cost it would take to replace that inventory.

17. **A** Analysts prefer LIFO for the income statement because the COGS is current.

18. **D** With rising prices, LIFO results in higher COGS. Higher costs mean lower income; lower income means lower taxes; and lower taxes mean higher cash flow.

19. **A** Firms using FIFO will have lower COGS, which means they will have higher net income when compared to a firm using LIFO when prices are rising.

20. **A** COGS per unit decline and profit margins increase.

21. **B** Falling prices for a firm using FIFO mean older, more expensive goods are going to COGS, thus lowering net income.

22. **D** If prices are rising, FIFO inventories will be higher. Because inventory is a current asset, this will result in a higher current ratio than firms using LIFO.

23. **D** LIFO COGS is the better measure of economic cost as long as inventory levels have not declined.

24. **C** If the LIFO firm is reporting higher net income, prices must be falling.

25. **D** With rising prices, all of the answers apply to LIFO compared to FIFO.

26. **C** All else equal, the FIFO firm has a higher level of assets due to the higher inventory. Since liabilities are assumed to be equal to total assets, the FIFO must have higher equity to finance those assets.

27. **A** FIFO COGS = LIFO COGS – (ending LIFO reserve – beginning LIFO reserve) = $125,000 – ($15,000 – $12,000) = $122,000.

28. **C** LIFO inventory is lower than FIFO, so add the LIFO reserve.

29. **D** Retained earnings must be increased by LIFO reserve, $60,000. No tax adjustment is necessary here.

30. **A** Accounts payable are not affected by inventory accounting methods.

31. **D** Decrease LIFO COGS by the change in the LIFO reserve.

32. **A** Because costs decrease by $10,000, pretax income would increase by $10,000, and after-tax net income would increase by $6,000. The change in LIFO reserve +$10,000, times (1 – 0.4) = $6,000.

33. **B** Costs can be estimated by adding the inflation rate multiplied by the beginning inventory.

34. **D** Inventory would increase, which means assets would increase, which means equity would increase to keep the balance sheet in balance.

35. **D** Either the change in a competitor's LIFO reserve as a percentage of BI_{FIFO} or industry statistics can be used to estimate the inflation rate.

36. **B** Market is equal to the replacement cost subject to replacement cost being within a specific range. The upper bound is net realizable value (NRV), which is equal to selling price ($50) less selling costs ($3) for an NRV of $47. The lower bound is NRV ($47) less normal profit (10% of selling price = $5) for a net amount of $42. Since replacement cost ($55) is greater than NRV ($47), market equals NRV ($47). Additionally, we have to use the lower of cost ($43) or market ($47) principle, so the shoes should be recorded at the cost of $43.

ANALYSIS OF LONG-LIVED ASSETS: PART I –THE CAPITALIZATION DECISION

Study Session 9

EXAM FOCUS

Firms must decide to either expense (write off immediately) or capitalize (place on the balance sheet) the costs of acquiring an asset. The decision is typically based on the longevity of the asset in accordance with the matching principle discussed earlier. For the Level 1 exam, know that the expensing versus capitalizing decision affects financial statement components and ratios.

Typically, firms that capitalize costs will have smoother net income, higher profitability in early years (lower in later years), higher cash flows from operations, lower cash flows from investing, and lower leverage ratios. Candidates should understand the circumstances and financial statement effects of capitalizing expenses in general, interest costs during construction, and intangible assets.

LOS 36.a: Demonstrate the effects of capitalizing versus expensing on net income, shareholders' equity, cash flow from operations, and financial ratios.

The costs (cash price plus all necessary expenditures made before an asset is ready for use) of acquiring resources that provide services over more than one operating cycle are capitalized and carried as assets on the balance sheet. The decision to **capitalize** or **expense** some items depends on management choices, and is subject to manipulation. These choices may affect the balance sheet, income statement, cash flow statement, and related financial ratios for the current period as well as over the life of the asset. When correctly employed, capitalization of expenses allows better matching of revenues with the expenses incurred to generate those revenues.

Issues that arise in capitalization include:

- Which components of cost are capitalized (e.g., interest charges, R&D).
- What method should be used to determine the amount capitalized.

Statement of Financial Accounting Concepts (SFAC) 6 defines accounting assets as those assets that provide probable future economic benefits. However, for the purpose of analysis, the term "asset" may represent:

- The initial investment outlays.
- Those parts of a firm that represent "wealth."
- One of the inputs in the production function.

Depending on the purpose of the analysis, the firm's assets may be evaluated by looking at:

- Profitability [by return on assets (ROA)].
- Solvency (protection for creditors).
- Operating efficiency and operating leverage.

Different types of analysis may require asset definitions different from those found in the accounting rules. For example, machinery acquired under an operating lease is not recognized as an asset on the balance sheet, but its recognition as an asset may be appropriate in security analysis. Research and development and advertising expenditures may provide future services, but are expensed when incurred and not recognized as an asset under accounting practices.

How Capitalization Affects Financial Statements and Ratios

The effects of capitalizing expenses on financial statements and ratios stem from the fact that capitalizing reduces current period expenses by the amount capitalized. The amount of capitalized expenses is added to assets, and the related cash flow is treated as an investing cash flow rather than an operating cash flow. The decision to capitalize expenses does not affect debt. Capitalizing expenses will increase equity, by increasing net income and retained earnings in the current period, and increase assets, because of the addition of the capitalized amount. The asset created by capitalizing expenses will be amortized—that is, the capitalized expenses will be spread over a period of years. The asset value is reduced by amortization each year, similar to depreciation of plant and equipment.

Financial statement effects. Although it may make no operational difference, the choice between capitalizing or expensing will affect reported income, cash flow from operations, and leverage ratios. Companies that capitalize expenses will show higher asset balances, greater cash flow from operations, and lower cash flow from investing. The capitalized expense is classified as an investing cash flow, rather than as an operating cash flow.

Income variability. Firms that capitalize costs and depreciate them over time *will show smoother reported income*. Firms that expense costs will tend to have greater variance in reported income. The expenditures that are candidates for capitalization are large in magnitude and tend to vary widely from year to year. When these amounts are expensed instead of capitalized, their variability causes a high degree of variability in net income.

Profitability. In the year in which an expense is capitalized, companies that capitalize expenses have higher profitability measures than expensing companies. When a company expenses large purchases, this decreases income. In later years, net income, ROA, and ROE will be lower for a company that capitalizes, because profits in later years will be lower than for expensing firms due to continuing depreciation, and because assets will be higher by the capitalized amount. Firms that expense have lower asset levels (and because of this, lower equity levels), so ROA and ROE will typically be higher over time than for firms that capitalize.

Cash flow from operations. Although *net* cash flows are not affected by the choice of capitalization or expensing (ignoring tax effects), the components of cash flow are

Study Session 9

Cross-Reference to CFA Institute Assigned Reading #36 – Analysis of Long-Lived Assets: Part I—The Capitalization Decision

affected. Because a firm that capitalizes outlays classifies those expenditures as investing cash flows, *cash flow from operations will be higher* and *investing cash flows will be lower* than that of a firm that expenses.

Leverage ratios. Capitalizing firms have higher asset and equity levels, while expensing firms report lower assets and equity levels. Therefore, *debt to equity and debt to asset ratios will appear worse for expensing firms* than for capitalizing firms.

The financial implications of capitalizing versus expensing are summarized in Figure 1.

Figure 1: Financial Statement Impacts: Capitalizing vs. Expensing

	Capitalizing	Expensing
Income variability	Lower	Higher
Profitability—early years (ROA & ROE)	Higher	Lower
Profitability—later years (ROA & ROE)	Lower	Higher
Total cash flows	Same	Same
Cash flow from operations	Higher	Lower
Cash flow from investing	Lower	Higher
Leverage ratios (debt/equity & debt/assets)	Lower	Higher

Example: Effect of capitalization

The figure below is a balance sheet for Soprano Company for 2005 and 2006 and its income statement for 2006.

Soprano Company Balance Sheet and Income Statement

Balance Sheet

	2006	2005
Assets		
Current assets		
Cash	$105	$95
Receivables	205	195
Inventories	310	290
Total current assets	$620	$580
Noncurrent assets		
Gross property, plant, and equipment	$1,800	$1,700
Accumulated depreciation	(360)	(340)
Net property, plant, and equipment	$1,440	$1,360
Total assets	$2,000	$1,940

Soprano Company Balance Sheet and Income Statement (Continued)

Liabilities		
Current liabilities		
Payables	$110	$90
Short-term debt	160	140
Current portion of long-term debt	55	45
Total current liabilities	$325	$275
Noncurrent liabilities		
Long-term debt	$610	$690
Deferred taxes	105	95
Stockholders' equity		
Common stock	$300	$300
Additional paid in capital	400	400
Retained earnings	620	180
Common shareholders' equity	1,020	880
Total liabilities & equity	$2,060	$1,940

Income Statement	2006
Sales	$4,000
Cost of goods sold	$3,000
Gross profit	1,000
Operating expense	650
Operating profit	350
Interest expense	50
Earnings before taxes	300
Taxes	100
Net income	$200
Common dividends	$60

During 2006, the company discovered that $150 of its operating expenses should have been capitalized, which would also have increased depreciation expense by $20.

Complete the following table, *assuming that there will be no impact on taxes:*

Soprano Company Answer Template

	Before Capitalization	After Capitalization
Net income	$200	
Profit margin	5.0%	
Return on capital	12.5%	
Cash flow from operations	220	
Cash flow from investing	(100)	
Total cash flow	10	
Debt/equity	59.8%	

Answer:

Net income: Cash operating expense decreases by $150, but depreciation increases by $20. New net income will be 200 + (150 − 20) = $330.

Profit margin: net income/sales = 330 / 4,000 = 8.3%. This ratio increased because the numerator, or net income, increased and the denominator remained constant.

Return on capital: 2006 total assets will increase by $150 less the depreciation of $20. New total assets = 2,060 + 150 − 20 = $2,190. Return on total capital = (net income + interest expense) / average total capital = (330 + 50) / [(2,190 + 1,940) / 2] = 18.4%. This ratio also increased. As will usually be the case, the relative net income (numerator) effect of the decreased expense was greater than the relative increase in average total capital (equity).

Cash flow from operations: Cash operating expense decreases by $150, so cash flow from operations will be 220 + 150 = $370. This is an increase.

Cash flow from investing: Outflows will increase by $150, so cash flow from investments will be −100 − 150 = −$250. This is a decrease, or a higher outflow.

Total cash flow will not change and will remain at $10.

Note: These cash flow calculations ignore any tax impact.

Debt-to-equity: Assets increased by $130, so equity will now increase by $130. New equity = 1,020 + 130 = $1,150. The debt-to-equity ratio = long-term debt / total equity = 610 / 1,150 = 53.0%. This ratio decreased because equity (the denominator) increased by the amount of the capitalized asset, and debt (the numerator) remained unchanged.

CAPITALIZED INTEREST

Capitalized interest is the interest incurred during the construction of long-lived assets. It is included in the initial cost of the asset on the balance sheet instead of being charged off as interest expense on the income statement.

The argument for interest capitalization is that the cost of the self-constructed asset should be identical to the cost of the asset purchased after completion. The argument against the capitalization of interest is that the interest expense is the result of a *financing* decision and not an *operating* or *investment* decision. Internationally, capitalization of interest is optional.

Computation of capitalized interest. In the United States, Statement of Financial Accounting Standards (SFAS) 34 requires the capitalization of interest costs incurred during the construction period.

- Interest incurred on borrowed funds during construction must be capitalized (i.e., included in cost of asset) and not expensed (SFAS 34), and the amount capitalized must be disclosed.
- If no specific borrowing is identified, the interest is estimated using the weighted average interest rate on outstanding debt up to the amount of the investment. Capitalized interest cannot exceed actual interest paid in any case.

When a firm constructs its own operating facilities (e.g., machinery or a building), then interest costs incurred during the period of construction are capitalized by adding that interest cost to the cost of the facility. To be capitalized, the interest must actually be paid by the firm (no opportunity costs are capitalized). The capitalized interest cost is based upon the average cost of the partially completed facility, first using the interest rate associated with borrowings to directly finance construction. Then the average interest rate of the firm's outstanding debt is applied to the excess of the investment in the project over these project-specific borrowings, if any. Thus, during construction, interest expense is total interest paid less capitalized interest.

> **Example: Capitalizing interest**
>
> During the current year, a firm has been constructing a building to be used for its production facility. The average cost of the building in process is $1,000,000. The firm has borrowed $500,000 at 5% interest to finance this construction. It has $3,000,000 of 10% debentures outstanding. Calculate the amount of interest that should be capitalized and the amount that should be expensed.

$500,000 x 1/2

Answer:

Interest on construction debt: [$500,000 (0.05)] $25,000   *Total.*
Interest on debentures [$500,000 (0.10)] $50,000
Total capitalized interest $75,000

Total interest expense = total interest paid – capitalized interest
                       = $25,000 + $300,000 – $75,000
                       = $250,000

Note: If the firm's only debt were the $500,000, 5% construction loan, then only the interest paid on that debt ($25,000) would be capitalized.

The Effects of Capitalizing Interest Costs

- During the current year, **capitalized interest decreases interest expense and increases net income.** For analysis purposes, capitalized interest should be added to interest expense and taken out of the fixed asset. When the capitalized interest is removed from fixed assets, depreciation expense will be reduced when that asset is placed in operations.

- **Capitalized interest distorts the classification of cash flows.** Interest capitalized as part of fixed assets is reported as a cash flow from investing (CFI), not a cash flow from operations (CFO). So CFO is overstated and CFI is understated. Therefore, cash flows should be adjusted by adding the capitalized interest back to the CFI and deducting it with the other interest payments from the CFO.

- For firms in an expansion phase, **capitalization of interest may result in a gain in earnings over an extended period** of time because the amount of interest amortized will not catch up with the amount of interest capitalized in the current period. Net income will be overstated.

 Professor's Note: Although the LOS for this topic does not explicitly state that you should understand potential analyst adjustments for capitalized interest, many analysts "undo" the effects of capitalized interest when analyzing and comparing firms.

An analyst should adjust income statements and balance sheets to reverse the impact of capitalized interest. Specifically, an analyst should make the following adjustments:

- Interest that was capitalized during the year should be added to interest expense. The amount of interest capitalized is disclosed in the financial statement footnotes.

- The amortization of interest capitalized in previous years should be deducted from depreciation expense. However, capitalized interest from previous years might not be disclosed in the financial statements. If this amount is small, the analyst can ignore it. If it is large, the analyst must estimate the adjustment by using the historical ratio of capitalized interest to total capital expenditures.

- The interest that was capitalized during the year should be added back to cash flow from investment and subtracted from cash flow from operations.

- Ratios such as interest coverage and profitability ratios should be recalculated with the restated figures. Interest coverage ratios and net profit margins are likely lower without capitalization.

Capitalization of Interest and Interest Coverage Ratios

The interest coverage ratio, often called times interest earned, is EBIT (operating earnings) divided by interest expense. This ratio gives an indication of the margin of safety the company has in regard to making interest payments on debt. When interest is capitalized, current period interest costs are decreased and the interest coverage ratio is increased. There is an effect of capitalizing interest on EBIT since capitalizing interest incurred during construction increases the asset value, and thereby increases depreciation expense. In the period of capitalization, the decrease in interest expense will be larger than any decrease in EBIT from increased depreciation, so that the interest coverage ratio is unambiguously increased by capitalization. Since capitalization of interest in a prior period has no effect on interest expense in subsequent periods, any decrease in subsequent period EBIT from greater depreciation will decrease the interest coverage ratio for that period. If interest is capitalized over a number of accounting periods, interest coverage ratios may be higher than without capitalization in each period.

LOS 36.b: Determine which intangible assets, including software development costs and research and development costs, should be capitalized, according to U.S. GAAP and international accounting standards.

An **intangible asset** is an asset that has no physical existence and has a high degree of uncertainty regarding future benefits.

When acquired in an arm's-length transaction, identifiable intangible assets (e.g., patents, trademarks, franchises) are recorded at acquisition cost. The expense of their use is recognized by amortization of cost over the shorter of estimated useful or legal lives.

The capitalize-versus-expense issue is relevant to intangible assets and resources such as patents, copyrights, licenses, brand names, goodwill, etc. The particular troubles with accounting for internally generated intangible assets are that the costs may not be easily separable, potential benefits may be difficult to measure (e.g., advertising), and economic life may be nearly impossible to establish (e.g., brand names).

Types of intangible assets include the following:

- *Research and development* (R&D): Although risky, R&D expenditures are clearly economic assets. (Empirical research suggests the average life is seven to ten years, depending on the assets and the industry). However, under Generally Accepted Accounting Principles (GAAP), specifically SFAS 2, it is required that *research and development expenditures be expensed* when incurred. Outside the United States, R&D expenditures may be capitalized if various conditions are met (e.g., International Accounting Standard 9 requires expensing research costs but capitalizing development costs).
- *Patents and copyrights* costs (except legal fees for registration, which are capitalized) incurred in developing patents and copyrights are expensed. However, if the patent or copyright is purchased, then the cost is capitalized.
- *Franchise and license* costs are typically capitalized by the purchasing firm.

- *Brands and trademarks:* If *acquired* in arm's-length transactions, the cost is capitalized.
- *Advertising costs,* like R&D expenditures, are expensed when incurred. However, direct-response (direct relation between marketing and sales, e.g., orders taken in response to a call) advertising costs are capitalized when the benefits will be realized over multiple accounting periods.
- *Goodwill* is an intangible asset representing the difference between the amount paid for an acquired firm and the fair market value of its net assets. Goodwill may be recognized and capitalized only in purchase transactions. Please note that expensing (amortizing) capitalized goodwill is no longer permitted under either U.S. GAAP or IFRS. Instead, an impairment exercise is performed each year to determine if purchased goodwill has been impaired relative to its balance sheet value. If an impairment has occurred, this impairment write off is recorded on the income statement as an expense.
- *Computer software development costs:* SFAS 86 requires that all costs incurred to *establish* the technological or economic feasibility of software intended to be sold to others be expensed (e.g., R&D). Subsequent costs may be capitalized as part of inventory. Disparate accounting for software development costs (e.g., Microsoft expenses all software costs) requires the analyst to *evaluate and eliminate the impact of capitalization* to facilitate company comparisons. SOP 98-1 *requires* expensing of development costs prior to establishing feasibility for software intended for internal use, and requires capitalization of development costs for internal-use software after technological feasibility has been established. Net income computed after "undoing" the effects of capitalizing software development cost will typically be lower. Reclassifying these costs as operating rather than investing cash flows can have a significant impact on cash flow classification, reducing CFO and increasing CFI.

Financial statement effects of intangibles: Consistent with the effects of expensing versus capitalizing, capitalizing development costs will increase current net income. If expenditures are increasing, future net incomes will be greater for the capitalizing firm. Thus, return on assets will be greater and debt-to-equity ratio lower (more income, more equity) for the capitalizing firm. If development expenditures are decreasing, then the amortization of the capitalized expenditures will result in lower future net incomes (and lower ROA) for the capitalizing firm.

Although total cash flows are unaffected, capitalizing development costs will result in lower cash flow from investing and greater cash flow from operations. This is summarized in Figure 2.

Figure 2: Impact of Capitalizing vs. Expensing Development Cost

Effect on …	If capitalized …	If expensed …
Current net income	Greater	Smaller
Future income (increasing capitalized expenditures)	Greater	Smaller
Future income (decreasing capitalized expenditures)	Smaller	Greater
Debt-equity ratio	Smaller	Greater
Return on assets (initial)	Greater	Smaller
Return on assets (future)	Smaller	Greater
Total cash flow	Same	Same
Cash flow from operations	Greater	Smaller
Cash flow from investing	Smaller	Greater

The effect of capitalizing expenditures of various types on ROE and ROA is sometimes confusing to students because the numerator (net income) as well as the denominators (equity and assets) both go up with capitalization. The key to the overall effect on the ratios is that we can safely assume in almost all cases that both equity and assets are significantly larger than net income. For a simple example, consider a non-capitalizing company with NI of 10, equity of 100, and assets of 200. ROE = 10% and ROA = 5%. If expenditures of 2 are capitalized rather than expensed,

$$\text{ROE} = \frac{12}{102} = 11.8\% \text{ and ROA} = \frac{12}{202} = 5.9\% \text{ in the year of capitalization.}$$

Capitalization Outside the United States

There are some significant differences between capitalization under U.S. GAAP and under accounting standards outside the United States.

Construction Interest Costs

Under International Accounting Standards (IAS 23), interest costs on corporate borrowing are typically expensed, as in the United States. With respect to interest costs that are specific to funds borrowed to acquire or construct assets, IAS permit, but do not require, capitalization. In many other countries, interest capitalization is allowed.

Research and Development Costs

International Accounting Standards require expensing of research expenses, but development expenses may be capitalized when several conditions are met. These conditions really just ensure that the costs are actually incurred in developing a clearly defined product that can and will be produced by the firm.

Study Session 9

Cross-Reference to CFA Institute Assigned Reading #36 – Analysis of Long-Lived Assets: Part I—The Capitalization Decision

KEY CONCEPTS

1. Capitalization of outlays, compared to expensing, causes lower variability of net income, higher net income, higher operating cash flow, and lower leverage ratios. Capitalization causes return on assets (ROA) and return on equity (ROE) to be higher in the year of capitalization and lower in later years unless capitalized expenditures are increasing.

2. Capitalization of interest causes interest expense to be lower, depreciation to be slightly higher, cash flow from operations to be higher, and the interest coverage ratio to be higher. Analysts often adjust financial statements to remove the effects of capitalized interest.

3. In general, intangible asset costs are capitalized when the assets are acquired from an outside entity. Under U.S. GAAP, only the legal fees to obtain a patent or trademark internally can be capitalized, and development costs for software for external sale may be capitalized after technical and economic feasibility have been established.

4. Under IFRS, development costs and interest costs associated with borrowing to acquire or construct specific assets may be capitalized.

CONCEPT CHECKERS

1. Which of the following statements about the capitalization decision is *most accurate*?
   A. The choice between capitalization and expensing makes no operational difference.
   B. Firms that capitalize costs will show more variability in reported income.
   C. Firms that capitalize costs will have lower assets and equity.
   D. Cash flow from operations is not affected by the capitalization or expensing choice.

2. For purposes of analysis, capitalized interest should be:
   A. added to fixed assets.
   B. added back to the cash flows for investment.
   C. added to interest expense and results in higher net income.
   D. subtracted from interest expense and results in higher net income.

3. With the exception of legal costs, generally accepted accounting principles (GAAP) require that costs incurred in:

	Developing patents are:	Purchased patents are:
A.	Expensed	Expensed
B.	Expensed	Capitalized
C.	Capitalized	Expensed
D.	Capitalized	Capitalized

4. Which of the following statements is *least accurate*? All other things being equal, firms that capitalize costs will:
   A. show smoother reported income than expensing firms.
   B. have higher operating cash flow and lower investment cash flow than expensing firms.
   C. have lower leverage ratios than expensing firms.
   D. have lower profitability ratios in the early years than expensing firms.

5. With the exception of legal costs, U.S. generally accepted accounting principles (GAAP) require that costs incurred in establishing the technological feasibility of software be:
   A. expensed, and interest expenses relative to the construction of a building must be expensed.
   B. expensed, and interest expenses relative to the construction of a building must be capitalized.
   C. capitalized, and interest expenses relative to the construction of a building must be expensed.
   D. capitalized, and interest expenses relative to the construction of a building must be capitalized.

Study Session 9

Cross-Reference to CFA Institute Assigned Reading #36 – Analysis of Long-Lived Assets: Part I—The Capitalization Decision

6.   Which of the following statements is *most accurate*? Accounting choices:
      A. never affect cash flows.
      B. always affect cash flows.
      C. may affect the classification of cash flow components without affecting total cash flow.
      D. never affect the classification of cash flow components without affecting total cash flow.

7.   Firm A expenses costs while Firm B capitalizes them. All other things being equal, which of the following choices *best* describes the relationship between the debt ratios of Firm A and Firm B?
      A. They will be equal.
      B. Firm A's will be lower.
      C. Firm A's will be higher.
      D. Cannot be determined without more information.

8.   Capitalizing construction interest costs leads to:
      A. a lower debt ratio.
      B. higher future depreciation expense.
      C. lower reported income after the first year.
      D. All of the above.

Use the following data to answer Questions 9 and 10.

Smokee Enterprises capitalizes most costs and Eb One Manufacturing expenses most costs.

9.   Which of the following choices *correctly* describes Smokee's financial results for current income, debt-to-equity ratio, and cash flow from operations as compared to Eb One's results?

	Current net income	Debt-to-equity ratio	Cash flows from operations
A.	Greater	Smaller	Smaller
B.	Greater	Smaller	Greater
C.	Smaller	Greater	Smaller
D.	Smaller	Smaller	Greater

10.   Which of the following choices *correctly* describes Eb One's financial results for initial return on assets, total cash flow, and cash flow from investing as compared to Smokee's results?

	Initial return on assets	Total cash flow	Cash flows from investing
A.	Smaller	Larger	Equivalent
B.	Larger	Equivalent	Smaller
C.	Smaller	Equivalent	Larger
D.	Equivalent	Larger	Smaller

11. Which of the following statements about the treatment of intangible assets is *least accurate*?
    A. Advertising costs are expensed when incurred.
    B. All software development costs may be capitalized.
    C. Internally developed patent and copyright costs are expensed when incurred.
    D. In the United States, research and development costs are expensed when incurred.

12. The interest costs during construction are:
    A. expensed as incurred.
    B. expensed at the completion of the construction project.
    C. capitalized and then, once construction is completed, amortized over the life of the loan.
    D. capitalized and then, once construction is completed, amortized over the life of the constructed asset.

13. Which of the following statements is *most accurate*?
    A. Research and development is capitalized according to U.S. GAAP.
    B. The costs associated with the creation of a brand name within a company are capitalized.
    C. In the case of a patent, the costs of developing the patent are expensed but legal costs can be capitalized.
    D. The difference between the purchase price and the fair value of identifiable net assets acquired in a purchase transaction is expensed in the period in which the acquisition is made.

©2008 Schweser

ANSWERS – CONCEPT CHECKERS

1. **A**   There is no operational difference.

2. **B**   For analysis purposes, interest expense should be added to cash flows for investment.

3. **B**   If a firm develops the patent as part of its own operations, the cost is expensed. Only costs for purchasing a patent are capitalized.

4. **D**   Firms that capitalize costs will show higher profitability ratios in early years due to the costs being spread out.

5. **B**   Establishing technological feasibility of software is an operational activity and costs must be expensed. Interest related to construction must be capitalized.

6. **C**   Overall cash flow may be the same even when accounting choices affect the classification of cash flow components. Accounting choices will affect cash flows if they affect taxes.

7. **C**   Firm A will have a lower level of assets, making the expensing firm's debt ratio appear higher.

8. **D**   All statements are true. The company will have a lower debt ratio because total equity (the denominator) will increase while the numerator is unchanged. The higher future depreciation expense results from the amortization of the capitalized interest, which an expensing firm would not have. This also results in lower reported income.

9. **B**   Capitalizing firms will have greater net incomes, smaller debt-to-equity ratios due to the larger amount of equity, and greater cash flow from operations due to the classification of expenditures as investment cash flows.

10. **C**   Firms that expense costs will have a smaller initial return on assets due to the effect of lower net income, the same total cash flows (only classification is different), and larger CFI due to expenses being considered CFO.

11. **B**   Software development costs are operational in nature and must be expensed.

12. **D**   Interest costs from construction are capitalized and amortized over the life of the asset.

13. **C**   R&D costs are expensed, only acquired brand names are capitalized, and goodwill is capitalized. Legal costs of securing a patent can be capitalized.

ANALYSIS OF LONG-LIVED ASSETS: PART II – ANALYSIS OF DEPRECIATION AND IMPAIRMENT

Study Session 9

EXAM FOCUS

Depreciation is allocating the cost of an asset to expense over time. In reality, depreciation is an allocation of past cash flows; depreciation expense appears on the income statement but has no impact on the statement of cash flows. There are multiple acceptable methods of calculating depreciation, and the method the firm chooses is its own decision. A firm using a slower method of depreciation will show higher net income. A firm may choose to use an accelerated method on its tax return to show lower taxable income and thus pay less in taxes. On the Level 1 exam, be prepared to calculate depreciation using all of the methods discussed in this topic review. Also know the effects of accelerated versus straight-line depreciation, as well as the effects on financial statements and ratios of taking a write-down on an impaired asset.

LOS 37.a: Demonstrate the different depreciation methods and explain how the choice of depreciation method affects a company's financial statements, ratios, and taxes.

The underlying *principle of depreciation* is that cash flows generated by an asset over its life cannot be considered income until provision is made for the asset's replacement. This means that the *definition of income* requires a subtraction for asset replacement.

The accounting problem is how to allocate the cost of the asset over time. Depreciation is the systematic allocation of the asset's cost over time.

Two important terms are:

- *Book value.* The net value of an asset or liability as it is listed on the balance sheet. For property, plant, and equipment, book value equals historical cost minus accumulated depreciation.
- *Historical cost.* The original purchase price of the asset including installation and transportation costs. The gross investment in the asset is the same as its historical cost.

Depreciation is a real and significant operating expense. Even though depreciation doesn't require current cash expenditures (the cash outflow was made in the past when the company invested in the depreciable assets), it is an expense that is just as important as labor or material expense. Therefore, analysis should *not* exclude depreciation expense. For financial statements, the analyst must decide whether the depreciation expense the firm reports is significantly more or less than the true decline in the value of the asset over the period, its *economic depreciation*. One chain of video rental stores was found to be overstating income by depreciating its stock of movies by equal amounts each year. In fact, a greater portion of the decrease in the value of newly released movies was realized in the first year. Depreciating this asset by a greater amount during the first year would have better approximated economic depreciation than depreciating it by equal amounts over three years.

Four methods of calculating depreciation are described here.

Straight-line (SL) depreciation is the dominant method of computing depreciation. It applies an equal amount of depreciation to each year over the asset's estimated depreciable life:

$$\text{depreciation expense} = \frac{\text{original cost} - \text{salvage value}}{\text{depreciable life}}$$

Example: Calculating straight-line depreciation expense

Melfi Co. has purchased a machine with a 4-year useful life. The machine cost $4,000 and has an estimated salvage value of $1,000. Using the SL method, calculate depreciation expense in year 1 and year 4. Note: This same example will be used throughout this discussion.

Answer:

The constant depreciation expense over all years will be:

$$\frac{\text{original cost} - \text{salvage value}}{\text{depreciable life}} = \frac{(\$4,000 - \$1,000)}{4} = \$750$$

There are some flaws with using straight-line depreciation.

- Straight-line depreciation is constant through time, while repair and maintenance expense will typically increase over the life of the asset. This will cause a decrease in reported income over time.
- This method yields an increasing rate of return over the life of the asset.

For example, assume the asset discussed above generates an annual income of $1,200 before the $750 depreciation charge. Net income will be $450 a year for each of the asset's four years of useful life. The book value (cost less accumulated depreciation) of the asset begins at cost, then decreases with the added depreciation expense each year. This decreasing book value and constant income results in an increasing rate of return on the asset, as shown in Figure 1.

Figure 1: ROA Calculation

Year	Beginning Carrying Value	Straight-Line Depreciation	Net Income	Rate of Return on Assets
1	$4,000	$750	$450	11.25%
2	$3,250	$750	$450	13.85%
3	$2,500	$750	$450	18.00%
4	$1,750	$750	$450	25.71%

The increase in maintenance generally does not negate the increase in return on assets (ROA) caused by the constant depreciation expense.

There are two **accelerated depreciation methods**, sum-of-year's digits (SYD) and double-declining balance (DDB), which recognize greater depreciation expense in the early part of an asset's life and less expense in the latter portion of its life.

The economic justifications of accelerated depreciation methods include increasing repair and maintenance costs, decreasing revenues and operating efficiency, and greater uncertainty about revenues due to obsolescence in the later years of the asset's life.

Accelerated depreciation methods are usually used on tax returns (when allowed) because greater depreciation expense in the early portion of the asset's life results in less taxable income and a smaller tax payment. A firm may use straight-line depreciation for its financial statements and an accelerated method on its tax returns. This initial saving on taxes is a deferral because a greater tax payment will be required in the latter part of the asset's life. Note that total depreciation is initial cost minus salvage value over the asset's life in either case; an accelerated method just moves some depreciation to earlier periods.

> **Example: Calculating sum of the year's digits depreciation expense**
>
> Melfi Co. has purchased a machine with a 4-year useful life that cost $4,000 and has an estimated salvage value of $1,000. Using the sum of the years' digits method, calculate depreciation expense in year 1 and year 4.

SL: High taxes

Ap: Low taxes

Answer:

$$SYD = 1 + 2 + 3 + 4 = 10, \text{ or } SYD = [(4)(5)]/2 = 20/2 = 10$$

$$\text{depreciation in year } x = \frac{(\text{original cost} - \text{salvage value}) \times (n - x + 1)}{SYD}$$

$$\text{depreciation in year } 1 = \frac{(\$4{,}000 - \$1{,}000) \times (4 - 1 + 1)}{10} = \$1{,}200$$

$$\text{depreciation in year } 4 = \frac{(\$4{,}000 - \$1{,}000) \times (4 - 4 + 1)}{10} = \$300$$

Note that the factors are simply 4/10, 3/10, 2/10, and 1/10 for the four years. Observe that the *total* depreciation expense calculated with the sum-of-years'-digits (SYD) method over the useful life of the asset is the same as that given by the straight-line method. That is, cost less salvage, which is $3,000.

The formula to calculate **double-declining balance** (DDB) depreciation is:

$$\text{depreciation in year } x = \frac{2}{\text{depreciable life}} \times \text{book value at beginning of year } x$$

The salvage value is not used in the formula. The remaining book value is not allowed to go below the salvage value. If the amount of depreciation in year x would take the book value below the salvage value, the depreciation in year x is equal to the difference between book value at the beginning of the year and the salvage value.

- The use of the *declining balance method* results in a constant percentage of an asset's carrying value (book value) being depreciated each period.
- The constant percentage can be any rate, but the most common are 200 DB (a.k.a. double-declining balance or DDB) and 150 DB. The rate is stated as a percentage of the straight-line rate. If the asset has a 10-year life, the straight-line rate is 10% per year and the 200DB rate is 20%; if the asset has a 20-year life, the straight-line rate is 5% and the 150DB rate is 150% of 5% or 7.5%.

Example: Calculating double declining balance depreciation expense

Melfi Co. has purchased a machine with a 4-year useful life that cost $4,000 and has an estimated salvage value of $1,000. Using the double-declining balance method, calculate depreciation expense in year 1 and year 4.

Answer:

$$\text{depreciation in year x} = \frac{2}{\text{depreciable life}} \times \text{book value at beginning of year x}$$

$$\text{depreciation in year 1} = \frac{2}{4} \times \$4,000 = \$2,000$$

$$\text{book value at the beginning of year 2} = \$4,000 - \$2,000 = \$2,000$$

$$\text{depreciation in year 2} = \frac{2}{4} \times \$2,000 = \$1,000$$

Book value at the end of year 2 is $2,000 – $1,000 = $1,000. Because book value at the end of year 2 is equal to salvage value, depreciation in years 3 and 4 will be zero.

The **units-of-production** and **service hours** methods apply depreciation at the rate at which an asset is being used. Either the production capacity or the service life of the asset is estimated when the asset is put into service. The cost of the asset minus the salvage value is divided by either the production capacity or service life to achieve either a rate per unit or a rate per hour. Depreciation is then charged based on the year's production or usage. Depreciation is never charged once the asset's book value reaches its estimated salvage value.

Example: Calculating units-of-production and service hours depreciation expense

Melfi Co. has purchased a machine with a 4-year useful life. The machine cost $4,000 and has an estimated salvage value of $1,000. The depreciable life is four years, and the machine is estimated to last 6,000 hours and produce 30,000 units. The machine is operated 1,200; 2,000; 2,000; and 1,500 hours in years 1 through 4; and the machine produces 12,000; 11,000; 10,000; and 9,000 units in years 1 through 4. Calculate depreciation expense in year 1 and year 4 using the units-of-production and service hours methods.

Answer:

Units of production:

$$\text{rate per unit} = \frac{\$4,000 - \$1,000}{30,000 \text{ units}} = \$0.10$$

$$\text{depreciation in year 1} = \$0.10 \times 12,000 = \$1,200$$

$$\text{depreciation in year 2} = \$0.10 \times 11,000 = \$1,100$$

$$\text{depreciation in year 3} = \$0.10 \times 10,000 = \$1,000$$

However, book value at the beginning of year 3 was $1,700 (= $4,000 – $1,200 – $1,100), so only $700 would be charged to depreciation in year 3 to make the book value equal to the salvage value of $1,000, and no depreciation would be charged in year 4.

Service hours:

$$\text{rate per hour} = \frac{\$4,000 - \$1,000}{6,000 \text{ hours}} = \$0.50$$

depreciation in year 1 = $0.50 × 1,200 = $600

depreciation in year 2 = $0.50 × 2,000 = $1,000

depreciation in year 3 = $0.50 × 2,000 = $1,000

depreciation in year 4 = $0.50 × 1,500 = $750

However, book value at the beginning of year 4 was $1,400 ($4,000 – $600 – $1,000 – $1,000), so only $400 would be charged to depreciation in year 4 to make book value equal to the salvage value of $1,000.

Sinking fund depreciation, sometimes called the annuity method, is seldom used and is prohibited in the U.S. and other countries. Depreciation expense actually *increases* each year so that the asset earns the same rate of return each year.

You can think about the rate of return on an asset or its return on investment as the net income generated from using the assets divided by its book value. If net income is changing over an asset's life only because depreciation is changing, both SL and accelerated depreciation methods lead to an increasing return on investment over time. With straight-line depreciation, the net income is the same each year, but the book value is decreasing, which produces an increasing return on investment. With accelerated methods, net income (net of depreciation) is increasing each year as well, and the return on investment increases even more in later years. With sinking fund depreciation, depreciation increases each year, so that net income decreases in proportion to the decrease in book value and keeps return on investment constant over the asset's life.

Effects of the Choice of Depreciation Method on Financial Statements, Ratios, and Taxes

Depreciation is an allocation of past investment cash flows, and the choice of depreciation method on the firm's financial statements has no impact on the statement of cash flows. It is important for the analyst to consider the capital expenditures to better understand the impact of the choice of depreciation methods.

In the early years of an asset's life, accelerated methods tend to depress net income and retained earnings and result in lower return measures [return on equity (ROE) and return on assets (ROA)]. At the end of the asset's life, the effect reverses. For firms with stable or rising capital expenditures, the early year effect will dominate, and depreciation expense on the total firm basis will be higher using accelerated methods.

A firm that chooses an accelerated depreciation method (e.g., DDB) instead of using straight-line will tend to have greater depreciation expense and lower net income. This will persist if the firm is investing in new assets such that the lower depreciation on old assets is more than compensated for by the higher depreciation on new assets. (If the firm is not investing in new assets, then the higher depreciation expense and lower net income are reversed in the later part of the asset's life.)

Although accelerated depreciation methods produce lower net assets and equity than straight-line, the lower net income causes a lower return on equity and return on assets. Regarding turnover ratios (e.g., sales over total assets), the lower asset levels for accelerated methods imply a higher ratio. There is no effect on cash directly caused by choice of depreciation methods, although the use of accelerated depreciation on tax returns reduces the cash paid for income taxes early in the asset's life and increases taxes paid in the later years of the asset's life. These relationships are summarized in Figure 2, assuming the firm is investing in a new asset.

Figure 2: Financial Statement Impact of Depreciation Methods*

	Straight Line	Accelerated (DDB & SYD)
Depreciation expense	Lower	Higher
Net income	Higher	Lower
Assets	Higher	Lower
Equity	Higher	Lower
Return on assets	Higher	Lower
Return on equity	Higher	Lower
Turnover ratios	Lower	Higher
Cash flow**	Same	Same

* The relationships indicated in the table are for the early years of an asset's life and are reversed in the latter years of the asset's life if the firm's capital expenditures decline.

** Assuming the depreciation method used for tax purposes is unchanged.

Study Session 9

Cross-Reference to CFA Institute Assigned Reading #37 – Analysis of Long-Lived Assets: Part II—Analysis of Depreciation and Impairment

LOS 37.b: Demonstrate how modifying the depreciation method, the estimated useful life, and/or the salvage value used in accounting for long-lived assets affect financial statements and ratios.

Depreciable Lives and Salvage Values

In general, a longer useful life estimate decreases annual depreciation and increases reported net income, while a shorter estimate of the asset's useful life will have the opposite effect. A higher estimate of the residual (salvage) value will also decrease depreciation and increase net income, while a lower estimate of the salvage value will increase depreciation and decrease net income.

The choice of estimated lives and residual values gives companies some ability to manage earnings, and an analyst should be alert to instances of excessively long depreciable life assumptions or excessively high residual (salvage) values, both of which will lead to an overstatement of net income. Although companies are required to disclose information on depreciable lives, such disclosures are often given as ranges and cover groups of assets rather than specific assets.

- Management could estimate a useful life longer than that warranted (thus reducing depreciation expense and increasing income) and then write down the overstated assets in a restructuring process.
- Management might also write down assets, taking an immediate charge against income, and then record less future depreciation expense based on the written-down assets. This results in higher future net income in exchange for a one-time charge to current income.
- Although not as significant as misspecifying the life of a depreciable asset, the residual value could be significantly overstated, thus understating depreciation expense during the life of the asset and overstating the loss when the asset is retired.

Changing Depreciation Methods or Changing the Estimated Useful Life or Salvage Value of an Asset

There are three ways that a company can change the way depreciation is applied.

Change in method for new assets. A company can change its method of depreciation for new assets but keep depreciating existing assets the same way it has done in the past. This will cause estimates of future income to be revised. The effect of this type of change on income will be gradual.

Change in method for existing assets. If the company changes its method of depreciation for all assets, several changes will occur:

- The firm must show the effect the change would have had on prior-period results.
- Existing depreciation expense will change.
- Because this change represents a change in an accounting principle, the cumulative effect of the change on past income will be shown net of tax on the income statement.
- Estimates of future income will be revised. These changes may be significant.

Changes in depreciable lives or salvage values. Changes in depreciable lives or salvage values are considered changes in accounting estimates and not changes in an accounting principle. Past income does not need to be restated. However, current income will change and estimates of future income will be revised, so the analyst should be alert to the possibility of earnings manipulation from such a change. Although no cumulative effect exists when estimated life is increased (change in estimate), a more liberal estimate of an asset's economic life will decrease depreciation and increase net income, ROA, and ROE. The opposite will occur if the firm reduces estimated asset life or changes to an accelerated depreciation method.

Effect of changes on financial statements. Switching from accelerated methods to straight-line will cause expenses to be lower and income to be higher. If a firm changes from an accelerated to straight-line depreciation method, the effect on financial statements is summarized in Figure 3.

Figure 3: Effect of Changing Depreciation Methods

Cumulative effect if applied to all assets	Increases net income—no change in income from continuing operations
Cumulative effect if applied only to newly acquired assets	No cumulative effect exists
Depreciation expense	Decreases
Net income from continuing operations	Increases
ROA and ROE	Although assets and equity increase, the larger net income will increase these ratios

---

LOS 37.c: Determine the average age and average depreciable life of a company's assets using the company's fixed asset disclosures.

The footnotes to the financial statements typically provide the analyst with a wealth of information regarding the structure of the company's fixed asset base. An analyst can use this data and other financial statement data to compute average age estimates. Average age data is useful for two reasons:

- It helps identify portfolios of older, less efficient assets, which may make the firm less competitive.
- An analyst can estimate when major capital expenditures will be required, which will help the analyst forecast when the firm will face significant financing requirements.

In addition:

- If a firm's average depreciable life is significantly greater than that of a similar firm, then one would expect it to have a lower depreciation expense and higher net income because it has used the longer useful life expectation.
- If the average age of assets is large and the cost of new PP&E has risen over time, then the firm's profit margins will be higher because depreciation expense is based on less costly, but potentially less efficient, PP&E.

There are three calculations that are useful concerning the quality of fixed assets on the balance sheet.

- **Average age** (in years) is approximated by:

$$\frac{\text{accumulated depreciation}}{\text{depreciation expense}}$$

This is only a rough estimate and can be significantly affected by changes in the asset mix.

- **Relative age**, or average age as a percentage of depreciable life is:

$$\frac{\text{accumulated depreciation}}{\text{ending gross investment}}$$

This calculation is more accurate when straight-line depreciation is being used and provides a better indication of whether the firm's assets are old or new.

- **Average depreciable life** is approximated by:

$$\frac{\text{ending gross investment}}{\text{depreciation expense}}$$

As is true for average age (in years), this is only an approximation and is affected by changes in the asset mix.

> **Example: Calculating average age and depreciable life**
>
> At the end of 2003, a company has gross fixed assets of $3 million and accumulated depreciation of $1 million. During the year, depreciation expense was $500,000.
>
> What is the average age in years and in percentage of the fixed assets, and what is the average depreciable life?
>
> **Answer:**
>
> $$\text{average age in years} = \frac{\text{accumulated depreciation}}{\text{depreciation expense}} = \frac{\$1,000,000}{\$500,000} = 2 \text{ years}$$
>
> $$\text{average age as a percentage} = \frac{\text{accumulated depreciation}}{\text{ending gross investment}} = \frac{\$1,000,000}{\$3,000,000} = 33\%$$
>
> $$\text{average depreciable life} = \frac{\text{ending gross investment}}{\text{depreciation expense}} = \frac{\$3,000,000}{\$500,000} = 6 \text{ years}$$

If a firm's relative age of plant and equipment is high, then the firm has not been adding to its capital stock. The firm is probably a less efficient and less competitive producer and will have to invest in PP&E in the future. However, the measure is sensitive to the estimated life and salvage value used—the shorter the estimated life, the greater the depreciation and the higher the average age percentage.

LOS 37.d: Explain and illustrate the use of impairment charges on long-lived assets, and analyze the effects of taking such impairment charges on a company's financial statements and ratios.

Financial reporting of impaired assets. Generally accepted accounting principles (GAAP) *require* that assets be carried at acquisition cost less accumulated depreciation. There is also a requirement that carrying amounts be reduced to market value when there is no longer an expectation that net balance sheet values can be recovered from future operations.

Assets carried at more than the recoverable amounts are considered *impaired*. For impaired assets retained by the firm, the issue is how to report the firm's inability to fully recover its carrying amount. Since management largely controls the timing and amount of impairment recognition, it is a potential tool for income manipulation. It is difficult to compare the impact of impairment and the resulting ratios over time and across companies.

 Professor's Note: Impairments are reported on the income statement pretax (above the line) as a component of income from continuing operations.

Impairment losses are sometimes reported as a component of restructuring, which also includes elements that affect cash flows (e.g., severance pay). It is, therefore, important to separate writedowns of assets that do not affect cash flow from those components of restructuring that do affect cash flow.

Loss from the impairment of assets must be recognized when there is evidence of a lack of recoverability of the carrying amount. Lack of recoverability may be signaled by:

- Changes in business environment or laws and regulations.
- A decline in the usage rate or market value of an asset.
- A forecast for a significant decline in profitability related to the asset.
- Significantly higher costs than expected.

The impairment of an asset cannot be restored under U.S. GAAP. However, some foreign countries and the IASB allow firms to recognize increases in value.

If an asset is held for disposition, it is carried on the balance sheet at the lower of cost or net realizable value.

Recoverability test. An asset is considered impaired if the carrying value (asset cost less accumulated depreciation) is more than the undiscounted cash flow from the asset's use and disposal.

Impaired if: carrying value of assets > undiscounted expected future cash flows

pd, cr, md,   *D: acure*

Study Session 9

Cross-Reference to CFA Institute Assigned Reading #37 – Analysis of Long-Lived Assets: Part II—Analysis of Depreciation and Impairment

Loss measurement. If a long-lived asset becomes permanently impaired, the relevant portion of its book value should be immediately recognized as a loss on the income statement. The loss is the excess of carrying value over the asset's fair market value (if known) or an estimate of present value of future cash flows if market value is unknown.

Professor's Note: The difference between the way cash flows are treated in testing for and measuring impairment can be confusing. In testing for impairment, undiscounted future cash flows are used. Once impairment has been detected, it should be estimated using discounted future cash flows.

Impact of Impairment on Financial Statements

- A writedown of assets affects the balance sheet categories of assets (PP&E), deferred tax liabilities, and stockholders' equity (retained earnings). Deferred tax liabilities result because financial statement depreciation is less than tax return depreciation. An impairment charge on the financial statements moves depreciation closer to tax return depreciation and reduces the future tax liability expected as these amounts come together. Deferred tax liabilities are fully described in the next study session.
- During the year of writedown, the loss from impairment decreases income from continuing operations. This decreases retained earnings. The assets and associated deferred taxes are reduced.
- Fixed asset turnover and total asset turnover both increase because asset values are lower.
- Writedowns increase a firm's debt-to-equity ratio as a result of the decrease in retained earnings and equity.
- Cash flow is not affected. Recognition of the impairment leads to a reduction in a deferred tax liability, not a current refund.
- In future years, less depreciation expense is recognized on the written-down asset, resulting in higher net income. Figure 4 relates the effects of impairments.

Figure 4: Impairment—Effects on Financial Statements

Impairment Effects	
Cash flow	No effect
Assets (PP&E)	Decrease
Deferred tax liabilities	Decrease
Stockholders' equity	Decrease
Current net income, ROA, ROE	Decrease
Future net income, ROA, ROE	Increase
Future depreciation expense	Decrease
Asset turnover ratio	Increase
Debt-to-equity ratio*	Increase

*Current D/E increases as equity goes down with the impairment charge and then decreases over time because lower depreciation going forward increases net income, retained earnings, and equity.

Analysis of Impairments

- Impairments may compensate for past underdepreciation or changes in market conditions and are quite difficult to forecast.
- Cash flow resulting from tax effects is difficult to determine, although generally there is none because impairments are not deductible for taxes.
- Impairments have resulted in diverse accounting practices, undermining comparability across firms and through time.

LOS 37.e: Discuss accounting requirements related to remedying environmental damage caused by operating assets and explain the financial statement and ratio effects that result from the application of those requirements.

Companies often own and operate assets that cause environmental damage, including strip mines, nuclear power plants, offshore oil platforms, and production plants that produce toxic waste as a by-product. Governments often require the company to clean up the site after the company ceases using the asset, and restore the asset or land to its original condition. Prior to the issuance of SFAS 143, companies took different approaches to the accounting for this asset retirement obligation (ARO).

SFAS 143 requires a consistent treatment of the ARO resulting from obligations related to remedying environmental damage caused by a company. The following rules apply:

- SFAS 143 applies to all companies and all legal and contractual obligations, including leased assets and legally enforceable contracts.
- The fair value of the ARO (liability) must be recognized. Fair value is either the liability's market value or, if market value is not available, the present value of the expected cash flows necessary to retire the liability (return the asset to the

condition required). An equal amount must be added to the carrying value of the asset.
- The company must recognize accretion of the liability on the income statement as part of interest expense. The liability on the balance sheet increases each year.
- Prior-period amounts are not adjusted for changes in the estimated amount of the liability.

The company is required to disclose the following information:

- A description of the ARO and the asset.
- A reconciliation of the ARO liability, including specific information on new liabilities incurred, old liabilities extinguished, accretion expense, and revisions to the ARO estimate.
- The fair value of funds set aside to retire the ARO obligation.

Most companies will experience the following financial statement effects from the implementation of SFAS 143:

- Fixed assets and liabilities reported on the balance sheet will increase.
- Net income will be lower because of the additional depreciation of the asset and the accretion of the liability. The accretion will increase each year.

In general, the implementation of SFAS 143 will make the financial statements of a firm with an ARO look worse. Figure 5 shows the ratio effects of implementation of SFAS 143.

Figure 5: Ratio Effects of SFAS 143

Ratio	Numerator	Denominator	Effect on Ratio
Asset turnover	Sales will not change.	Assets will increase because of higher fixed assets.	Decrease
Liabilities-to-equity	Liabilities will increase because of ARO liability.	Equity will decrease because of lower net income.	Increase
Return on assets	Net income will decrease.	Assets will increase.	Decrease
Interest coverage	EBIT will decrease because of higher depreciation.	Interest expense will increase because of accretion of ARO liability.	Decrease

KEY CONCEPTS

1. Depreciation methods include straight-line and accelerated methods, units of production and service hours methods, and the sinking fund method.

2. Compared to straight-line methods, accelerated methods decrease operating earnings and net income in the early years of an asset's life and increase them in the later years.

3. The choice of depreciation method on the firm's financial statements does not affect the firm's cash flow, but the use of accelerated depreciation methods for tax reporting lowers taxable income and taxes due, increasing the firm's cash flow by the reduction in taxes.

4. A change in accounting method requires a restatement of prior income and an adjustment on the income statement for the cumulative after-tax effect of the change.

5. Longer estimates of useful lives and higher estimates of residual asset values both reduce depreciation expense and increase reported earnings.

6. Using balance sheet items, an analyst can estimate average age and average depreciable asset lives (both are approximate and affected by asset mix) and can estimate the relative age of the assets when straight-line depreciation is used.

7. Impairment must be recognized when the carrying value of an asset is higher than the sum of the future cash flows (undiscounted) from their use and disposal. Impairments will cause income, asset value, deferred taxes, equity, and future depreciation to decline, resulting in an increase in future net income.

8. SFAS 143 requires capitalization of environmental remediation expenses and for most firms will lead to higher assets, liabilities, depreciation expense, and interest expense, which will tend to decrease net income. ROA, asset turnover, and interest coverage ratios will all decrease, and liabilities-to-equity will increase.

©2008 Schweser

CONCEPT CHECKERS

1. Which of the following accounts is *least likely* to be affected by an asset impairment?
    A. Inventory.
    B. Fixed assets.
    C. Deferred taxes.
    D. Stockholders' equity.

2. Which of the following will *least likely* enable a firm to report higher income in the future?
    A. Changing from sum of the years' digits to straight-line while capital expenditures are increasing.
    B. Declaring an asset impairment.
    C. Resetting the salvage values of all of its assets to zero.
    D. Increasing the depreciable life of all of its assets.

Use the following data to answer Questions 3 through 6.

Acquisition cost of asset	$25,000
Salvage value	$3,000
Useful life	4 years
Cash flow per year	$8,000
Expected output of machine	25,000 units

3. Based on the straight-line (SL) method, the first year's depreciation will be:
    A. $4,460.
    B. $5,500.
    C. $6,250.
    D. $8,800.

4. Based on the sum-of-years' digits (SYD) method, the first year's depreciation will be:
    A. $4,460.
    B. $5,500.
    C. $6,250.
    D. $8,800.

5. Based on the double-declining balance (DDB) method, the first year's depreciation will be:
    A. $4,400.
    B. $5,500.
    C. $8,800.
    D. $12,500.

6.   If the actual usage of the asset in the first year is 7,200 units, then depreciation under the units-of-production method will be:
      A. $4,400.
      B. $5,500.
      C. $6,336.
      D. $7,200.

7.   Compared to firms using the sum-of-years' digits (SYD) method, a firm using straight-line (SL) depreciation will initially report earnings that are:
      A. lower.
      B. equal.
      C. greater.
      D. dependent on usage.

Use the following data to answer Questions 8 through 10.

Tofu Products, Inc., has purchased a new soybean processor for $300,000 (shipping and installation included).

*   The processor has a useful life of 15 years.
*   The expected salvage value is $10,000.
*   Their corporate tax rate is 39%.
*   They expect to earn $500,000 before depreciation and taxes.

8.   What is the depreciation expense for year 3 if the sum-of-years' digits (SYD) depreciation method is used?
      A. $19,333.
      B. $29,604.
      C. $31,417.
      D. $36,250.

9.   What is the depreciation expense for year 2 if the double-declining balance (DDB) method is used?
      A. $19,333.
      B. $24,242.
      C. $34,667.
      D. $40,000.

10. Which of the three methods—SL, SYD, or DDB—will produce the *most* year-1 net income?
      A. Straight-line.
      B. Sum-of-years' digits.
      C. Double-declining balance.
      D. They all will produce the same level of net income.

Use the following data to answer Questions 11 through 13.

Gross plant and equipment $1,500,000
Depreciation expense $225,000
Accumulated depreciation $675,000
The firm uses SL depreciation.

11. The average depreciable life of plant and equipment is:
    A. 3.00 years.
    B. 3.67 years.
    C. 6.67 years.
    D. 10.33 years.

12. The average age, given as percent, of the plant and equipment is:
    A. 40%.
    B. 45%.
    C. 50%.
    D. 55%.

13. The average age in years of plant and equipment is:
    A. 2.67 years.
    B. 3.00 years.
    C. 3.67 years.
    D. 6.67 years.

14. Which of the following statements about depreciation methods is *least likely* correct?
    A. Sinking fund depreciation is a common depreciation method in the U.S.
    B. The cost of plant and equipment includes all necessary expenditures made prior to placing the asset into service.
    C. When using the DDB method, depreciation is ended when book value is reduced to salvage value.
    D. Accelerating deductions by using SYD for tax purposes and SL for financial reporting will result in the creation of a deferred tax liability.

15. Which of the following statements is *least likely* correct? Assuming the firm continues to invest in new assets, firms that choose accelerated depreciation over straight-line (SL) depreciation will tend to have lower:
    A. equity.
    B. net income.
    C. return on assets.
    D. depreciation expense.

16. Which of the following statements is *most likely* correct? When a company changes the salvage values of an asset:
    A. past earnings must be restated.
    B. the company must report a change in accounting principles.
    C. current and future income will be slightly affected.
    D. an impairment is declared.

17. Which of the following statements about how inflation affects the measurement of economic depreciation is *least likely* correct? In an inflationary period:
    A. reported ROAs and ROEs will be too low.
    B. reported income will be too high.
    C. depreciation based on historical costs will not be sufficient to replace the asset.
    D. depreciation based on the current cost of the asset (rather than historical costs) will create superior future net income estimates.

18. A change in depreciation method is:
    A. not allowed under GAAP.
    B. considered a change in accounting estimates.
    C. considered a change in accounting principles.
    D. required when an asset is judged to be impaired.

19. An asset is impaired when:
    A. accumulated depreciation exceeds acquisition costs.
    B. the firm can no longer fully recover the carrying amount of the asset through operations.
    C. accumulated depreciation plus salvage value exceeds acquisition costs.
    D. the present value of future cash flows exceeds the carrying amount of the asset.

20. Which of the following statements is *least likely* correct? During the year of a writedown, the loss from impairment will decrease:
    A. cash flows.
    B. asset values.
    C. retained earnings.
    D. income from continuing operations.

21. Which of the following choices describes a *benefit* of calculating average age of assets?
    A. Firms with low average age of assets typically are inefficient.
    B. An analyst can use the data to help forecast future capital expenditures.
    C. Average age multiplied by asset turnover will be equal to the DuPont ROE.
    D. Risk arbitrage analysts view companies with low average age as takeover candidates.

22. To determine whether an asset is impaired, an analyst should use:
    A. discounted cash flows and should use discounted cash flows to calculate the amount of the impairment.
    B. discounted cash flows and should use undiscounted cash flows to calculate the amount of the impairment.
    C. undiscounted cash flows and should use discounted cash flows to calculate the amount of the impairment.
    D. undiscounted cash flows and should use undiscounted cash flows to calculate the amount of the impairment.

Study Session 9

Cross-Reference to CFA Institute Assigned Reading #37 – Analysis of Long-Lived Assets: Part II—Analysis of Depreciation and Impairment

23. Which of the following statements about SFAS 143 on environmental remediation is *least likely* correct?
    A. Implementation of SFAS 143 inflates depreciation expense.
    B. Ratio impacts include lower asset turnover and higher debt-to-equity ratios.
    C. The periodic interest accretion increases expenses and decreases cash flow from operations.
    D. The asset and liability are recorded at the time of asset acquisition and include the costs to return the land to the condition required.

24. Which depreciation method will *least likely* lead to an increasing return on investment when net asset cash flows are level over the asset's life?
    A. Sum-of-year's-digits.
    B. Straight line.
    C. Double-declining balance.
    D. Sinking fund.

ANSWERS – CONCEPT CHECKERS

1. **A** Inventory will not be affected.

2. **C** Decreasing salvage values to zero would result in higher depreciation expense and, thus, decreased income. To increase income, the company would need to increase salvage values. The other choices would result in less depreciation expense and, thus, higher income.

3. **B** Straight-line (SL) depreciation is equal for all years.

$$\text{year 1 SL depreciation} = \frac{\text{original cost} - \text{salvage value}}{\text{depreciable life}}$$

$$\frac{\$25,000 - \$3,000}{4} = \$5,500$$

4. **D** Sum-of-years' digits (SYD) depreciation for year 1

$$= (\text{original cost} - \text{salvage value}) \times \frac{(\text{useful life} - \text{year of interest} + 1)}{\text{sum of the useful life's digits}}$$

$$= \frac{(\$25,000 - \$3,000)(4 - 1 + 1)}{(4 + 3 + 2 + 1)} = \$8,800$$

5. **D** Using the double-declining balance method:

$$\text{year 1 depreciation} = \frac{2}{\text{useful life}} \times \text{original cost} = \frac{2}{4} \times \$25,000 = \$12,500$$

6. **C** Using the units of production method, the year 1 depreciation = rate per unit × number of units. Rate per unit = (original cost − salvage value) / expected output = (25,000 - 3,000 / 25,000) = 0.88. Thus, year 1 depreciation = 0.88 × (7,200) = $6,336.

7. **C** The sum-of-years' digits (SYD) method will report greater depreciation early on, thus reporting lower earnings. A firm using straight-line (SL) depreciation will report greater earnings. Neither method considers usage.

8. **C** SYD depreciation for year 3 = (original cost − salvage value) × $\dfrac{\text{useful life} - \text{year of interest} + 1}{\text{sum of the useful life's digits}}$

$$\text{SYD} = 1 + 2 + \dots + 15 = 120$$

$$\text{depreciation} = \frac{(15 - 3 + 1)}{120} \times 290,000 = \$31,417$$

9. **C** Depreciation in year 1: $\dfrac{2}{15} \times 300,000 = \$40,000$.

Book value in the beginning of the second year = 300,000 − 40,000 = $260,000.

Depreciation in year 2: $\dfrac{2}{15} \times 260,000 = \$34,667$.

10. **A** Because straight-line (SL) depreciation reports the lowest expense, it will report the highest year-1 income. The other two methods accelerate depreciation expense.

11. **C** $\text{Average depreciable life} = \dfrac{\text{ending gross investment}}{\text{depreciation expense}} = \dfrac{1,500,000}{225,000} = 6.67$ years.

12. **B** $\text{Average age as a percentage of plant and equipment} = \dfrac{\text{accumulated depreciation}}{\text{ending gross investment}}$
$$= \dfrac{675,000}{1,500,000} = 45\%$$

13. **B** $\text{Average age} = \dfrac{\text{accumulated depreciation}}{\text{depreciation expense}} = \dfrac{675,000}{225,000} = 3.00$ years

14. **A**   Sinking fund depreciation is prohibited in the U.S.

15. **D**   A firm that continues to invest in new assets will have higher depreciation expense due to the use of accelerated methods.

16. **C**   Changing the salvage value of an asset is considered a change in accounting estimate; past income does not need to be restated.

17. **A**   Inflation causes ROA and ROE to be too high because the true cost of replacing the asset is not reflected by depreciation.

18. **C**   A change in depreciation method is a change in the method of accounting. The cumulative effect on past income should be noted.

19. **B**   This statement correctly describes an impaired asset.

20. **A**   The loss from impairment does not affect cash flow.

21. **B**   Average age calculations can be useful because they allow an analyst to assess the quality of a company's assets and help the analyst forecast when major capital expenditures will be required.

22. **C**   Don't let this confuse you. In testing for impairment, undiscounted cash flows are used. Once impairment has been detected, it should be measured using discounted cash flows.

23. **C**   Cash flow is not decreased by SFAS 143 since the annual accretion is not a cash charge. The other statements are true. The debt-equity ratio is higher because debt will be higher and equity will be lower. Asset turnover ratios are lower because assets are higher. The present value of the liability added to the asset's balance at the time of purchase is depreciated over the asset's useful life, thus increasing depreciation expense.

24. **D**   Sinking fund depreciation is calculated to produce a constant return on investment.

ANALYSIS OF INCOME TAXES

EXAM FOCUS

Legally, companies are permitted to keep two sets of financial records in the United States—one for financial reporting and one for tax reporting. Candidates should be aware of the terminology that relates to each set of records, notably taxes payable, which are the taxes actually due to the government; and income tax expense, which is reported on the income statement and reflects taxes payable plus any deferred income tax expense. Because tax reporting uses a modified cash basis and financial reporting uses accrual accounting according to Generally Accepted Accounting Principles,

differences in income can result. This leads to the creation of deferred tax liabilities, which the company may have to pay in the future, or deferred tax assets, which may provide benefits in the future. For the exam, you should know that some differences between taxable and pretax income are temporary, while some are permanent and will never reverse. Be prepared to calculate taxes payable, tax expense, deferred tax liabilities and assets, and be able to adjust financial statements for permanent income differences.

LOS 38.a: Explain the key terms related to income tax accounting and the origin of deferred tax liabilities and assets.

Professor's Note: Accounting definitions are not usually included directly in an LOS. You should expect to see questions involving tax terminology and definitions on the exam. To understand the material, pay particular attention to the difference between the definitions of taxable income (on the tax return) and pretax income (on the income statement) and the difference between the definitions of taxes payable (on the tax return) and income tax expense (on the income statement).

Tax Return Terminology

- **Taxable income.** Income subject to tax based on the tax return.
- **Taxes payable.** The tax liability on the balance sheet caused by taxable income. This is also known as current tax expense, but do not confuse this with income tax expense (see below).
- **Income tax paid.** Actual cash flow for income taxes, including payments or refunds for other years.
- **Tax loss carryforward.** The current net taxable loss that is used to reduce taxable income (thus, taxes payable) in future years and can generate a deferred tax asset.

Financial Reporting Terminology

- **Pretax income.** Income before income tax expense.
- **Income tax expense.** The expense recognized on the income statement that includes taxes payable and deferred income tax expense. It is extremely important to note that income tax expense is composed of taxes payable plus noncash items such as changes in deferred tax assets and liabilities (DTA and DTL).

     Income tax expense = taxes payable + ΔDTL – ΔDTA

- **Deferred tax expense.** The difference between taxes payable and income tax expense. This results from changes in deferred tax assets and liabilities.
- **Deferred tax asset.** Balance sheet amounts that result from an excess of taxes payable over income tax expense that are expected to be recovered from future operations.
- **Deferred tax liability.** Balance sheet amounts that result from an excess of income tax expense over taxes payable that are expected to result in future cash outflows. Deferred tax liabilities are created when more expense is applied to the tax return relative to the income statement (e.g., more depreciation). This results in lower taxable income and lower taxes payable on the tax return relative to the pretax income and tax expense that are shown on the income statement.
- **Valuation allowance.** Reserve against deferred tax assets based on the likelihood that those assets will not be realized.
- **Timing difference.** The difference between the treatment of expenditures on the tax return and for financial reporting.
- **Temporary difference.** The differences between tax and financial reporting that will reverse in the future and will affect taxable income when they reverse, including the differences in the carrying cost of depreciable assets on tax and accounting records.
- **Permanent difference.** The differences between tax and financial reporting that are not expected to reverse in the future.

The Origin of Deferred Tax Liabilities and Assets

A *deferred tax liability* is created when an income or expense item is treated differently on financial statements than it is on the company's tax returns, and that difference results in greater tax expense on the financial statements than taxes payable on the tax return.

Deferred tax liabilities are accounted for because the differences arising from unique accounting treatments for tax and financial reporting purposes are expected to reverse themselves (i.e., they are temporary differences) and they result in future cash outflows related to the payment of taxes.

The most common way that deferred taxes are created is when different depreciation methods are used on the tax return and income statement.

Let's look at how a DTL is created.

  Situation: Asset cost $600,000, 3-year life, zero salvage value

  Tax return depreciation is sum-of-years' digits (SYD), year 1 $300,000, year 2 $200,000, year 3 $100,000.

Income statement depreciation is straight line (SL), $200,000 each year.

EBITDA is $500,000 each year.

Figure 1: Tax Return (40% Rate, SYD Depreciation)

	Year 1	Year 2	Year 3	Total 1-3
EBITDA	$500,000	$500,000	$500,000	1,500,000
Depreciation	–300,000	–200,000	–100,000	600,000
Taxable income	$200,000	$300,000	$400,000	$900,000
Tax Rate	× 0.40	× 0.40	× 0.40	× 0.40
Tax Payable	$80,000	$120,000	$160,000	$360,000

Figure 2: Income Statement (40% Tax Rate, SL Depreciation)

	Year 1	Year 2	Year 3	Total 1-3
EBITDA	$500,000	$500,000	$500,000	1,500,000
Depreciation	–200,000	–200,000	–200,000	600,000
Pre-Tax Income	$300,000	$300,000	$300,000	$900,000
Tax Rate	× 0.40	× 0.40	× 0.40	× 0.40
Income Tax Expense	$120,000	$120,000	$120,000	$360,000

In year 1, taxes payable = $80,000 and income tax expense is $120,000, so $40,000 of the tax expense is deferred to a future period by using an accelerated depreciation method for tax purposes. We note this on the balance sheet by creating a deferred tax liability of $40,000, and income tax expense = taxes payable + change in DTL ($120,000 = $80,000 + $40,000).

In year 2, depreciation is equal for tax and income statements, taxable income equals pretax income, and there is no change in the deferred tax liability. DTL remains at $40,000.

In year 3, depreciation for tax purposes ($100,000) is less than depreciation on the income statement ($200,000); taxable income is greater than pretax income; and the DTL is reduced from $40,000 to zero. Income tax expense = taxes payable + change in DTL [$120,000 = $160,000 + (–$40,000)].

Note that over the useful life of the asset, total depreciation, total taxable (and pre-tax) income, and total taxes payable (income tax expense) are all equal. By using accelerated depreciation for tax purposes we *deferred* $40,000 of taxes from year 1 to year 3.

A *deferred tax asset* is created when an income or expense item is treated differently on financial statements than it is on the company's tax returns, and that difference results in lower income tax expense on the financial statements than on the tax return.

Similar to deferred tax liabilities, deferred tax assets are expected to reverse themselves through future operations and provide tax savings and, therefore, are accounted for on the balance sheet.

Warranty expenses and *tax-loss carry forwards* are typical causes of deferred tax assets.

LOS 38.b: Demonstrate the liability method of accounting for deferred taxes.

The **liability method** of accounting for deferred taxes starts from the premise that differences between taxes calculated on the income statement [Generally Accepted Accounting Principles (GAAP) accounting] and taxes from the income tax return (determined by the Internal Revenue Code) will be reversed at some future date. When income tax expense based on GAAP is greater than taxes payable on the income tax return, a deferred tax liability in the amount of the difference is entered on the balance sheet. Activities in the current period have caused the company to incur a tax liability that must be paid in a future period.

If a company has an expense item (e.g., estimated warranty expense) on its financial statements that is not deductible for tax purposes currently, a deferred tax asset will be created. This represents the future tax savings that will result when the deduction is taken (e.g., when warranty expense is actually paid).

Both deferred tax assets and liabilities are adjusted for changes in the tax rate expected for the period(s) in which the deferred tax asset/liability is expected to be reversed (usually the current tax rate). Additionally, deferred tax assets are adjusted for the probability that they will actually be realized in future periods. This adjustment is made by creating or adjusting a "valuation allowance" on the balance sheet. This item serves to reduce the DTA to reflect the probability that the DTA will not actually be realized in future periods.

LOS 38.c: Discuss the use of valuation allowances for deferred tax assets, and their implications for financial statement analysis.

Deferred tax assets can have a valuation allowance, which is a contra account (offset) against deferred tax assets based on the likelihood that these assets will not be realized.

For deferred tax assets to be beneficial, the firm must have future taxable income. If it is more likely than not (> 50% probability) that a portion of deferred tax assets will not be realized (insufficient future taxable income to take advantage of the tax asset), then the deferred tax asset must be reduced by a valuation allowance.

It is up to management to defend the recognition of all deferred tax assets. If a company has order backlogs or existing contracts which are expected to generate future taxable income, a valuation allowance would not be necessary. However, if a company has cumulative losses over the past few years or a history of an inability to use tax credit carryforwards, then the company would need to use a valuation allowance to reflect the likelihood that the deferred tax asset would never be realized.

A valuation allowance reduces income from continuing operations. Because an increase (decrease) in the valuation allowance will serve to decrease (increase) operating income, changes in the valuation allowance are a common means of managing or manipulating earnings.

Whenever a company reports substantial deferred tax assets, an analyst should review the company's financial performance to determine the likelihood that those assets will be realized. Analysts should also scrutinize changes in the valuation allowance to determine whether those changes are economically justified.

 Professor's Note: The valuation allowance applies exclusively to deferred tax assets.

LOS 38.d: Explain the factors that determine whether a company's deferred tax liabilities should be treated as a liability or as equity for purposes of financial analysis.

If deferred tax liabilities are expected to reverse in the future, then they are best classified as liabilities. If, however, they are not expected to reverse in the future, they are best classified as equity. The key question is, "when or will the total deferred tax liability be reversed in the future?" In practice, the treatment of deferred taxes for analytical purposes varies. An analyst must decide on the appropriate treatment on a *case-by-case basis*. Some guidelines follow:

- In many cases, it may be unlikely that deferred tax liabilities will be paid. For example, if a company has deferred tax liabilities occurring solely because of the use of accelerated depreciation for tax purposes and the company's capital expenditures are expected to continue to grow in the foreseeable future, the deferred tax liability will not reverse and should be considered as equity. However, if growth is expected to stop or slow considerably, the liability will reverse and it should be considered as a true liability.
- If it is determined that deferred taxes are not a liability (i.e., non-reversal is certain), then the analyst should reduce the deferred tax liability and increase stockholders' equity by the same amount. This decreases the debt-to-equity ratio, sometimes significantly.
- Sometimes, instead of reclassifying deferred liabilities as stockholders' equity, the analyst might just ignore deferred taxes altogether. This is done if non-reversal is uncertain or financial statement depreciation is deemed inadequate and it is therefore difficult to justify an increase in stockholders' equity. Some creditors, notably banks, simply ignore deferred taxes.

Let's work through an example of the impact of growth on deferred tax liabilities using the following assumptions:

- A firm purchases an asset each year for three years: Asset 1 in the first year, Asset 2 in the second year, and Asset 3 in the third year.
- The cost of each of these assets is $3,000 with no salvage value and a 3-year life.
- Double-declining balance (DDB) method is used on tax returns and SL for financial statements.
- The tax rate is 30%.

Figures 3 through 5 reveal total tax deduction and total depreciation expense for these assets purchased in each of the first three years.

Figure 3: Tax Return Calculations—Double-Declining Balance (tax deduction)

	Year 1	Year 2	Year 3
Asset 1	$2,000	$667	$333
Asset 2	0	2,000	667
Asset 3	0	0	2,000
Total DDB depreciation	$2,000	$2,667	$3,000

Figure 4: Financial Statement Calculations—Straight-line (financial statements)

	Year 1	Year 2	Year 3
Asset 1	$1,000	$1,000	$1,000
Asset 2	0	1,000	1,000
Asset 3	0	0	1,000
SL depreciation	$1,000	$2,000	$3,000

Figure 5: Cumulative Deferred Tax Liability

	Year 1	Year 2	Year 3
Deferred liability	$300	$500	$500

In year 1, the change in deferred tax liability is $(2,000 - 1,000)(0.30) = +\$300$. In year 2, the change is $(2,667 - 2,000)(0.30) = +\$200$.

Note: There is no reversal of the deferred liability. The cumulative deferred liability will continue to increase as long as the firm continues to grow.

LOS 38.e: Distinguish between temporary and permanent items in pretax financial income and taxable income.

Temporary differences are differences in taxable and pretax incomes that will reverse in future years. That is, current lower (higher) taxes payable will mean future higher (lower) taxes payable. These differences result in deferred tax assets or liabilities. Various examples and how they are classified on the financial statements are as follows:

- *Current liabilities.* The temporary difference that results from using the installment sales method for taxes and the sales method for pretax income. Recall that the installment sales and sales basis methods are used in revenue recognition.
- *Long-term liabilities.* The long-term tax liability that results from using the declining balance depreciation for the tax returns and SL depreciation for the financial statements.
- *Current assets.* The deferred tax assets created when warranty expenses are accrued on the financial statements but are not deductible on the tax returns until the warranty claims are paid.
- *Long-term assets.* The deferred tax asset created when post-retirement benefits expense in pretax income exceeds that allowed for a deduction on tax returns.
- *Stockholders' equity.* The gains or losses from carrying marketable securities at market value are deferred tax adjustments to stockholders' equity.

Permanent differences are differences in taxable and pretax incomes that will not reverse.

- Tax-exempt interest income and the proceeds from life insurance on key employees are not taxable but are recognized as *revenue* on the financial statements.
- Tax-exempt interest expense, premiums paid on life insurance of key employees, and goodwill amortization are examples of *expenses* on the financial statements, but they are not deductions on the tax returns. Remember that goodwill amortization is no longer permitted under U.S. GAAP or International Financial Reporting Standards (IFRS).
- Tax credits for some expenditures directly reduce taxes and, unlike accelerated recognition of expenses for tax purposes, will not reverse in the future.

Permanent differences do not result in deferred tax liabilities or assets. Permanent differences between taxable income and pretax income are reflected in a difference between a firm's effective tax rate and its statutory tax rate. A firm's *reported* effective tax rate is simply $\dfrac{\text{income tax expense}}{\text{pretax income}}$.

The statutory tax rate is the marginal tax rate in the jurisdiction in which the firm operates. Income recognized on the financial statements (e.g., tax-exempt interest income) that is not included in taxable income, will result in an effective tax rate lower than the statutory rate. Expenses recognized on the income statement that are not deductible for tax purposes (e.g., premiums paid on key employee life insurance) will tend to increase the effective tax rate relative to the statutory tax rate. Differences between the statutory rate and the effective rate can also arise when a firm's operations are in different geographic locations and subject to different tax laws. Sometimes the income of a foreign subsidiary is reinvested in the subsidiary and not remitted to the parent company, postponing taxation at the statutory rate. Remitting accumulated subsidiary income from prior periods would, of course, have an opposite effect on the difference between statutory and effective rates.

Indefinite reversals. There is uncertainty about whether some differences will reverse in the future. The most common of these differences is the undistributed earnings of unconsolidated subsidiaries or joint ventures. If income is earned but not distributed back to the parent company in the form of dividends, the income will be reflected on the income statement as pretax income but will not appear on the tax return. The parent may consider this income to be permanently reinvested in the subsidiary. In that case, the difference will never be reversed. The company can treat this difference as permanent if the parent controls the subsidiary or joint venture.

LOS 38.f: Calculate and interpret income tax expense, income taxes payable, deferred tax assets, and deferred tax liabilities.

Calculations of deferred taxes require going through the tax returns and the income statement and noting the differences between taxable income on the tax return and pretax income on the income statement.

Example: Deferred tax liabilities

An asset costs $200,000, has a depreciable life of four years, and has zero salvage value. It is expected to produce $150,000 in annual revenue. It is depreciated by the DDB method for tax purposes and by SL for financial reporting purposes. The firm has a tax rate of 40%. Calculate the deferred tax liability stemming from the asset at the end of each of the next four years.

Answer:

Using the DDB method, depreciation will be $100,000, $50,000, $25,000, and $25,000 in each of the next four years. Year 1 = $100,000 = ($200,000 – 0)(2/4); Year 2 = $50,000 = ($200,000 – $100,000)(2/4); Year 3 = $25,000 = ($200,000 – $150,000) (2/4); Year 4 depreciation is the remaining $25,000 of book value.

The firm will report the following *for tax reporting:*

Tax Reporting—Deferred Tax Liability (Continued)

	Year 1	Year 2	Year 3	Year 4	Total
Revenue	$150,000	$150,000	$150,000	$150,000	$600,000
Depreciation	$100,000	$50,000	$25,000	$25,000	$200,000
Taxable income	$50,000	$100,000	$125,000	$125,000	$400,000
Taxes payable	$20,000	$40,000	$50,000	$50,000	$160,000
Net income	$30,000	$60,000	$75,000	$75,000	$240,000

Depreciation using SL will be $50,000 per year.

The tax expense is calculated as the tax rate times pretax income, so for *financial reporting:*

Financial Reporting—Deferred Tax Liability

	Year 1	Year 2	Year 3	Year 4	Total
Revenue	$150,000	$150,000	$150,000	$150,000	$600,000
Depreciation	$50,000	$50,000	$50,000	$50,000	$200,000
Pretax income	$100,000	$100,000	$100,000	$100,000	$400,000
Tax expense	$40,000	$40,000	$40,000	$40,000	$160,000
Net income	$60,000	$60,000	$60,000	$60,000	$240,000

Total tax ($160,000) and total net income ($240,000) are the same for tax and financial reporting.

This approach to reporting taxes is based on an income statement approach. Income taxes are treated as a cost of operations and the matching principle implies tax expenses should be based on pretax income. The accelerated depreciation allowed for tax purposes results in lower taxes in the early years that are then reversed (or paid off) in later years.

The difference between pretax income on the financial statements and taxable income on the tax return is attributable to the different accounting treatments. For example, in year 1 the difference between tax expense and taxes payable is $40,000 – $20,000 = $20,000. Because the differences are expected to reverse, a *balance sheet perspective* recognizes a *liability* in the early years equal to the amount of tax that must eventually be paid back in later years. Note that the differences accrue over the life of the asset.

The firm will report the following deferred tax liabilities (represented as the cumulative figure) on the balance sheet shown in Figure 6.

Figure 6: Deferred Tax Calculation—Deferred Tax Liability

	Year 1	Year 2	Year 3	Year 4
Tax expense	$40,000	$40,000	$40,000	$40,000
Taxes payable	$20,000	$40,000	$50,000	$50,000
Annual deferred taxes	$20,000	$0	–$10,000	–$10,000
Deferred taxes (cumulative)	$20,000	$20,000	$10,000	$0

Example: Deferred tax assets

Consider warranty guarantees and associated expenses. Pretax income (financial reporting) includes an accrual for warranty expense, but warranty cost is not deductible for taxable income until the firm has made actual expenditures to meet warranty claims. Suppose:

- A firm has sales of $5,000 for each of two years.
- The firm estimates that warranty expense will be 2% of annual sales ($100).
- The actual expenditure of $200 to meet all warranty claims was not made until the second year.
- Assume a tax rate of 40%.

For tax reporting, taxable income and taxes payable for two years are:

Tax Reporting—Deferred Tax Asset

	Year 1	Year 2
Revenue	$5,000	$5,000
Warranty expense	0	200
Taxable income	$5,000	$4,800
Taxes payable	2,000	1,920
Net income	$3,000	$2,880

For financial reporting, pretax income and tax expense are:

Financial Reporting—Deferred Tax Asset

	Year 1	Year 2
Revenue	$5,000	$5,000
Warranty expense	100	100
Pretax Income	$4,900	$4,900
Tax expense	1,960	1,960
Net Income	$2,940	$2,940

In this example, year 1 and year 2 tax expense (on financial statements) is $1,960. Year 1 and year 2 taxes payable are $2,000 and $1,920. The year 1 difference of $40 (taxes paid greater than tax expense) is a deferred tax asset. In the second year, the temporary difference associated with warranties is reversed when the tax expense of $1,960 is $40 more than the taxes payable of $1,920.

Professor's Note: To summarize deferred tax asset and liability creation, if taxable income (on the tax return) is less than pretax income (on the income statement) and the cause of this difference is expected to reverse in future years, then a deferred tax liability is created, and if taxable income is more than pretax income and the difference is expected to reverse in future years, then a deferred tax asset results.

LOS 38.g: Calculate and interpret the adjustment(s) to the deferred tax accounts related to a change in the tax rate.

Besides the impact on current period taxes payable and income tax expense, under the liability method, *all balance sheet deferred tax assets and liabilities are revalued* when the tax rate the firm will face in the future changes. An increase (decrease) in the tax rate increases (decreases) both deferred tax assets and liabilities.

If the *tax rate increases*, the increase in deferred tax liabilities increases the income tax expense, and the increase in deferred tax assets decreases the income tax expense. As long as deferred tax liabilities exceed deferred tax assets (the most common occurrence), the net impact of the increase in the tax rate will be to increase tax expense, which will cause net income and stockholders' equity to decline.

If the *tax rate decreases*, the decrease in deferred tax liabilities decreases income tax expense, and the decrease in deferred tax assets increases income tax expense. As long as deferred tax liabilities exceed deferred tax assets (the most common occurrence), the net impact of the decrease in the tax rate will be to decrease the tax expense, which will cause net income and stockholders' equity to rise. The basic equation is:

$$\text{income tax expense} = \text{taxes payable} + \Delta DTL - \Delta DTA$$

Let's work through an example of financial statements and a change in tax rates.

Consider a firm that has a DTL of $16,000 and a DTA of $4,000 on the balance sheet at year-end, based on a tax rate of 40%. For the current year, accelerated depreciation used on the tax return is $20,000 more than straight line (income statement) depreciation, *and* warranty expense on the tax return is $5,000 less than warranty expense shown on the income statement. During the year the firm's tax rate is reduced from 40% to 30%.

Initially ignoring the balance sheet amounts, the current year calculations are:

	Tax Return	Income Statement	
Taxable income before depreciation & warranty expense	$100,000	$100,000	
−Depreciation	−30,000	−10,000	adds 0.3 × 20,000 = +6,000 to DTL
−Warranty expense	−5,000	−10,000	adds 0.3 × 5,000 = +1,500 to DTA
	Taxable inc 65,000	Pretax inc 80,000	
	× 0.3	× 0.3	
	Tax payable 19,500	Tax expense 24,000	ΔDTL − ΔDTA = $4,500

Income tax expense = tax payable + ΔDTL − ΔDTA

$24,000 = $19,500 + $6,000 − $1,500

There are additional effects, however, from the adjustments to the DTL and DTA already on the balance sheet at the beginning of the year. The existing DTL of $16,000 must be reduced to $12,000 because the tax rate has decreased by 25%, from 40% to

30% $\left(\dfrac{0.30}{0.40} \times \$16,000 = \$12,000 \right)$. The existing DTA is reduced to

$\dfrac{0.30}{0.40} \times \$4,000 = \$3,000$. So the change in tax rate requires changes to existing balance

sheet amounts:

ΔDTL = −$4,000 and ΔDTA = −$1,000

The calculation of income tax expense for the year will take all these effects into account.

For the current year, we had income tax expense = taxes payable + ΔDTL − ΔDTA which was $24,000. When we also adjust income tax expense for the changes in existing balance sheet DTL and DTA amounts as computed above, we have:

$24,000 − $4,000 − (−$1,000) = $21,000

The net effect of the change in balance sheet deferred taxes on income tax expense is −($4,000 − $1,000) = −$3,000. Since the DTL was greater than the DTA, the decrease in the tax rate reduced the liability by more than it reduced the asset, resulting in a decrease in the current year income tax expense.

LOS 38.h: Interpret a deferred tax footnote disclosure that reconciles the effective and statutory tax rates.

The disclosure requirements of SFAS 109 include separate disclosure of the following information:

- Deferred tax liabilities, deferred tax assets, any valuation allowance, and the net change in the valuation allowance over the period.
- Any unrecognized deferred tax liability for undistributed earnings of subsidiaries and joint ventures.
- Current-year tax effect of each type of temporary difference.
- Components of income tax expense.
- Reconciliation of reported income tax expense and the tax expense based on the statutory rate.
- Tax loss carryforwards and credits.

Analyzing Effective Tax Rates

The firm's effective tax rate is an important input to valuation models because the forecast of future after-tax cash flows depends on the tax rate applied to those cash flows. The reported effective tax rate uses income tax expense and pretax income from the firm's financial statements (f/s):

$$\text{reported effective tax rate} = \frac{\text{income tax expense}\left(\text{from the f/s}\right)}{\text{pretax income}\left(\text{from the f/s}\right)}$$

There are two alternatives to this measure, however, which use items in the numerator derived from the firm's tax returns: taxes payable or income tax paid. Taxes payable is the tax liability on the balance sheet caused by taxable income. Income tax paid is the actual cash flow for income taxes, including payments or refunds from other years. These measures may be more useful for analysis because they are less affected by management's choice of accounting methods.

$$\text{effective tax rate measure \#1} = \frac{\text{taxes payable}\left(\text{from the tax return}\right)}{\text{pretax income}\left(\text{from the f/s}\right)}$$

$$\text{effective tax rate measure \#2} = \frac{\text{income tax paid}\left(\text{from the tax return}\right)}{\text{pretax income}\left(\text{from the f/s}\right)}$$

Low effective tax rates according to either of these measures (relative to effective tax rates of comparable companies) are a potential red flag indicating possible earnings manipulation.

When analyzing the firm's income tax disclosures, watch for these other warning signals:

- Companies that generate significant pretax income on their financial statements while reporting low taxes payable (i.e., low effective tax rates as measured with the alternative definitions previously discussed) are likely to be employing aggressive accounting methods and have low-quality earnings.
- A decrease in capital spending may signal a reversal of past temporary differences related to depreciation methods, resulting in higher taxes payable.
- Restructuring charges typically have no tax cash flow effects in the year they are recorded but may have significant effects in future years as the restructured operations and impaired assets are sold.
- Temporary differences may reverse because of changes in tax law, causing higher taxes payable.

Analyzing the Effective Rate Reconciliation

Some firms' reported income tax expense differs from the amount based on the statutory income tax rate. This is referred to as the difference between the effective tax rate and the statutory rate. The differences are generally the result of:

- Different tax rates in different tax jurisdictions (countries).
- Permanent tax differences: tax credits, tax-exempt income, nondeductible expenses, and tax differences between capital gains and operating income.
- Changes in tax rates and legislation.
- Deferred taxes provided on the reinvested earnings of foreign and unconsolidated domestic affiliates.
- Tax holidays in some countries (watch for special conditions such as termination dates for the holiday or a requirement to pay the accumulated taxes at some point in the future).

Accounting standards require a disclosure reconciling the difference between reported income tax expense and the amount based on the statutory income tax rate. Understanding this difference will enable the analyst to better estimate future earnings and cash flow.

When estimating future earnings and cash flows, the analyst should understand each element of the reconciliation, including its relative impacts, how each has changed with time, and how each is likely to change in the future. Often the analyst will need additional information from management to determine the future direction of each element.

In analyzing trends in tax rates, it is important to only include reconciliation items that are continuous in nature rather than those that are sporadic. There are no general rules for the kinds of items that are continuous or sporadic. The disclosures of each financial statement should be reviewed based on the footnotes and management discussion and analysis.

Nevertheless, items including different rates in different countries, tax-exempt income, and non-deductible expenses tend to be continuous. Others items are almost always sporadic, such as the occurrence of large dollar amounts of asset sales and tax holiday savings.

Example: Analyzing the tax rate reconciliation

Novelty Distribution Company (NDC) does business in the United States and abroad. The company's reconciliation between effective and statutory tax rates for three years is provided in the following figure.

Statutory U.S. Federal Income Tax Rate Reconciliation

	2003	2004	2005
Statutory U.S. federal income tax rate	35.0%	35.0%	35.0%
State income taxes, net of related federal	2.1%	2.2%	2.3%
Benefits and taxes related to foreign	(6.5%)	(6.3%)	(2.7%)
Tax rate changes	0.0%	0.0%	(2.0%)
Capital gains on sale of assets	0.0%	(3.0%)	0.0%
Special items	(1.6%)	8.7%	2.5%
Other, net	0.8%	0.7%	(1.4%)
Effective income tax rates	29.8%	37.3%	33.7%

	2003	2004	2005
Taxable income	$2,330.00	$1,660.00	$2,350.00
Statutory U.S. federal income tax	815.50	581.00	822.50
State income taxes, net of related federal	48.93	36.52	54.05
Benefits and taxes related to foreign	(151.45)	(104.58)	(63.45)
Tax rate changes	–	–	(47.00)
Capital gains on sale of assets	–	(49.80)	–
Special items	(37.28)	144.42	58.75
Other, net	18.64	11.62	(32.90)
Effective income taxes	$694.34	$619.18	$791.95

Analyze the trend in effective tax rates over the three years shown.

Answer:

For some trend analysis, the analyst may want to convert the reconciliation from percentages to absolute numbers. However, for this example, the trends can be analyzed simply by using the percentages. Nevertheless, both percentages and the absolute numbers are provided.

The effective tax rate is upward trending over the 3-year period. Contributing to the upward trend is an increase in the state income tax rate and the loss of benefits related to taxes on foreign income. In 2004, a loss related to the sale of assets partially offset an increase in taxes created by special items. In 2003 and 2005, the special items and the other items also offset each other. The fact that the special items and other items are so volatile over the 3-year period suggests that it will be difficult for an analyst to forecast the effective tax rate for NDC for the foreseeable future without additional information. This volatility also reduces comparability with other firms.

LOS 38.i: Analyze disclosures relating to, and the effect of, deferred taxes on a company's financial statements and financial ratios.

LOS 38.j: Compare and contrast a company's deferred tax items and effective tax rate reconciliation (1) between reporting periods and (2) with the comparable items reported by other companies.

Companies are required to disclose details on the source of the temporary differences that cause the deferred tax assets and liabilities reported on the balance sheet. Changes in those balance sheet accounts are reflected in deferred income tax expense on the income statement. Here are some common examples of temporary differences you may encounter on the exam.

- A long-term deferred tax liability results from using the MACRS *depreciation* schedule for the tax returns and straight-line depreciation for the financial statements. The analyst should consider the firm's growth rate and capital spending levels when determining whether the difference will actually reverse.
- *Impairments* generally result in a deferred tax asset since the writedown of assets is recognized immediately for financial reporting, but not for tax purposes until the asset is sold.
- *Restructuring* generates a deferred tax asset because, for financial reporting purposes, the costs are recognized when restructuring is completed, but not expensed for tax purposes until actually paid. Note that restructuring usually results in significant cash outflows (net of the tax savings) in the years following when the restructuring costs are reported.
- In the United States, firms that choose to use LIFO for financial statement purposes are required to use LIFO for tax purposes, so no temporary differences result. However, in countries for which this is not a requirement, temporary differences can result from the *choice of inventory accounting method*.
- *Post-employment benefits* and *deferred compensation* are both recognized when earned by the employee for book purposes but not expensed for tax purposes until actually paid. This will result in a current deferred tax asset or liability.
- A deferred tax adjustment is made to stockholder's equity to reflect gains or losses from carrying *available-for-sale marketable securities* at market value.

Example: Analyzing deferred tax item disclosures

WCCO Inc.'s income tax expense has consistently been larger than taxes payable over the last three years. WCCO disclosed in the footnotes to its 2005 financial statements the major items recorded as deferred tax assets and liabilities (in millions of dollars), as shown in the following table.

Deferred Tax Disclosures in Footnotes to WCCO Inc. Financial Statements

	2005	2004	2003
Employee benefits	$278	$310	$290
International tax loss carryforwards	101	93	115
Subtotal	379	403	405
Valuation allowance	(24)	(57)	(64)
Deferred tax asset	355	346	341
Property, plant and equipment	452	361	320
Unrealized gains on available-for-sale securities	67	44	23
Deferred tax liability	519	405	343
Deferred income taxes	$164	$59	$2

Use the figure above to explain why income tax expense has exceeded taxes payable over the last three years. Also explain the effect of the change in the valuation allowance on WCCO's earnings for 2005.

Answer:

The company's deferred tax asset balance results from international tax loss carryforwards and employee benefits (most likely pension and other post-retirement benefits) offset by a valuation allowance. The company's deferred tax liability balance results from property, plant, and equipment (most likely from using accelerated depreciation methods for tax purposes and straight-line on the financial statements) and unrealized gains on securities classified as available-for-sale (because the unrealized gain is not taxable until realized).

Income tax expense is equal to taxes payable plus deferred income tax expense. Because the deferred tax liabilities have been growing faster than the deferred tax assets, deferred income tax expense has been positive, resulting in income tax expense being higher than taxes payable.

Management decreased the valuation allowance by $33 million in 2005. This resulted in a reduction in deferred income tax expense and an increase in reported earnings for 2005.

Estimating Taxable Income from Deferred Tax Expense

Recall that deferred tax expense results from the difference between taxable income on the tax returns and pretax income on the financial statements. We can use the deferred tax expense and the statutory tax rate to estimate the difference between taxable income and pretax income attributable to specific temporary differences:

$$\left(\text{pretax income} - \text{taxable income}\right) = \frac{\text{deferred tax expense}}{\text{statutory tax rate}}$$

Example:

In 2005 WCCO reported depreciation expense on the statement of cash flows of $426 million. The deferred tax liability related to depreciation increased from $361 million in 2004 to $452 million in 2005. Assuming a statutory tax rate of 35%, compute the tax basis depreciation for 2005 and the cumulative financial reporting tax difference for net property, plant, and equipment as of fiscal year end 2005.

Answer:

The additional depreciation expense under tax reporting is equal to the change in the deferred tax liability divided by the statutory rate: ($452 − $361) / 0.35 = $260. Total tax basis depreciation for 2005 was $426 + $260 = $686.

The reporting difference in accumulated depreciation is approximately $1,291 ($452 / 0.35). The tax basis for property, plant, and equipment is $1,291 million less than the net amount reported on the balance sheet.

Effect of Disclosures on Financial Statements and Ratios

If the deferred tax liability or asset is expected to reverse, it is valued for accounting purposes at its undiscounted value. Because the payments may occur far into the future, an analyst should revalue the liability or asset at its present value. The difference between the stated value and the present value of deferred taxes should be treated as equity.

Example: Adjusting deferred taxes

Company A and Company B each have debt of $1,000,000, deferred tax liabilities of $200,000, and equity of $2,000,000. The deferred tax liabilities were created as a result of depreciation for tax purposes being greater than depreciation for financial reporting purposes. For Company A, there is no slowdown in capital expenditures expected, while for Company B, the growth in capital expenditures will stop. Therefore, it is reasonable to expect $75,000 of Company B's deferred tax liabilities to reverse. These deferred tax liabilities have a present value of $50,000.

Answer:

Analysis of Company A:

The unadjusted debt-to-equity ratio for Company A is:

$$\text{unadjusted debt-to-equity for Company A} = \frac{\$1,000,000 + \$200,000}{\$2,000,000} = 0.60$$

Since the deferred tax liabilities are not expected to reverse, they should be treated as equity. Therefore, the revised debt-to-equity ratio is:

$$\text{adjusted debt-to-equity for Company A} = \frac{\$1,000,000}{\$2,000,000 + \$200,000} = 0.45$$

This is a significant improvement over the unadjusted debt-to-equity ratio.

The right-hand side of the balance sheet (liabilities plus equity) stays constant. There is no additional wealth created or lost, and there has only been a reclassification between liabilities and equity.

Analysis of Company B:

The initial debt-to-equity ratio for Company B is also 0.60. Since some of the deferred tax liabilities are expected to reverse, the portion expected to reverse will be treated as a liability and the remaining amount treated as equity. Therefore, $50,000 of the deferred tax liability will remain as a liability, and $150,000 will be reclassified as equity. The revised debt-to-equity ratio is:

$$\text{adjusted debt-to-equity for Company B} = \frac{\$1,000,000 + \$50,000}{\$2,000,000 + \$125,000 + \$25,000} = 0.49$$

As with Company A, there is no change to the total value of the right-hand side of Company B's balance sheet because it still has to equal the total value of the assets. However, the reclassification of the deferred tax liabilities under present value assumptions means that the analyst has to increase the value of the equity by the amount of deferred tax liabilities that are not expected to reverse plus the difference between the absolute value and the present value of the deferred tax liabilities that are expected to reverse. Therefore, the value of equity is $2,000,000 + $125,000 + ($75,000 − $50,000) = $2,150,000.

Generally, if a company's deferred tax liabilities are not expected to reverse (and are therefore reclassified as equity), there will be a corresponding reduction in the firm's debt-to-equity ratio.

KEY CONCEPTS

1. Taxable income on the tax return is equivalent to pretax income on the income statement; taxes payable on the tax return is equivalent to tax expense on the income statement.

2. Deferred tax assets are balance sheet amounts that result from an excess of taxes payable over income tax expense that are expected to be recovered from future operations. Deferred tax liabilities are balance sheet amounts that result from an excess of income tax expense over taxes payable that are expected to result in future cash outflows.

3. Deferred tax assets and liabilities are calculated using the liability method, in which the assets and liabilities are calculated at any one time to reflect the current tax rate.

4. A valuation allowance reduces the value of a deferred tax asset when its eventual recoverability is in doubt.

5. Deferred tax liabilities that are expected never to reverse, typically because of expected growth in capital expenditures, should be treated for analytical purposes as equity. If deferred tax liabilities are expected to reverse, they should be treated for analytical purposes as liabilities, but calculated at their present value.

6. Permanent differences between taxable income and pretax income should not create a deferred asset or liability but should be used to adjust the effective tax rate.

7. If the tax rate increases, the increase in deferred tax liabilities increases the income tax expense, and the increase in deferred tax assets decreases the income tax expense. A tax rate decrease has the opposite effect.

8. Firms are required to disclose a reconciliation between a company's effective income tax rate and the applicable statutory rate in the country where the business is domiciled. Looking at the trend of the individual items of the reconciliation can aid in understanding past earnings trends and in predicting future tax rates. Where adequate data is provided, they can also be helpful in predicting future earnings, cash flows, and in adjusting financial ratios.

CONCEPT CHECKERS

1. Which of the following statements is *most accurate*? The difference between taxes payable for the period and the tax expense recognized on the financial statements results from differences:
    A. in management control.
    B. between basic and diluted earnings.
    C. between financial and tax accounting.
    D. between state and federal tax policies.

2. Which of the following tax definitions is *least accurate*?
    A. Taxable income is income based upon IRS rules.
    B. Taxes payable is the amount due to the government.
    C. Pretax income is income tax expense divided by one minus the statutory tax rate.
    D. Income tax expense is the amount listed on the firm's financial statements.

Use the following data to answer Questions 3 through 10.

-   A firm acquires an asset for $120,000 with a 4-year useful life and no salvage value.
-   The asset will generate $50,000 of cash flow for all four years.
-   The tax rate is 40% each year.
-   The firm will depreciate the asset over three years on a straight-line (SL) basis for tax purposes and over all four years on a SL basis for financial reporting purposes.

3. Taxable income in year 1 is:
    A. $6,000.
    B. $10,000.
    C. $20,000.
    D. $50,000.

4. Taxes payable in year 1 are:
    A. $4,000.
    B. $6,000.
    C. $8,000.
    D. $20,000.

5. Pretax income in year 4 is:
    A. $6,000.
    B. $10,000.
    C. $20,000.
    D. $50,000.

6. Income tax expense in year 4 is:
    A. $4,000.
    B. $6,000.
    C. $8,000.
    D. $20,000.

7. Taxes payable in year 4 are:
   A. $4,000.
   B. $6,000.
   C. $8,000.
   D. $20,000.

8. At the end of year 2, the firm's balance sheet will report a deferred tax:
   A. asset of $4,000.
   B. asset of $8,000.
   C. liability of $4,000.
   D. liability of $8,000.

9. Suppose tax rates rise during year 2 to 50%. At the end of year 2, the firm's balance sheet will show a deferred tax liability of:
   A. $5,000.
   B. $6,000.
   C. $8,000.
   D. $10,000.

10. Suppose tax rates rise during year 2 to 50%. What will be the income tax expense in year 2?
    A. $5,000.
    B. $8,000.
    C. $10,000.
    D. $11,000.

11. In its first year of operations, a firm produces taxable income of –$10,000. The prevailing tax rate is 40%. The firm's balance sheet will report a deferred tax:
    A. asset of $4,000.
    B. asset of $10,000.
    C. liability of $4,000.
    D. liability of $10,000.

12. An analyst is comparing a firm to its competitors. The firm has a deferred tax liability and is expected to continue to grow in the foreseeable future. How should the liability be treated for analysis purposes?
    A. It should be treated as equity at its full value.
    B. It should be treated as a liability at its full value.
    C. The present value should be treated as a liability with the remainder being treated as equity.
    D. It should be considered neither a liability nor equity.

13. An analyst is comparing a firm to its competitors. The firm has a deferred tax liability and is expected to have capital expenditures decline in the future. How should the liability be treated for analysis purposes?
    A. It should be treated as equity at its full value.
    B. It should be treated as a liability at its full value.
    C. The present value should be treated as a liability with the remainder being treated as equity.
    D. It should be considered neither a liability nor equity.

14. Which one of the following statements is *most accurate*? Under the liability method of accounting for deferred taxes, a decrease in the tax rate at the beginning of the accounting period will:
    A. increase taxable income in the current period.
    B. reduce income tax expense for the current period.
    C. reduce the deferred tax liability.
    D. increase the beginning-of-period deferred tax asset.

15. An analyst gathered the following information about a company:
    - Taxable income is $40,000.
    - Pretax income is $50,000.
    - Current tax rate is 50%.
    - Tax rate when the reversal occurs will be 40%.

    What is the company's deferred tax liability at the end of year 1?
    A. $3,500.
    B. $4,000.
    C. $4,500.
    D. $5,000.

16. While reviewing a company, an analyst identifies a permanent difference between taxable income and pretax income. Which of the following statements *most accurately* identifies the appropriate financial statement adjustment?
    A. The amount of the tax implications of the difference should be added to the deferred tax liabilities.
    B. The present value of the amount of the tax implications of the difference should be added to the deferred tax liabilities.
    C. The effective tax rate for calculating tax expense should be adjusted.
    D. Taxes payable should be reduced.

17. An analyst is reviewing a company with a large deferred tax asset on its balance sheet. In reviewing the company's performance over the last few years, the analyst has determined that the firm has had cumulative losses for the last three years and has a large amount of inventory that can only be sold at sharply reduced prices. Which of the following adjustments should the analyst make to account for the deferred tax assets?
    A. Record a deferred tax liability to offset the effect of the deferred tax asset on the firm's balance sheet.
    B. Recognize a valuation allowance to reflect the fact that the deferred tax asset is unlikely to be realized.
    C. Do nothing. The difference between taxable and pretax income that caused the deferred tax asset is likely to reverse in the future.
    D. Decrease tax expense by the amount of the deferred tax asset unlikely to be realized.

ANSWERS – CONCEPT CHECKERS

1. **C** The difference between taxes payable for the period and the tax expense recognized on the financial statements results from differences between financial and tax accounting.

2. **C** Pretax income and income tax expense are not always linked because of temporary and permanent differences.

3. **B** Annual depreciation expense for taxes is ($120,000 – 0) / 3 = $40,000. Taxable income is $50,000 – $40,000 = $10,000.

4. **A** Taxes payable is taxable income × tax rate = $10,000 × 40% = $4,000. (The $10,000 was calculated in question #3).

5. **C** Annual depreciation expense for financial income is ($120,000 – 0)/ 4 = $30,000. Pretax income is $50,000 – $30,000 = $20,000.

6. **C** Because there has been no change in the tax rate, income tax expense is pretax income × tax rate = $20,000 × 40% = $8,000. (The $20,000 was calculated in question #5).

7. **D** Note that the asset has been fully depreciated for tax purposes after year 3, so taxable income is $50,000. Taxes payable for year 4 = taxable income × tax rate = $50,000 × 40% = $20,000.

8. **D** The difference between pretax income (calculated in question #5) and taxable income (calculated in question #3) each year is $20,000 – $10,000 = $10,000. The cumulative difference after two years is (2 × $10,000) = $20,000. The deferred tax liability is $20,000 × 40% = $8,000. It is a liability because pretax income exceeds taxable income.

9. **D** The deferred tax liability is now $20,000 × 50% = $10,000. (Multiply the cumulative income difference by the new tax rate.)

10. **D** Taxes payable in year 2 is now taxable income × 50% = $10,000 × 50% = $5000. The deferred tax liability at the end of year 1 was $4,000 (before restatement under the new tax rates). Tax expense = taxes payable + increase in deferred taxes = $5,000 + ($10,000 – $4,000) = $11,000.

11. **A** Tax loss carryforwards are deferred tax assets and would be equal to the loss multiplied by the tax rate.

12. **A** The firm has a deferred tax liability and is expected to continue to grow in the foreseeable future. The liability should be treated as equity at its full value.

13. **C** The firm has a deferred tax liability and is expected to have capital expenditures decline in the future. The present value should be treated as a liability with the remainder being treated as equity.

14. **C** If the tax rate falls, balance sheet DTL and DTA are both reduced. Taxable income is unaffected. Income tax expense could increase if the balance sheet DTA is greater than the DTL.

15. **B** The tax rate that should be used is the expected tax rate when the liability reverses. The deferred tax liability will be $10,000 × 40% = $4,000.

16. C   If a permanent difference between taxable income and pretax income is identifiable, the effective tax rate for calculating tax expense should be adjusted.

17. B   A valuation allowance is used to offset deferred tax assets if it is unlikely that those assets will be realized. Because the company has a history of losses and inventory that is unlikely to generate future profits, it is unlikely the company will realize its deferred tax assets in full.

ANALYSIS OF FINANCING LIABILITIES

EXAM FOCUS

One crucial point in this topic review is that when a company issues a bond, the initial liability posted to the balance sheet is the amount received, not the par amount, and the effective interest rate is the market rate, not the coupon rate. The discount or premium is amortized over the bond's life so that the liability is equal to par at maturity. Candidates should understand the difference between cash interest costs and interest expense, how cash flow from operations is distorted by discount/premium bonds, and why market values of debt are more appropriate than book values for calculating leverage and for valuation purposes. Some advantages of various types of debt would be good to know, as would the balance sheet treatment of convertible bonds and bonds with attached warrants.

BOND TERMINOLOGY

The various forms of debt and financing activities are important aspects of the analysis of a firm's short-term liquidity and long-term solvency.

This review emphasizes balance sheet debt, including current liabilities, long-term liabilities from financing activities, various debt instruments, and the effect of interest rate changes.

- The **face value** is also known as the bond's maturity value, or par value. This is the value of the bond if market interest rates equal the coupon rate on the date of bond issuance.
- The **coupon rate** is multiplied by the face value to calculate the periodic *coupon payments* to be made to investors.
- The **market rate of interest** is used to value debt obligations. Do not confuse the market rate of interest, which is the compensation required by financial markets for default risk, liquidity, the time value of money, etc., with the coupon rate, which is the rate of interest stated on the debt contract. For fixed-rate debt, the coupon rate does not change over the life of the contract. However, the market rate changes every day and will cause differences between the book value of the debt and the market value of the debt. This concept is explained in greater detail later in this topic review.

TYPES OF BALANCE SHEET DEBT

Current liabilities are defined as those liabilities due within one year or operating cycle.

Current liabilities are reported on the balance sheet according to their: (1) order by maturity, (2) descending order by amount, or (3) order in the event of liquidation. Current liabilities are reported at their full maturity value. Current liabilities may result from operating activities (e.g., trade credit) or from financing activities (e.g., current portion of long-term debt).

Long-term debt contracts are obligations that are not payable within one year or one operating cycle, whichever is longer. Long-term debt may be obtained from many sources and may differ in the structure of interest and principal payments and the claims creditors have on the assets of the firm. Some creditors may have a claim on specific assets and other creditors may have only a general claim. Some creditors may have claims that rank below (are *subordinated* to) the claims of other creditors whose claims have priority (are *senior* to the other claims).

- Debt is equal to the present value of the future interest and principal payments. For *book values*, the discount rate is the interest rate in effect when the debt was incurred. For *market values*, the rate is the current market interest rate.
- Interest expense is the amount paid to the creditor in excess of the amount received. Although the total amount of interest to be paid is known, the allocation to specific time periods may be uncertain.

Bonds are a contract between the borrower and the lender that obligates the bond issuer to make payments to the bondholder over the life of the bond. Two types of payments are involved:

1. Periodic payment of interest [affects cash flows from operations (CFO)].

2. Repayment of principal at maturity [affects cash flow from financing (CFF)].

   interest expense each period = interest rate at issuance × balance sheet liability

The interest expense of bonds issued at a discount rises over time because of the increasing value of the liability. The interest expense of bonds issued at a premium will fall over time because of the decreasing value of the liability, and the interest expense of par bonds will remain constant.

The **balance sheet liability** is the present value of the remaining cash payments using the market rate when the bonds were issued. At maturity, the value of the liability will equal the par value of the bond.

The bond contract does not determine the amount the borrower receives or the allocation between interest and principal. That depends on the current market rate of interest. The market interest rate depends on the maturity and risk of the bond and may be equal to, less than, or greater than the coupon rate on the date of issue.

- When the market rate equals the coupon rate, the bond is called a *par* bond.
- When the market rate is greater than the coupon rate, the bond is called a *discount* bond.
- When the market rate is less than the coupon rate, the bond is called a *premium* bond.

LOS 39.a: Distinguish between operating and trade debt related to operating activities and debt generated by financing activities, and discuss the analytical implications of a shift between the two types of liabilities.

There are two types of current liabilities that arise from operating (as opposed to financing) activities.

1. *Trade debt* (payables) arises when a firm purchases inputs from its suppliers on credit. *Wages payable* arise when wages are owed for work performed during the period, but have not yet been paid.

2. *Advances from customers* are shown as a current liability even though they are satisfied by delivering goods or services, rather than being paid in cash.

Even though these current liabilities must be paid in the future (within one accounting cycle), they are carried on the balance sheet at the value that must be paid in the future, rather than the present value of the expected future payment.

There are two types of entries for current liabilities that arise from financing activities rather than from operating activities.

1. *Short-term debt* results from borrowings for periods less than one accounting cycle and typically includes all interest-bearing debt with maturities of one year or less.

2. The *current portion of long-term debt* records the principal amount on long-term debt that is scheduled to be paid within the next year. Each year the liability for long-term debt is reduced by the portion of the principal due within the next year that is moved to current liabilities.

When the analyst is examining the firm's liquidity, the treatment of these various current liabilities differs. As noted above, advances from customers need not be paid in cash. An increase in advances from customers indicates an increase in (future) sales and does not indicate a deteriorating liquidity position. A growing reliance on short-term borrowings as opposed to trade payables often indicates that the risk of liquidity problems is increasing. Such would be the case if the firm's suppliers began to limit the credit they extend to the firm.

In general, operating liabilities will increase as the firm's business grows. Trade liabilities that grow more rapidly than sales indicate a heavier reliance on suppliers as a source of cash to fund operations, but this is not necessarily a bad thing. It is the shift from operating liabilities to financing liabilities that typically signals greater potential for liquidity problems.

LOS 39.b: Determine the effects of debt issuance and amortization of bond discounts and premiums on financial statements and financial ratios.

Bonds Issued at Par

When a bond is issued at par, its effects on the financial statements are very straightforward.

- **Balance sheet impact**. Bonds are always initially listed as liabilities equal to the amount of the proceeds received at issuance. For a par bond the proceeds are equal to face value, so the bond liability remains at face value over the life of the bond.
- **Interest expense**. Interest expense is always equal to the book value of the bonds at the beginning of the period multiplied by the market rate of interest *at issuance.* In the case of par value bonds, this is the same as the coupon rate of the bond.
- **Cash flow**. CFO includes a deduction for interest expense. For bonds issued at par, the interest expense is equal to the coupon payment. CFF is increased by the amount received. Upon repayment of the bond at maturity, CFF is reduced by the bond's par value.

Bonds Issued at a Premium or Discount

When the market rate of interest is not equal to the coupon rate, the present value of the coupon payments plus the present value of the face value is not equal to par value, and a *premium* or *discount* occurs. The premium or discount is usually relatively small for coupon bonds.

If the market rate of interest is less than the coupon rate, the proceeds received will be greater than face value, and a premium results. Recall from our basic bond valuation that if the market rate of interest is less than the coupon rate, investors will *pay more* to obtain the higher coupon payment attached to the bond in question. Hence, the bond will sell at a premium.

If the market rate of interest is greater than the coupon rate, the proceeds received will be less than the face value, and a discount results. Here, the coupon rate is low relative to bonds that are being issued at par value. Hence, individuals will *pay less* than face value for bonds with low coupons relative to the current market rate. These are called discount bonds.

Balance sheet impact

- Bonds are always initially listed as liabilities based on the proceeds received from the bonds, which is the present value of all future payments. At any point in time, the book value of the bonds can be calculated as the present value of all future payments at the market rate of interest.

    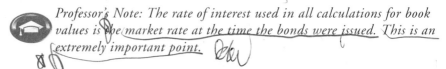 *Professor's Note: The rate of interest used in all calculations for book values is the market rate at the time the bonds were issued. This is an extremely important point.*

- Bonds that were originally sold at a premium will always be shown at a premium on the balance sheet. This premium will be amortized toward zero over the life of the bond.

- Bonds that were originally sold at a discount will always be recorded on the balance sheet at a discount. This discount will be amortized toward zero over the life of the bond. Hence, the book value of both premium and discount bonds will *converge* to the bonds' par or face values at maturity.

Interest expense

- Interest expense is always equal to the book value of the bonds at the beginning of the period multiplied by the market rate of interest. Market rate of interest refers to the rate in effect when the bonds are issued.
- In the case of premium bonds, the interest expense will be lower than the coupon. The amortization of the bond's premium will serve to *reduce* the interest expense that is shown on the income statement. In general, interest expense will equal the coupon payment less the premium amortization.
- In the case of discount bonds, the interest expense will be higher than the coupon. Here, the amortization of the bond's discount will serve to *increase* the interest expense that is reported on the income statement. In general, interest expense will equal the coupon payment plus the discount amortization.

> *Professor's Note: In the case of a discount bond, the coupon is too low relative to the market's required rate of return. The purpose of amortizing the discount is to (1) increase the bond's book value over time and (2) increase interest expense so that the coupon + discount amortization is approximately equal to the interest expense that would have prevailed had the bond been issued at par with a higher coupon. This argument is easily reversed for premium bonds.*

Cash flow

- The coupon represents the cash flow component of the bond and is the amount deducted in calculating CFO for accounting purposes. However, from an analytical perspective, the interest expense and the amortization of the premium or discount should be separated. Amortization should be included in CFF, not CFO.
- *For premium bonds*, the cash coupon is higher than interest expense; consequently, CFO is understated and CFF is overstated relative to a company that does not have premium bonds in its capital structure.
- *For discount bonds*, the cash coupon is lower than interest expense; consequently, CFO is overstated and CFF is understated relative to a company that does not have discount bonds.
- Analysts can make adjustments to CFO by correcting for the difference between the coupon payment and the interest expense—this adjustment will be positive for premium bonds and negative for discount bonds.
- Upon issuance, CFF is increased by the amount of the proceeds, and upon repayment at maturity, CFF is reduced by the par value or payoff amount.
- In our review of the statement of cash flows, it is argued that all debt-related cash flow should be excluded from CFO and included in CFF. This takes the adjustments just discussed one step further. From an economic perspective, this approach is desirable because it separates investment decisions from financing decisions and gives a clearer picture of the profitability of operations.

Example: Book values and cash flows

On December 31, 2002, a company issued a 3-year, 10% annual coupon bond with a face value of $100,000.

Part A: Calculate the book value of the bond at year-end 2002, 2003, and 2004, and the interest expense for 2003, 2004, and 2005, assuming the bond was issued at a market rate of interest of (1) 10%, (2) 9%, and (3) 11%.

Part B: The financial statements for 2003 show that cash flow from operations was $50,000. Assuming that the market rate of interest was 9% when the bond was issued, how should this cash flow be analyzed when comparing it to other companies?

Answer: Part A

Bond issued at par. If the market rate of interest at issuance is 10%, the book value of the bonds will always be $100,000, and the interest expense will always be $10,000, which is equal to the coupon payment of 0.10 × $100,000. There is no discount or premium to amortize.

Premium bonds. If the market rate of interest is 9%, the present value of the cash payments (a 3-year annuity of $10,000 and a payment in three years of $100,000) is $102,531.

N = 3; PMT = 10,000; FV = 100,000; I/Y = 9; CPT → PV = $102,531

 Professor's Note: The present value computed in this manner will have a minus sign.

The following figure shows the interest expense (IE) and book value (BV) at the end of each year.

Interest Expenses and Book Value for a Premium Bond

Year	(1) Beginning Book Value	(2) Interest Expense (1) × 9%	(3) Coupon	(4) Ending Book Value (1) + (2) – (3)
2003	$102,531	$9,228	$10,000	$101,759
2004	101,759	9,158	10,000	100,917
2005	100,917	9,083	10,000	100,000

The premium amortization for 2003 is 10,000 – 9,228 = $772. For 2004, the amortization is 10,000 – 9,158 = $842. Finally, for 2005, premium amortization is $917. Note that the premium has been fully amortized upon maturity such that the book value of the bond equals par value.

Discount bonds. If the market rate of interest is 11%, the present value of the cash payments (a 3-year annuity of $10,000 and a payment in three years of $100,000) is $97,556.

N = 3; PMT = 10,000; FV = 100,000; I/Y = 11; CPT → PV = $97,556

The following figure shows the interest expense and book value at the end of each year.

Interest Expense and Book Value for a Discount Bond

Year	(1) Beginning Book Value	(2) Interest Expense (1) x 11%	(3) Coupon	(4) Ending Book Value (1) + (2) – (3)
2003	$97,556	$10,731	$10,000	$98,287
2004	98,287	10,812	10,000	99,099
2005	99,099	10,901	10,000	100,000

Again, the pattern of discount amortization is such that the discount is fully amortized upon maturity, when the book value of the bond equals par value.

Answer: Part B   CFO understaten

For the premium bond (9% market rate at issuance), the cash component of interest expense was overstated. CFO was understated in 2003 because CFO is reduced by the coupon of $10,000 instead of by the true interest expense of $9,228. For analysis, cash flow from operations should be adjusted by adding $772 ($10,000 – $9,228). Note that since CFO is understated, CFF will be overstated over the life of a premium bond. While the proceeds of issuance are a positive CFF (+$102,531), the negative CFF at maturity is only the face value ($100,000). Over the life of the bond, net CFF (+2,531) is positive, by the same amount that CFO is understated.

Summary of Financial Statement Effects of Issuing a Bond

Statement of Cash Flows

Figure 1: Cash Flow Impact of Issuing a Bond

	Cash Flow from Financing	Cash Flow from Operations
Issuance of debt	Increased by cash received (Present value of the bond at the market interest rate)	No effect
Periodic interest payments	No effect	Decreased by interest paid [(coupon rate) × (face or par value)]
Payment at maturity	Decreased by face (par) value	No effect

Figure 2: Economic or Analytic Perspective of Interest Payments

	Cash Flow from Financing	Cash Flow from Operations
Premium bonds	Overstated	Understated
Discount bonds	Understated	Overstated

Income Statement

$$\text{interest expense} = \left(\begin{array}{c}\text{the market rate}\\\text{at issue}\end{array}\right) \times \left(\begin{array}{c}\text{the balance sheet value}\\\text{of the liability at}\\\text{the beginning of the period}\end{array}\right)$$

Figure 3: Income Statement Impact of Issuing a Bond

Issued at Par	Issued at a Premium	Issued at a Discount
Market rate = coupon rate Interest expense = coupon rate × face value = cash paid	Market rate < coupon rate Interest expense = cash paid – amortization of premium	Market rate > coupon rate Interest expense = cash paid + amortization of discount
Interest expense is constant	Interest decreases over time	Interest increases over time

Balance Sheet

Long-term debt is carried at the present value of the remaining cash payments discounted at the market rate existing when the debt was issued.

Figure 4: Balance Sheet Impact of Issuing a Bond

Issued at Par	Issued at a Premium	Issued at a Discount
Carried at face value	Carried at face value plus premium The liability decreases as the premium is amortized to interest expense	Carried at face value less discount The liability increases as the discount is amortized to interest expense

LOS 39.c: Analyze the effect on financial statements and financial ratios of issuing zero-coupon debt.

Zero-coupon debt is debt issued with no periodic payments of interest and principal is paid back with one lump sum payment upon maturity. Zero-coupon bonds are also known as *pure discount* instruments because they are issued at a discount from par value, and their annual interest expense is *implied.* Actual interest is all paid at maturity when the bonds are paid off (at their par value). The effects of zero-coupon debt on financial statements are qualitatively the same as those of discount debt—only the impact is larger because the discount is larger.

For discount bonds, the coupon understates the cash component of interest expense and CFO is overstated. With zero-coupon bonds, there is no coupon, so for operating cash flow purposes there is no interest expense deducted. This *severely overstates CFO.* The difference shows up at maturity when the zero-coupon bond is paid off. The cash flow when the bond is paid off is charged to CFF, and for discount debt this negative cash flow is greater than the positive CFF at issuance. Thus CFF is understated over the life of the bond.

Example: Effect of zero-coupon debt on CFO

Two companies have an identical value for cash sales less cash inputs and cash operating expenses of $50,000. The only difference between the two companies is their financing. At the beginning of this year, Company A sold $1,000,000 of face value zero-coupon bonds maturing in three years. Company B sold $750,000 of 10% coupon bonds maturing in three years. Assume the market rate of interest on these bonds is 10%.

- How much did Company A receive for its bonds?
- What would interest expense be for Company A over the three years of the bond's life?
- Compute the cash flow from operations for Company A and Company B for year 1 (ignore taxes).

Assume that both bonds are *annual pay* and are valued using annual pay assumptions.

 Professor's Note: For the exam, know that most zero-coupon bonds in the United States are valued using a semiannual pay convention.

Answer:

The present value of $1,000,000 in three years is $1,000,000 / (1.1)^3 = 751,315.

$$N = 3; \ I/Y = 10; \ FV = 1,000,000; \ PMT = 0; \ CPT \rightarrow PV = \$751,315$$

Interest expense in year 1 is $751,315 \times 10\% = \$75,131$.

Book value in year 1 is $751,315 + $75,131 = \$826,446$.

Interest expense in year 2 is $826,446 \times 10\% = \$82,645$.

Book value in year 2 is $826,446 + $82,645 = $909,091.

Interest expense in year 3 is $909,091 \times 10\% = $90,909.

Book value at the end of year 3 = $909,091 + $90,909 = \$1,000,000$.

Note that the "interest expense" for Company A is entirely composed of *discount amortization*. There is no cash interest component to Company A's interest expense.

CFO for Company A = $50,000 because there is no cash interest expense.

CFO for Company B = $50,000 − $75,000 = −$25,000. Company B's cash coupon payment reduces CFO significantly.

Without any adjustments, Company A's CFO appears significantly higher than Company B's CFO. An analyst should either adjust B's cash flow upward or A's downward when comparing the companies. Note that at issuance CFF is approximately +$750,000 for both A and B (A was issued for $751,315), but at maturity CFF is −$750,000 for Company B and −$1,000,000 for Company A.

LOS 39.d: Classify a debt security with equity features as a debt or equity security and demonstrate the effect of issuing debt with equity features on the financial statements and ratios.

Convertible Bonds

When convertible bonds are issued, under U.S. Generally Accepted Accounting Principals (U.S. GAAP), they are recorded on the balance sheet as if there were no conversion feature, and interest expense is recorded exactly as it is for option-free bonds. A change in this treatment is currently under consideration.

From an analytic perspective, however, the equity feature of convertible bonds can be an important distinction. In general, when the stock price is significantly above the conversion price, it should be treated like equity for the purposes of calculating the debt ratios. Such treatment will decrease debt to equity and debt to total capital. At the other extreme, when the stock price is significantly lower than the conversion price, convertible debt should be treated like debt in calculating ratios.

When the stock price is close to the conversion price, the classification is not as clear and the effect on the debt to total capital ratio is uncertain. The analyst should compute debt ratios treating the convertible bonds alternatively as debt and as equity to gauge the impact of the assumption used. Choosing one treatment over the other should depend on the purpose of the analysis and the analyst's estimate of the probability of conversion over the relevant time horizon.

Bonds With Warrants

When bonds are issued with warrants attached, the proceeds are allocated between the two components. The bond portion is recognized (at a discount) as a liability at fair market value and the discount is amortized over the life of the issue. The warrants are recognized as equity at fair market value, and the cash received when the warrants are exercised is added to equity capital. Overall, debt ratios will be increased less by the issuance of bonds with warrants attached than by the issuance of convertible bonds.

Non-convertible preferred shares are treated by the analyst as equity unless they are redeemable by the holder, in which case they should be treated as debt and the dividends treated as interest. This treatment is required by International Financial Reporting Standards (IFRS) and under consideration by the Financial Accounting Standards Board (FASB).

The liability recorded for conventional bonds and convertible bonds is greater than for an equivalent amount of bonds with warrants attached. Because a portion of the proceeds of a bond with attached warrants is classified as equity, both debt-to-equity and debt-to-total capital will be *lower* than if conventional or convertible debt were issued.

LOS 39.e: Describe the disclosures relating to financing liabilities, and discuss the advantages/disadvantages to the company of selecting a given financing instrument and the effect of the selection on a company's financial statements and ratios.

There are various disclosures related to financing liabilities that will aid an analyst.

- On the balance sheet, we will find the present value of the promised future liability payments, discounted at the rate in effect at issuance.
- On the income statement or in a footnote, we will find interest expense for the period.
- On the cash flow statement, we will find cash interest expense and we can compare this to interest expense to see the effect of the issuance of zero-coupon or discount debt.
- For a publicly-traded firm, filings with the SEC will detail all outstanding securities and their relevant terms.
- For off-balance-sheet liabilities, such as leases, take-or-pay contracts, and other material financial obligations of the firm, we will find details of each liability in the footnotes to the financial statements.

When raising funds, the firm must decide which instrument it will use among a wide variety of security types. Each instrument has advantages and disadvantages. Which is most advantageous for the firm will depend on the specific circumstances of the firm. Some key points will help you to understand which instrument would be the best choice, given the firm's circumstances.

As noted previously, *zero-coupon debt* reduces the firm's cash interest costs and may be advantageous when near-term cash flow is low or quite uncertain. If the firm faces restrictions on its cash interest coverage ratio or has financing costs tied to this ratio, zero coupon debt could offer the most advantages.

Variable-rate debt (also called floating-rate debt) carries an interest rate that is periodically reset to market rates. This typically has the effect of keeping the market value of the debt close to its par value. If a firm has operating cash flows that tend to go up (down) when short-term interest rates increase (decrease), then issuing variable-rate debt can reduce stress on net cash flows. On the other hand, when this is not the case, issuing variable-rate debt can increase the variability of net cash flows as interest rates rise and fall.

When management believes that interest rates will fall in the future, the issuance of variable-rate debt may be based on speculation. If management is right, the variable-rate debt can be replaced with fixed-rate debt in the future after rates have fallen. Thus, we can draw a distinction between managements that issue variable-rate debt for valid business purposes and those that issue for speculative reasons.

One final advantage can arise when short-term interest rates are significantly lower than longer term rates. If this situation persists, the firm can reduce total interest costs over the planning horizon by issuing variable-rate debt, since the variable rate is typically a short-term rate. Be aware, however, that the firm will be accepting cash interest variability along with a potential reduction in total interest costs and that often, higher long-term rates may be an indication that short-term rates will be significantly higher in the future.

Firms can issue **debt denominated in a foreign currency**. This type of liability can be advantageous if the firm has future cash flows in that currency. By matching the currency of this cash flow to future liabilities, the firm may hedge (reduce) some currency risk that they would otherwise have. If a firm, for some reason, has a lower borrowing cost in foreign markets, this could make the issuance of debt denominated in a foreign currency attractive.

Each of the types of debt securities with equity features discussed previously has its own potential advantages. Issuing **convertible debt** will decrease borrowing costs, reducing both interest expense and cash interest expense. The trade-off here is simply the value of the option to convert into common stock that is included in the security. There are no specific balance sheet differences between issuing convertible debt and issuing an equivalent amount of non-convertible debt.

Issuing **bonds with warrants attached** can also reduce interest costs relative to conventional corporate bonds but, given the balance sheet treatment of the liability, interest expense will be greater than for equivalent convertible bonds. When warrants are attached, the value attributed to the warrants is treated as a bond discount at issuance and is amortized over the term of the bond. The balance sheet liability is less than both a conventional and convertible bond for this same reason. This will, of course, affect related debt ratios. Assuming the stated coupon rate is the same for a convertible bond and an equivalent bond with warrants attached, the cash interest will be the same for both, and less than the cash interest costs for a conventional bond.

Debt convertible into the shares of a company other than the issuing company is referred to as **exchangeable debt**. There are several potential advantages to issuing exchangeable debt. As with convertible debt, the exchange option will decrease the required yield, and therefore interest expense, of the borrowing. At the same time, the exchange price will typically be some premium over the current market value of the shares. A holding of the shares of the other company may, at the same time, offer some strategic business advantage. If there is a significant capital gain in the shares, the firm may be avoiding significant tax consequences of selling the position and at the same time realizing its value. If the block of exchangeable shares is relatively large, the firm can reduce the market impact of a sale of the entire block by calling the exchangeable debt periodically, releasing shares to the market in a piecemeal manner.

Commodity-linked bonds may reduce (hedge) cash flow risk for producers of the commodity. Consider an oil company that issues bonds with a coupon rate tied to the price of oil. Presumably, when oil prices are high, operating cash flows are relatively high and more cash is available to pay interest costs. More importantly, cash interest expense would fall when oil prices are low. In this case, the times interest earned and cash interest coverage ratios will tend to be more stable over an economic cycle than if conventional debt were issued.

The issuance of **perpetual debt** or conventional bonds with very long maturities (e.g., 100 years) issued at par will not have balance sheet, income statement, or cash flow effects appreciably different from those of conventional fixed-rate bonds with more typical maturities. The analyst, however, may choose to treat these securities more like equity, given their similarity to a preferred stock. The idea here is that perpetual debt is more similar to permanent capital than to conventional debt. Just as issuing variable-rate debt has a potential advantage over fixed rate debt if rates subsequently decrease, issuing perpetual debt has a potential advantage if it is timed to coincide with low market interest rates.

Conventional **preferred shares** have no set maturity and pay a dividend that can be omitted without forcing bankruptcy, so they are treated as equity. However, the distinction between debt and equity securities is often not clear in the case of preferred stock. Just as perpetual debt has characteristics similar to equity, some preferred shares have characteristics more similar to debt than to equity. When preferred shares are redeemable by the shareholder or required to be redeemed by a sinking fund provision, their value should be treated like debt. Also, preferred shares that pay an adjustable short-term interest rate (so-called adjustable-rate or market-rate preferred) have the characteristics of short-term debt and should be treated as such by the analyst.

LOS 39.f: Determine the effects of changing interest rates on the market value of debt and on financial statements and ratios.

Under U.S. GAAP, balance sheet values for outstanding debt must be based on the market rate on the date of issuance.

Changes in market interest rates lead to changes in the market values of debt. *Increases (decreases) in the market rate of interest decrease (increase) the market value of debt.* These gains (from the decrease in market value of debt) or losses (from the increase in market value of debt) are not reflected in the financial statements. Hence, the book value of debt will not equal the market value.

With variable-rate debt, neither balance sheet values nor market values of the debt change with market rates, but interest expense does. Rising market rates increase interest expense on variable-rate debt and decrease net income.

For purposes of analysis, market values may be more appropriate than book values. For example, firms that issue debt when interest rates are low are relatively better off when interest rates increase. This increase should be reflected in a higher value of equity and a lower value of debt. Adjusting the firm's debt down to market value will reduce it to the amount the firm would currently have to pay to retire the debt, and will decrease the debt-to-equity ratio. If interest rates decrease, adjusting the debt to market value will have the opposite effects.

SFAS 107 requires disclosures about the fair value of outstanding debt based on year-end or quarter-end prices. These disclosures are made in the notes to the financial statements.

Note: Market value disclosures are not required for non-U.S. firms.

Estimating market values for publicly traded debt is easy. For debt that is not publicly traded, we can find the present value of the future cash flows. Typically, these cash flows are disclosed by the company. The relevant market rate for finding the present values can be found by considering the maturity and other terms of the debt and then using:

- Other similar issues of the company which are publicly traded.
- Rates on publicly traded debt of similar companies.
- A risk premium added to the U.S. bond rate for that maturity.

LOS 39.g: Calculate and describe the accounting treatment of, and economic gains and losses resulting from, the various methods of retiring debt prior to its maturity.

A firm may choose to retire debt because interest rates have fallen, because it has generated a surplus of operating cash flow, or because funds from the issuance of equity make it possible (and desirable). When debt is retired prior to maturity at its book value, no gain or loss is reported on the transaction. When the payment to retire the debt is greater than or less than its book value, a gain or loss is recorded. Unless the debt retirement specifically qualifies for treatment as an extraordinary item, the gains and losses recorded affect income from continuing operations, which is the typical treatment.

If a firm is simply showing a gain because interest rates have risen, and is replacing previously issued low-coupon debt with higher coupon debt, there is no economic gain on the transaction. The gains reported in the current period are offset by the higher interest charges on the new debt that must be paid in the future. In this case the analyst is advised to treat the gain as extraordinary; that is, back it out of net income from continuing operations.

The same can be said of losses from retiring premium debt that was issued when interest rates were higher. From an economic standpoint, the current loss is offset by a reduction in future interest charges on the newly issued lower-coupon debt. The analyst should ignore this loss in calculating operating earnings.

Callable Debt

There are circumstances in which the company actually realizes an economic benefit from early debt retirement. With callable debt the firm may retire premium debt for less than its present value. Consider a callable bond that allows the issuer to retire it prior to maturity for 101 (percent of face value). If interest rates have fallen since the debt was issued, the firm has incurred an (unreported) economic loss because the present value of the future interest and principal payments on the debt has risen. If rates have fallen such that the present value of the bond liability is 105% of face value, retiring the bond issue at 101% of face value actually generates an economic gain for the firm. From an accounting standpoint, however, a loss will be recorded since the redemption price of 101 is greater than the book value of 100 (assuming the debt was originally issued at par).

It is up to the analyst, therefore, to evaluate whether the early retirement of debt results in an economic gain or loss to the firm, which will not necessarily be the same as the accounting gain or loss on the transaction reported under GAAP. One suggestion is that the analyst always ignore both gains and losses that result from debt retirement.

Defeasance

If a firm has generated sufficient funds to retire non-callable debt prior to maturity, it may choose to invest those funds in riskless (e.g. Treasury) securities to be held in trust. The riskless securities are purchased in amounts that will generate the periodic interest and principal amount due at maturity (or the call date) on the existing liability. This is referred to as *in-substance defeasance*. Under current GAAP, no accounting gain or loss is recorded for such pre-refunding. Only the actual termination of the liability to the debt holders generates such treatment.

LOS 39.h: Analyze the implications of debt covenants for creditors and the issuing company.

Debt covenants are restrictions imposed by the bondholders on the issuer in order to protect the bondholders' position. The bondholder can demand repayment of the bonds after a violation of one of the covenants (this is called a technical default). An analysis of the bond covenants is a necessary component of the credit analysis of a bond. Bond covenants are typically disclosed in the footnotes.

Examples of covenants include restrictions on:

- Dividend payments and share repurchases.
- Mergers and acquisitions, and sale, leaseback, and disposal of certain assets.
- Issuance of new debt.
- Repayment patterns (e.g., sinking fund agreements and priority of claims).

Other covenants require the firm to maintain ratios or financial statement items, such as equity, net working capital, current ratio, or debt-to-equity ratio at certain levels. Covenants will specify whether GAAP is to be used when calculating the ratios or whether some adjustment is required. Covenants protect bondholders from actions the firm may take that would negatively affect the value of the bondholders' claims to firm assets and earnings (i.e., decrease credit quality). To the extent that covenants restrict, for example, the firm's ability to invest, take on additional debt, or pay dividends, an analysis of covenants can be important in valuing the firm's equity (especially involving its growth prospects) as well as in analyzing and valuing its debt securities.

KEY CONCEPTS

1. Early retirement of debt may result in gains or losses in income from continuing operations which do not represent actual economic gains or losses.
2. Issuance of discount bonds will lead to an understatement of CFF and an overstatement of CFO, and issuance of premium bonds will have the opposite effect because coupon interest (cash) payments are not equal to interest expense.
3. The amortization of bond premiums and discounts will provide the correct interest expense for the period since the coupon payment does so only for bonds issued at par.
4. The issuance of zero-coupon (pure discount) bonds causes the most severe overstatement of CFO and eventual understatement of CFF.
5. Debt with equity features should be treated for analytical purposes as having both a debt and equity component.
6. The following table summarizes the key issues related to financing liabilities in this topic review:

Financing Liability	Advantages (from the perspective of the issuer)	Analyst Treatment
Discount/ zero-coupon debt	• CFO overstated • Cash interest reduced	• Increase interest expense and decrease CFO by amount of discount amortization
Convertible debt	Versus conventional debt: • Lower interest expense • Higher operating cash flow • Same balance sheet liability	• Treat as equity if stock price > conversion price • Treat as debt if stock price < conversion price
Exchangeable debt	• Lower interest expense • Generate cash without selling investment • Reduce market impact of selling investment • Delay tax impact of gain and control timing of gain	• Similar to convertible
Bonds with warrants	Versus conventional debt: • Lower interest expense • Higher operating cash flow • Lower balance sheet liability	• Classify bond value as debt, warrant value as equity
Commodity bonds	• Converts interest expense from fixed to variable cost • Can reduce interest coverage variability	• May reduce risk compared to conventional debt
Perpetual debt	• Lock in long-term rates when rates are low	• Treat as equity

Financing Liability	Advantages (from the perspective of the issuer)	Analyst Treatment
Preferred stock	• Create a debt/equity hybrid security	• Classify redeemable preferred shares as debt and dividends as interest • Classify variable-rate shares as short-term liabilities

7. Market values of fixed-rate debt change as interest rates change, but reported book values do not. Use market values for analysis and valuation purposes, with the offsetting adjustment to equity.

8. Evaluation of a firm's credit risk and growth prospects should include an analysis of bond covenants.

CONCEPT CHECKERS

1. The book value of debt equals the present value of interest:
    A. payments at the current discount rate.
    B. payments using the discount rate at the time of issue.
    C. and principal payments using the current discount rate.
    D. and principal payments using the discount rate at the time of issue.

2. Annual interest expense is the:
    A. sum of the annual coupon payments.
    B. amount paid to creditors in excess of par.
    C. book value of the debt times the current interest rate.
    D. book value of the debt times the market interest rate when it was issued.

Use the following data to answer Questions 3 through 10.

A firm issues a $10 million bond with a 6% coupon rate, 4-year maturity, and annual interest payments when market interest rates are 7%.

3. The bond can be classified as a:
    A. discount bond.
    B. zero-coupon bond.
    C. par bond.
    D. premium bond.

4. The annual coupon payments will each be:
    A. $600,000.
    B. $676,290.
    C. $700,000.
    D. $723,710.

5. Total cash payment due the bondholders is:
    A. $12,400,000.
    B. $12,738,721.
    C. $12,800,000.
    D. $13,107,960.

6. The initial book value of the bonds is:
    A. $9,400,000.
    B. $9,661,279.
    C. $10,000,000.
    D. $10,338,721.

7. For the first period the interest expense is:
    A. $600,000.
    B. $676,290.
    C. $700,000.
    D. $723,710.

8. If the market rate changes to 8%, the book value of the bonds at the end of the first period will be:
   A. $9,484,581.
   B. $9,661,279.
   C. $9,737,568.
   D. $9,745,959.

9. The total interest expense reported by the issuer over the life of the bond will be:
   A. $2,400,000.
   B. $2,738,721.
   C. $2,800,000.
   D. $3,107,960.

10. How much will cash flow from operations (CFO) in year 1 be understated or overstated by these bonds?
    A. Overstated by $76,290.
    B. Overstated by $100,000.
    C. Understated by $76,290.
    D. Understated by $100,000.

11. Interest expense reported on the income statement is based on the:
    A. market rate at issuance.
    B. coupon payment.
    C. current market rate.
    D. unamortized discount.

12. The actual coupon payment on a bond is:
    A. reported as an operating cash outflow.
    B. reported as a financing cash outflow.
    C. reported as a financing cash inflow and operating cash outflow.
    D. not reported since only the interest expense is reported.

13. A 2-year bond is carried on the books at a premium because it was issued at a coupon rate of 0.25% higher than the market rate. After one year, market rates have gone down by 0.5%. The bond will now be listed on the books as having:
    A. the same premium it had when originally issued.
    B. a lower premium than when it was originally issued.
    C. par value.
    D. a discount.

14. Wolfe Inc. had a capital structure consisting of $10 million of liabilities and $15 million of equity. Wolfe then issued $0.7 million of preferred shares and $1.0 million of bonds with warrants attached (debt component comprises 80% of the value) for total cash proceeds of $1.7 million. Which of the following amounts is the revised debt to total capital ratio upon the issuance of the two new financial instruments?
    A. 0.404.
    B. 0.431.
    C. 0.679.
    D. 0.757.

15. A company has convertible bonds on its books with a conversion price of $20 per share. The stock price is currently $40 per share. For analytical purposes, the bonds should be treated as:
    A. debt.
    B. preferred stock.
    C. equity.
    D. a hybrid of debt and common stock.

16. The relative effects on interest expense and operating cash flow from issuing convertible bonds versus conventional bonds are:

	Interest expense	Operating cash flow
A.	Lower	Lower
B.	Lower	Higher
C.	Higher	Higher
D.	Higher	Lower

17. Which of the following is *least likely* a motivation for issuing exchangeable debt?
    A. The issuing firm reports an immediate gain when the debt is issued.
    B. Interest expense is lower than issuing conventional debt.
    C. The market impact of selling the underlying shares all at once is mitigated.
    D. The issuing firm generates cash while retaining control of the underlying shares.

ANSWERS – CONCEPT CHECKERS

1. **D** The book value of debt is equal to the present value of interest and principal payments. Book value is based on the market interest rate in effect at the time the debt was issued.

2. **D** Annual interest expense is the book value of the debt times the interest rate at the time of issuance.

3. **A** This bond is issued at a discount since the coupon rate < market rate.

4. **A** Coupon payment = (coupon rate × face value of bond) = 6% × $10,000,000 = $600,000.

5. **A** Four coupon payments and the face value = $600,000 × 4 + $10,000,000 = $12,400,000.

6. **B** The present value of a 4-year annuity of $600,000 plus a 4-year lump sum of $10 million, all valued at a discount rate of 7%, equals $9,661,279. C and D can be eliminated because the bond is selling at a discount.

7. **B** Market interest rate × book value = 7% × $9,661,279 = $676,290.

8. **C** The change in interest rates is ignored. The new book value = beginning book value + interest expense – coupon payment = $9,661,279 + $676,290 – $600,000 = $9,737,569. The interest expense was calculated in Concept Checker 7. Alternatively, changing N from 4 to 3 and calculating the PV will yield the same result.

9. **B** Coupon payments + amortized interest = coupon payments + (face value – issue value) = $2,400,000 + ($10,000,000 – $9,661,279) = $2,738,721.

10. **A** The true interest expense is $676,290, while the coupon being deducted to calculate CFO is only $600,000. This means CFO is overstated by the difference of $76,290.

11. **A** Interest expense reported on the income statement is based on the market rate at issuance and reflects the coupon rate plus or minus the amortization of the discount or premium.

12. **A** The actual coupon payment on a bond is reported as operating cash outflow.

13. **B** The premium will be lower because of the amortization of the premium over time. The change in interest rates has no impact.

14. **A** The $0.7 million of preferred shares are treated as equity. For the warrants, $0.8 million would be treated as debt and $0.2 million as equity.

    liabilities = $10 million + $0.8 million = $10.8 million

    equity = $15 million + $0.7 million + $0.2 million = $15.9 million

    debt to total capital ratio = liabilities / (liabilities + equity) = $10.8 million / ($10.8 million + $15.9 million) = 0.404

15. **C** The bonds should be treated as equity for analytical purposes because the stock price is significantly above the conversion price.

16. **B** Issuing convertible bonds instead of conventional bonds reduces interest expense (because convertibles carry lower yields, all else equal) and increases operating cash flow.

17. **A** One of the advantages of issuing exchangeable debt is to *delay the income tax impact of a potential gain* from selling the shares until the investors exchange the shares. The other three choices are motivations for issuing exchangeable debt.

LEASES AND OFF-BALANCE-SHEET DEBT

Study Session 9

EXAM FOCUS

The key to this topic review is differentiating between an operating lease and a capital lease. With an operating lease, there is no recognition of an asset or liability on the balance sheet. The lease payment is charged to the income statement as rent expense and reduces cash flow from operations. With a capital lease, a depreciable asset and a liability are reported on the balance sheet, much as if the asset were purchased and financed with debt. Each lease payment is composed of interest expense and amortization of the lease liability. For the Level 1 exam, be prepared for questions asking for the differences in financial statements and ratios depending on whether an operating lease or a capital lease is used. You should also be able to make lease accounting calculations. Finally, expect questions about how off-balance-sheet financing activities, such as take-or-pay contracts, throughput arrangements, and sales of receivables, affect the financial statements.

LOS 40.a: Discuss the incentives for leasing assets instead of purchasing them, and the incentives for reporting the leases as operating leases rather than capital leases.

Leases are classified as either capital leases or operating leases. A lessee must classify a lease as a **capital lease** if *any one* of the following criteria is met:

- The title to the leased asset is transferred to the lessee at the end of the lease period.
- A bargain purchase option exists. A bargain purchase option is a provision that permits the lessee to purchase the leased asset for a price that is significantly lower than the fair market value of the asset on the date that the purchase option becomes exercisable.
- The lease period is at least 75% of the asset's economic life.
- The present value of the lease payments is equal to or greater than 90% of the fair value of the leased asset. The interest rate used to discount the lease payments is the *lower* of the lessee's incremental borrowing rate or the interest rate implicit in the lease.

Professor's Note: The implicit interest rate in the lease is the discount rate that the lessor used to determine the lease payments. It is the lease's internal rate of return because it is the interest rate that equates the present value of lease payments to the fair value of the leased asset. Using the lower of the two discount rates increases the present value of the lease payments and increases the likelihood that the lease will satisfy the 90% criterion and therefore be classified as a capital lease.

A lease not meeting any of these criteria is classified as an operating lease.

To have the use of assets in production, a firm can buy the asset, rent it for a short term, or lease it for a longer term. There are two different accounting treatments for leases, one for operating leases and one for capital leases. We will address these different treatments shortly, but first let's look at some reasons for leasing rather than purchasing an asset that are not related to the differences in accounting treatment. The **lessee** is the firm that is leasing the asset for use. The **lessor** is the firm from which they are leasing the asset.

Reasons for leasing rather than purchasing an asset include:

- The period of use is short relative to the asset's useful life. For example, a construction company may lease some equipment for the duration of a 1- or 2-year construction project.
- The lessor may be better able to resell the asset. For example, a lessor of copy machines may be well equipped to refurbish and sell a used machine.
- The lessee may not want the risk of resale (the uncertainty about the value of the asset at the end of the period of use, when it will be sold). For example, with high technology equipment, whether it will still be the best technology at the end of the lease period can have a large effect on its resale value.
- If the lessor has market power, the lessor may maximize profits through leasing the asset and maintaining more control of its use. For example, the sole manufacturer of specialized machinery may want to set lease terms based on the intensity of use of the machine, which it could not control or charge for under an outright sale.
- Assets less specialized to the firm are more likely to be leased. For example, office space is often leased.
- There may be risk reduction benefits, especially to privately held firms, from leasing when firm assets have highly correlated values over time. Some of the risk of changes in asset value are effectively borne by the lessor who, in effect, retains ownership of the asset.

Capital Vs. Operating Leases

As we will discuss in more detail shortly, an operating lease is accounted for like a rental—no asset or liability is shown on the firm's balance sheet and the periodic lease payments are simply an expense in the current period. In contrast, a capital lease is treated like a purchase of the asset, with the present value of future minimum lease payments treated as a balance sheet liability and the (equal) value of the asset for the lease period shown as an asset on the balance sheet.

Professor's Note: Most of the "incentives" below favor the operating lease. There are very few (if any) incentives for the lessee to classify a lease as a capital lease.

The **incentives for structuring a lease as an operating lease** are:

- If the lessor is in a higher marginal tax bracket than the lessee, the lease should be structured as an operating lease so that the lessor can take advantage of the depreciation of the leased equipment to reduce its taxable income and, thereby, the taxes it pays.
- An operating lease avoids recognition of an asset and a liability on the lessee's balance sheet. Relative to a company that uses capital leases, the operating lease company will have higher profitability ratios (e.g., return on assets) and lower leverage ratios. The lessee may have bond covenants governing its financial policies (e.g., a maximum debt-to-equity ratio).
- Management compensation can be linked to returns on invested capital and operating leases will result in lower invested capital than capital leases.

Capital leases involve the effective transfer of all the risk and benefits of the property to the lessee. Capital leases are economically equivalent to sales (i.e., to a purchase with a transfer of title) and for accounting purposes are treated as sales. Advantages of a capital lease (to the lessee) include the following:

- In the early years of the lease, total expense is greater, potentially leading to tax savings.
- Operating cash flow is higher under a capital lease relative to an operating lease.

LOS 40.b: Contrast the effects of capital and operating leases on the financial statements and ratios of lessees and lessors.

Reporting by Lessee

Operating lease: At the inception of the lease, no entry is made. During the term of the lease, *rent expense,* the lease payment, is charged to income and to *cash flow from operations.* Footnote disclosure of the lease payments for each of the next five fiscal years is required.

Capital lease: At the inception of the lease, the *present value* of minimum lease payments is recognized as an asset and as a liability on the lessee's balance sheet. During the term of the lease, the leased asset is *depreciated* on the income statement. (The depreciation period is the lease period if there is no title transfer or bargain purchase option; if there *is* a title transfer or bargain purchase option, the leased asset is depreciated over its estimated economic life.)

- The lease payment is separated into *interest expense* (the discount rate times the lease liability at the beginning of the period) and *principal payment* on the lease liability (the lease payment less the interest expense).
- *Cash flow from operations* is reduced by the interest expense and *cash flow from financing* is reduced by the principal payment on the lease liability.

Example: Effects of a capital lease

Affordable Leasing Company leases a machine for its own use for four years with annual payments of $10,000. At the end of the lease, the lessor regains possession of the asset, which will be sold for scrap value. The lessor's implicit rate on the lease is 6%, and Affordable Leasing's incremental borrowing rate is 7%. Calculate the impact of the lease on Affordable Leasing's balance sheet and income statement for each of the four years, including the immediate impact. Affordable Leasing depreciates all assets on a straight-line (SL) basis. Assume the lease payments are made at the end of the year.

Answer:

The lease is classified as a capital lease because the asset is being leased for at least 75% of its useful life (we know this because at the end of the lease term, the asset will be sold for scrap). The discount rate that should be used to value the lease is 6%, which is the lower of the lessor's implicit rate on the lease and Affordable Leasing's incremental borrowing rate. The present value of the lease payments at 6% is $34,651.

$$N = 4; \ I/Y = 6; \ PMT = 10,000; \ FV = 0; \ CPT \rightarrow PV = \$34,651$$

This amount is immediately recorded as both an asset and a liability.

Over the next four years, depreciation will be $34,651 / 4 = \$8,663$ per year.

The asset value will decline each year by the depreciation amount and will be: $25,988; $17,326; $8,663; and $0 at the end of each of the next four years, respectively.

The interest expense and liability values are shown in the following figure. Note that the *principal repayment* equals the lease payment minus interest expense.

Affordable Leasing Example: Capitalized Lease Calculations

Year	(1) Beginning Leasehold Value	(2) Interest Expense (1) × 6%	(3) Lease Payment	(4) Ending Leasehold Value (1) + (2) − (3)	(5) Book Value of the Asset
0				$34,651	$34,651
1	$34,651	$2,079	10,000	26,730	25,988
2	26,730	1,604	10,000	18,334	17,326
3	18,334	1,100	10,000	9,434	8,663
4	9,434	566	10,000	0	0

Column 5 contains the annual book value of the asset. Notice that because the asset is being depreciated at a rate that is different from the rate of amortization for the liability, the two values are equal only at the inception and termination of the lease.

Financial Statement and Ratio Effects of Operating and Capital Leases

Balance sheet. Capital leases create an asset and a liability. Consequently, turnover ratios that use total or fixed assets in their denominator will appear lower for capital leases relative to operating leases. Return on assets will also be lower for capital leases. Most importantly, leverage ratios such as the debt-to-assets ratio and the debt-to-equity ratio will be higher with capital leases because of the recorded liability. The next lease payment is recognized as a current liability on the lessee's balance sheet. This reduces the lessee's current ratio and its working capital (current assets minus current liabilities).

Since operating leases do not affect the lessee's liabilities, they are sometimes referred to as *off-balance-sheet financing.*

Income statement. *All else held constant, operating income* will be higher for companies that use capital leases relative to companies that use operating leases. This is because the depreciation expense for a capital lease is lower than the lease payment. Interest expense is not included in the calculation of operating income.

Let's assume Affordable Leasing can treat the lease as either an operating or a capital lease. The table in Figure 1 compares the income statement (IS) effects for operating and capital leases.

Figure 1: Affordable Leasing: Leasing Decision Impact on Cash Flow

	Operating Lease	Capital Lease		
	Operating Expense = Total Expense	Operating Expense	Nonoperating Expense	
Year	Rent	Depreciation	Interest	Total Expense
1	$10,000	$8,663	$2,079	$10,742
2	10,000	8,663	1,604	10,267
3	10,000	8,663	1,100	9,763
4	10,000	8,663	566	9,229
Total	40,000			40,000

Total expense over the life of the lease will be the same for operating and capital leases because the sum of the depreciation plus the interest expense will equal the total of the lease payments. However, although the lease payments and depreciation are constant, the interest expense is higher in the first few years (this behavior of interest expense is typical of an amortizing loan). Consequently, net income in the first few years of the lease will be lower for capital leases because the sum of depreciation and interest expense exceeds the lease payment early in the lease's life.

Cash flow. Total cash flow is unaffected by the accounting treatment of a lease as either a capital or operating lease. In our example, total cash outflow is $10,000 per year. However, if the lease is an *operating lease* (rent expense = $10,000), then the *total cash payment* reduces cash flow from *operations*. If the lease is a *capital lease*, then *only* the portion of the lease payment that is considered *interest expense* reduces cash flow from operations. The part of the lease payment considered *payment on principal* reduces cash flow from *financing* activities. The data in Figure 2 illustrate that if a lease is a capital lease, there is greater cash flow from operations (CFO) and less cash flow from financing (CFF).

Figure 2: Affordable Leasing: Leasing Decision Impact on Cash Flow

| Year | Capital Lease | | Operating Lease |
	CF Operations	CF Financing	CF Operations
1	−$2,079	−$7,921	−$10,000
2	−1,604	−8,396	−10,000
3	−1,100	−8,900	−10,000
4	−566	−9,434	−10,000

For example, assume that Affordable Leasing reports CFO of $15,000. If it reports the lease as a capital lease, CFO equals $12,921 (15,000 − 2,079). If it reports the lease as an operating lease, CFO equals $5,000 (15,000 − 10,000). Hence, companies with capital leases will show higher levels of CFO relative to firms that use operating leases (all else the same).

The tables in Figure 3 and Figure 4 summarize the differences between the effects of capital leases and operating leases on the financial statements of the lessee.

Figure 3: Financial Statement Impact of Lease Accounting

Financial Statement Totals	Capital Lease	Operating Lease
Assets	Higher	Lower
Liabilities (current and long term)	Higher	Lower
Net income (in the early years)	Lower	Higher
Net income (later years)	Higher	Lower
Total net income	Same	Same
EBIT (operating income)	Higher	Lower
Cash flow from operations	Higher	Lower
Cash flow from financing	Lower	Higher
Total cash flow	Same	Same

Figure 4: Ratio Impact of Lease Accounting

Ratios	Capital Lease	Operating Lease
Current ratio (CA/CL)	Lower	Higher
Working capital (CA – CL)	Lower	Higher
Asset turnover (Sales/TA)	Lower	Higher
Return on assets* (EAT/TA)	Lower	Higher
Return on equity* (EAT/E)	Lower	Higher
Debt/assets	Higher	Lower
Debt/equity	Higher	Lower

* In the early years of the lease.

In sum, all the ratios in Figure 4 are worse when the lease is capitalized. The only improvements in financial statement items and ratios from capitalization are an improvement in EBIT (because interest is not subtracted), an increase in CFO (because principal reduction is CFF), and higher net income in the later years of a lease (because interest plus depreciation is less than the lease payment in the later years).

 Professor's Note: For the lessor, a lease can be classified as an operating lease or a capital lease. If it is a capital lease it can be classified as a sales-type lease or as a direct financing lease. The effects on the financial statements of the lessor of these various classifications are covered in the final LOS of this review.

LOS 40.c: Describe the types of off-balance-sheet financing and analyze their effects on selected financial ratios.

 Professor's Note: Operating leases are the most prevalent type of off-balance-sheet financing.

Operating leases are just one example of contractual obligations that are not recognized as liabilities on the balance sheet. All financial statements should be adjusted to reflect the economic reality of the following off-balance-sheet financing activities.

Under a **take-or-pay contract** or **throughput arrangement**, the purchasing firm commits to buy a minimum quantity of an input (usually a raw material) over a specified period of time. Prices may be fixed or related to market prices. Neither the asset nor any borrowings used to secure the commitment are recognized on the balance sheet. However, the purchaser must disclose the nature and minimum required payments in the footnotes to the financial statements.

For analysis purposes, the present value of the assets and debt commitments should be added to the balance sheet assets and debt to compute leverage ratios.

Under a **sale of receivables with recourse**, a firm may sell its accounts receivable to unrelated parties, but the firm continues to service the original receivables and transfers any collections to the new owner of those receivables. Although such transactions are recorded as a sale, thereby decreasing accounts receivable and increasing operating cash flow, the buyer usually has limited exposure (the risk of not collecting a receivable is borne by the seller). Therefore, the transaction is nothing more than a collateralized borrowing.

For analysis purposes, accounts receivable and current liabilities should be increased by the amount of receivables that were sold before computing ratios (e.g., the current ratio, receivables turnover, and leverage ratios). Also, cash flow from operations should be adjusted by classifying the sale of the receivables as cash from financing instead of cash from operations.

Although all majority-owned subsidiaries must be consolidated (their assets and liabilities added to the parent's balance sheet), **financial subsidiaries** for which the parent owns less than 50% are not consolidated. For example, if a firm owns 49% of a financial company, the investment in that company on the parent's balance sheet represents 49% of the subsidiary's assets and liabilities. But those liabilities (and an equal amount of assets) are not recognized on the parent's balance sheet.

For analysis purposes, the proportionate share of receivables and liabilities in the subsidiary should be added back to the parent's accounts when computing consolidated debt-to-equity, receivables turnover, and interest coverage ratios. You'll learn more about proportionate consolidations at Level 2.

Firms may obtain operating capacity through **investments in affiliated firms** (suppliers and end users). **Joint ventures** may provide economies of scale and disperse risks. Financing is frequently acquired through take-or-pay or throughput contracts. Direct or indirect debt guarantees may also be present in joint ventures. These guarantees will be disclosed in footnotes to the financial statements.

For analysis, the debt guarantees should be added to the debt of the company. If there are no guarantees, the proportionate share of the debt of the joint venture or affiliate should be added to the debt of the company.

Off-Balance-Sheet Financing and Financial Ratios

Because the debt on take-or-pay contracts and throughput arrangements is off-balance-sheet, it has the effect of lowering leverage ratios such as the debt ratio and the debt-to-equity ratio. That is why, for analytical purposes, the present value of the minimum purchase obligation should be added to both long-term liabilities and long-term assets before calculating leverage ratios.

The sale of receivables artificially reduces the receivables balance and short-term borrowings. Consequently, leverage ratios are too low, receivables turnover is too high, and the current ratio (assuming it is greater than 1.0) is too high. That is why, for analytical purposes, the receivables and short-term debt should be added back to the book value balances and the ratios should be calculated with these restated values.

Let's work through an example of the sale of receivables. Assume that a firm reports selling $170,000 of receivables, and footnote disclosures reveal the sale has not transferred the risk (i.e., the receivables were sold with recourse). In addition, the reported debt is $1,300,000, the reported equity is $580,000, and the interest rate associated with the receivables sale is 9%.

For purposes of analysis, we should *treat the sale as a borrowing, reinstate the receivables, and treat the proceeds of the sale as debt.* We can adjust the end-of-period balance sheet as shown in Figure 5.

Figure 5: Balance Sheet Adjustments

	As Reported	Adjusted
Debt	$1,300,000	$1,470,000
Equity	$580,000	$580,000
Debt-to-equity ratio	2.24	2.53

We also need to make an adjustment to the income statement to show the change in interest. We add interest on the receivables to both income and expense. (Assuming a 9% interest rate, interest expense would be $15,300.) Hence, net income will not be affected, but the coverage ratios will be lower than reported. EBIT increases because the discount (implicit interest) on the sale of the receivables is taken as an operating loss.

Figure 6: Income Statement Adjustments

	As Reported	Adjusted
EBIT	$265,000	$280,300
Interest expense	$102,000	$117,300
Coverage ratio	2.60	2.39

The cash flow statements also need to be adjusted by reducing the cash flow from operations and increasing the cash flow from financing by the amount of the receivables sold. CFI and total cash flows are not affected.

LOS 40.d: Distinguish between sales-type leases and direct financing leases and explain the effects of these types of leases on the financial statements of lessors.

Sales-Type and Direct-Financing Leases

If the lease is a capital lease and the lessor is a dealer or seller of the leased equipment, then the lease is a **sales-type lease** on the books of the lessor. This means that the implicit interest rate is such that the present value of the minimum lease payments is the *selling price* of the leased asset. Thus, *at the time of the lease's inception, the lessor recognizes a gross profit* equal to the present value of the minimum lease payments (MLPs) less the cost of the leased asset. Interest revenue is equal to the implicit interest rate times the net lease receivable at the beginning of the period.

If the lease is a capital lease and the lessor is not a dealer in the leased asset (e.g., a finance company), then the lease is a **direct financing lease**. *No gross profit is recognized at lease inception*, and all profit is interest revenue. The implicit rate is such that the present value of the minimum lease payments equals the *cost* of the leased asset. Interest revenue equals the implicit interest rate times the net lease receivable at the beginning of the period.

Professor's Note: The lessor always uses the implicit rate on the lease to calculate the interest revenue and determine the net investment in the lease. The lessee uses the lower of the lessor's implicit rate and the lessee's incremental borrowing rate.

Accounting for Sales-Type Leases

Accounting at sale. When the sale is made, two transactions are set up.

- First, the sale is recorded as the present value of the lease payments, with the cost of goods sold being equal to the net difference between the cost of the asset being leased and the present value of the estimated future salvage value of the asset (its terminal value). The profit shows up on the income statement. That same amount is reported as an operating cash inflow and an investment cash outflow, so net cash flow is zero.

- The second transaction sets up an asset account called the *net investment in the lease*, which is the present value of all future lease payments and the estimated salvage value.

Periodic transactions. Interest income is calculated each year by multiplying the year's beginning value of the net investment in the lease by the discount rate on the lease. The interest income affects both the income statement and cash flow from operations. The net investment in the lease at the end of each year is calculated by subtracting the difference between the lease payment and interest income from the beginning net investment balance. The reduction in net investment on the lease is an investing cash flow, not an operating cash flow.

Ending balance. After the lease is completed, the salvage value remains as an asset. If the asset is sold, this cash inflow is an investing cash flow.

Accounting for Direct Financing-Type Leases

There is no sales or manufacturing profit in a direct financing-type lease, so the only profit element is interest income. Compared to a sales-type lease, a direct financing lease will result in lower net income, lower retained earnings, and lower equity by the amount of the profit on sale that is recorded for a sales-type lease.

Example: Direct financing type leases

Assume Johnson Company purchases an asset for $69,302 to lease to Carver, Inc. for four years with an annual lease payment of $20,000 at the end of each year. At the end of the lease, Carver will own the asset for no additional payment. The implied discount rate on the lease is therefore 6% (N = 4, PV = –69,302, PMT = 20,000, FV = 0, CPT → I/Y = 6). Determine how Johnson should account for the lease payments from Carver.

Answer:

Because ownership of the asset transfers for no additional payment at the end of the lease, Johnson (the lessor) treats this as a direct financing-type capital lease. Johnson would record an asset—net investment in the lease—in the amount of $69,302. The lease payments would be recorded as follows:

Accounting for Lease Payments to Lessor

Year	(1) Beginning Investment in Lease	(2) Interest Income (1) × 6%	(3) Lease Payment	(4) Ending Investment in Lease (1) + (2) – (3)
0				$69,302
1	$69,302	$4,158	$20,000	53,460
2	53,460	3,208	20,000	36,668
3	36,668	2,200	20,000	18,868
4	18,868	1,132	20,000	0

Interest income received each year would increase income and cash flow from operations as lease payments are received. The principal reduction amount (column 3 – column 2) reduces the asset net investment in lease and is treated as an inflow to CFI.

KEY CONCEPTS

1. A lease is classified as a capital lease by a lessee if any one of the following holds:
   - If the title is transferred to the lessee at the end of lease period.
   - A bargain purchase option exists.
   - The lease period is at least 75% of the asset's life.
   - The present value of the lease payments is at least 90% of the fair value of the asset.

   Otherwise, it is classified as an operating lease.

2. Capital leases are recorded on the lessee's financial statements as assets and liabilities—the assets are depreciated, and the lease payments are split into principal repayments and interest expense. The recorded liability is amortized over the life of the lease.

3. Relative to operating leases, capital leases provide a lessee with higher assets, higher liabilities, deferred net income, and higher operating cash flow.

4. Relative to operating leases, capital leases provide a lessor with earlier recognition of profit, larger assets, and lower cash flow from operations.

5. Various off-balance-sheet financing methods include take-or-pay and throughput arrangements, sales of receivables, finance subsidiaries, and joint ventures.

6. Off-balance-sheet financing methods make debt balances look artificially low, and receivables sales and finance subsidiaries make receivables look artificially low. For analytical purposes, the debt and receivables should be restated before calculating ratios.

7. Capital leases are sales-type leases if the lessor is a manufacturer or dealer of the asset being leased and allow the lessor to record the sale at the beginning of the lease, while with direct financing leases, only interest income is recorded as lease payments are received.

CONCEPT CHECKERS

1. Compared to a capital lease, a firm with an equivalent operating lease will show higher:
   A. return on assets if a lessee and higher profitability ratios if a lessor.
   B. initial leverage ratios if a lessee and avoid recognition of debt on the balance sheet.
   C. profitability ratios if a lessee and avoid recognition of debt on the balance sheet, and higher cash flow from operations if a lessor.
   D. return on assets if a lessor, higher profitability ratios and initial leverage ratios if a lessee, and avoid recognition of debt on a lessee's balance sheet.

2. Which of the following statements about leases is *least accurate*?
   A. A lease is considered a capital lease if the lease period is at least 75% of the asset's economic life.
   B. In a capital lease, substantially all benefits and risks of ownership are transferred to the lessee.
   C. The lessee should book capital leases to the leased asset and lease obligation accounts, and then amortize the lease obligation and depreciate the leased assets.
   D. To record leased assets, the lessee determines the present value of the lease payments using the greater of the implicit rate in the lease or the lessee's incremental borrowing rate.

3. A firm leases a machine for ten years.
   • Lease payments are $3,500 per year at the end of each year.
   • The firm has an option to buy the machine for $15,000 at the end of the lease term.
   • The fair market value of the machine is $30,000.
   • The machine's economic life is 15 years.
   • There will be zero salvage value in 15 years.
   • The implicit rate in the lease is 8.25%.

   The firm should:
   A. treat the lease as an operating lease.
   B. capitalize the lease because it involves a bargain purchase.
   C. capitalize the lease because the lease term is less than 75% of the economic life of the asset.
   D. capitalize the lease because the present value of future lease payments exceeds 90% of fair market value.

4. For a lessee:

Operating leases are accounted for like:	Operating lease payments are reported as:
A. Contracts	Lease expense
B. Asset purchases	Lease expense
C. Contracts	Interest expense
D. Asset purchases	Interest expense

---

5. For a lessee, a capital lease results in:
    A. an asset.
    B. a short-term liability.
    C. a long-term liability.
    D. all of the above.

6. For a company that has sold receivables but retained the credit risk, which of the following *least likely* has to be adjusted?
    A. Accounts receivable.
    B. Inventory turnover.
    C. Current ratio.
    D. Debt-to-equity.

7. Which of the following is *least likely* an off-balance-sheet financing method?
    A. Sale of receivables.
    B. Finance subsidiaries.
    C. Throughput arrangements.
    D. Convertible bonds.

8. Which of the following statements about capital and operating leases is *least accurate* for a lessee?
    A. Total cash flows are not affected by the accounting treatment of the lease.
    B. When a capital lease is initiated, the present value of the leased asset is treated as a financing cash flow.
    C. As compared to an operating lease, a capital lease will report higher operating cash flows and lower financing cash flows.
    D. Over the life of a capital lease the total expenses will equal those of a similar operating lease; but the operating lease will have lower expenses in the earlier years, while the capital lease will have lower expenses in the later years.

9. A capital lease results in the following net income to a lessee compared to a comparable operating lease:

	Early years	Later years
A.	Lower	Lower
B.	Lower	Higher
C.	Higher	Lower
D.	Higher	Higher

10. For a lessee, capital lease interest expense is equal to the:
    A. interest rate multiplied by the beginning leasehold liability.
    B. interest rate multiplied by the lease payment.
    C. lease payment.
    D. depreciation expense.

11. Compared to an operating lease, the lessee's debt-to-equity ratio for a capital lease is:
    A. higher.
    B. lower.
    C. not affected.
    D. higher in the early years and lower in the later years.

12. For a lessee, an operating lease compared to a capital lease will *least likely* result in a:
    A. lower debt-to-equity ratio.
    B. higher financing cash flow.
    C. lower cash flow from operations.
    D. lower net income in the earlier years of the lease.

13. Which of the following statements concerning a lessee is *least accurate*?
    A. All else equal, when a lease is capitalized, income will rise over time.
    B. Lease capitalization increases a firm's operating cash flows and decreases the firm's financing cash flows relative to cash flows for an operating lease.
    C. In the first years of a capital lease, the firm's debt-to-equity ratio will be greater than if the firm had used an operating lease.
    D. In the first years of a capital lease, the firm's current ratio will be greater than it would have been had the firm used an operating lease.

Use the following data to answer Questions 14 through 18.

- A firm has just signed a 5-year lease on a new machine.
- Lease payments are $20,000 per year, payable at the end of the year.
- The machine has no salvage value at the end of the lease term.
- The machine has a 5-year useful life.
- The firm's incremental borrowing cost is 11%.
- The lessor's implicit rate on the lease is 10%.
- The lease is classified as a capital lease.

14. What will be the leasehold asset at the inception of the lease?
    A. $0.
    B. $20,000.
    C. $73,918.
    D. $75,816.

15. What will the firm report as interest expense in the first year?
    A. $7,582.
    B. $8,131.
    C. $12,418.
    D. $20,000.

16. What will be straight-line (SL) depreciation expense in the first year?
    A. $10,000.
    B. $12,418.
    C. $15,163.
    D. $20,000.

17. How much of the first-year lease payment will be deducted from cash flow from operations?
    A. $0.
    B. $7,582.
    C. $12,418.
    D. $20,000.

18. How much of the first-year lease payment will be deducted from cash flow from financing?
    A. $0.
    B. $7,582.
    C. $12,418.
    D. $20,000.

COMPREHENSIVE PROBLEMS

1. Consider the effects on the following financial statement items and ratios of capitalizing a lease rather than treating it as an operating lease. Indicate the effect of capitalizing the lease on the following during the first year of the lease (circle one).

	higher	lower	no change
CFF	higher	lower	no change
CFO	higher	lower	no change
CFI	higher	lower	no change
Total cash flow	higher	lower	no change
EBIT	higher	lower	no change
Net income	higher	lower	no change
D/A	higher	lower	no change
D/E	higher	lower	no change
ROA	higher	lower	no change
ROE	higher	lower	no change
Total asset turnover	higher	lower	no change

2. Babson Corp. sold $550,000 of receivables during the most recent period. Meg Jones, CFA, is adjusting balance sheet items and some ratios for this sale of receivables because significant credit risk on these remains with Babson. Indicate increase, decrease, or unchanged to reflect the effect of adjustment on the indicated items and ratios.

Debt   Cash   Current ratio (= 1)

Debt-to-equity   Receivables   Working capital

Receivables turnover   Cash conversion cycle   Interest coverage

CFO   CFF   CFI

3.   Ed's Supply Corp. is examining the effects on the financial statements of classifying the lease of equipment to Excavations Inc. If Ed's (the lessor) classifies this 4-year lease as a sales-type capital lease rather than as an operating lease, the effects on the following in the first year and the third year of the lease are (indicate +, –, or = for no change):

	1st year of lease	3rd year of lease
Revenues		
Interest income		
Net income		
Retained earnings		
CFO		
CFI		
Assets		

ANSWERS – CONCEPT CHECKERS

1. **C** Structuring a lease as an operating lease results in higher profitability ratios for the lessee and avoidance of recognition of debt on the lessee's balance sheet, and higher cash flow from operations for the lessor. The other statements each have an incorrect component. As compared to a capital lease, an operating lease results in lower profitability ratios for a lessor, lower initial leverage ratios for the lessee, and a lower return on assets for the lessor.

2. **D** Lease payments are valued using the *lower* of the implicit lease rate or lessee's incremental borrowing rate.

3. **A** The purchase option is not a bargain because it is one-half the original price when only one-third of the asset life remains; title is not transferred at the end of the lease term; lease period is only 2/3 of the asset's life; 90% of fair value is $27,000, while the present value of lease payments at the implicit rate is $23,222. Because none of the capital lease criteria hold, the lease is treated as an operating lease.

4. **A** Operating leases are accounted for like contracts (capital leases are like purchases), and operating lease payments are reported as lease expense.

5. **D** For a lessee recording a capital lease, both a long-term asset and long-term liability will be recognized, as well as a short-term liability being recognized for next year's lease payment.

6. **B** The inventory turnover ratio does not need to be adjusted.

7. **D** Convertible bonds are not an off-balance-sheet financing method.

8. **B** The accounting treatment of a lease affects the classification of cash flows but not the total cash flows. Also, a capital lease will report higher operating cash flows and lower financing cash flows than an operating lease. For a lessee there is typically no cash flow at initiation. The principal portion of each lease payment is treated as a cash flow from financing.

9. **B** In the early years, a capital lease results in lower net income because interest plus depreciation expense is greater than rent expense under an operating lease. This effect reverses in the later years of the lease.

10. **A** Interest expense is calculated each year by multiplying the year's beginning value of the leasehold liability by the discount rate on the lease. This *interest expense* is charged to income and operating cash flow.

11. **A** A capital lease will cause the debt-to-equity ratio to increase due to the ratio's denominator effect when adding assets and liabilities to the balance sheet. No debt is booked related to the operating lease.

12. **D** A capital lease results in lower net income in the early years of the lease due to the capital lease recognizing interest expense and depreciation expense. A capital lease will also have a *higher* operating cash flow due to payments being split between operating and financing cash flows.

13. **D** A firm's current ratio will be less when using a capital lease due to the next year's lease payment being classified as a current liability.

©2008 Schweser

14. **D** The appropriate discount rate is the 10% rate implicit in the lease (it's less than the lessee's incremental borrowing rate of 11%). The present value of the lease payments at a 10% discount rate is $75,816. Using a financial calculator:

I/Y = 10; PMT = 20,000; N = 5; CPT → PV = $75,816

15. **A** Interest expense is the leasehold value multiplied by 10%, which is $7,582.

16. **C** Depreciation is the leasehold value divided by 5, or 75,816 / 5 = $15,163.

17. **B** Only the interest expense is deducted from CFO.

18. **C** The financing cash flow is the principal component of the lease, which is the lease payment of $20,000 less the interest component of $7,582.

ANSWERS – COMPREHENSIVE PROBLEMS

1. With a capital lease:
    - CFF is lower.
    - CFO is higher.
    - CFI is unchanged.
    - Total cash flow is unchanged.
    - EBIT is higher.
    - Net income is lower in the early years.
    - D/A is higher.
    - D/E is higher.
    - ROA is lower.
    - ROE is lower.
    - Asset turnover is lower.

2. To adjust these items, we treat the sale of receivables as if it were a short-term borrowing and add back the amount of receivables sold. This will increase debt and the D/E ratio. Receivables increase and current liabilities increase by the same amounts so that working capital, the current ratio (because it's equal to 1), and cash position are unchanged by the adjustment. The receivables turnover is decreased by adding back AR so the cash conversion cycle is longer. The cash generated by the sale is CFF after adjustment rather than CFO, so CFF increases and CFO decreases. The increase in interest from adjusting debt upward will decrease the interest coverage ratio, assuming EBIT > interest expense. CFI is unaffected.

3.

	1st year of lease	3rd year of lease
Revenues	+	–
Interest income	+	+
Net income	+	–
Retained earnings	+	+
CFO	+	–
CFI	–	+
Assets	+	+

In the first year of the lease, capitalization of a sales-type lease increases revenues because it is reported as a sale. The profit on the sale increases net income and retained earnings. The recognition of the sale also increases CFO in the first year and decreases CFI by the investment in the lease. Assets are higher for the capitalized lease until the end of the lease term because of the recognition of the profit on the sale at lease inception. Interest income is recognized for the capital lease but not for the operating lease (payments are all rental income), so interest income is always higher for the capital lease.

Revenues are lower for the sales-type lease after the first year because only interest income is recognized and this is lower than the lease payment. Net income is lower in later years for the lessor with a sales-type lease. The income on the sales-type lease is CFI and CFO. For the operating lease, the entire rental payment is CFO. The interest portion of the sales-type lease is CFO, so it goes down each year and the difference between sales-type lease CFO and operating lease CFO is greater each year.

Retained earnings are higher for a sales-type lease in the initial year because of the profit recognition, and will remain higher until the end of the lease term, when total net income over the lease is equal for both treatments.

The following is a review of the Financial Statement Analysis principles designed to address the learning outcome statements set forth by CFA Institute®. This topic is also covered in:

FINANCIAL ANALYSIS TECHNIQUES

EXAM FOCUS

This topic review presents a "tool box" for an analyst. It would be nice if you could calculate all these ratios, but it is imperative that you understand what firm characteristic each one is measuring, and even more important, that you know whether a higher or lower ratio is better in each instance. Different analysts calculate some ratios differently. It would be helpful if analysts were always careful to distinguish between total liabilities, total interest-bearing debt, long-term debt, and creditor and trade debt, but they do not. Some analysts routinely add deferred tax liabilities to debt or exclude goodwill when calculating assets and equity; others do not. Statistical reporting services almost always disclose how each of the ratios they present was calculated. So do not get too tied up in the details of each ratio, but understand well what each one represents and what factors would likely lead to significant changes in a particular ratio. The DuPont formulas have been with us a long time and were on the test when I took it back in the 1980s. The extended form here is different that the one presented in the Study Session on Corporate Finance, making it less likely that you need to memorize it. Either way, decomposing ROE into its components is an important analytic technique and it should definitely be in your tool box.

LOS 41.a: Evaluate and compare companies using ratio analysis, common-size financial statements, and charts in financial analysis.

Common-size statements normalize balance sheets and income statements and allow the analyst to more easily compare performance across firms and for a single firm over time.

- A vertical common-size balance sheet expresses all balance sheet accounts as a percentage of total assets.
- A vertical common-size income statement expresses all income statement items as a percentage of sales.

In addition to the comparison of financial data across firms and time, common-size analysis is appropriate for quickly viewing certain financial ratios. For example, the gross profit margin, operating profit margin, and net profit margin are all clearly indicated within a common-size income statement.

- Vertical common-size income statement ratios are especially useful in studying trends in costs and profit margins.

$$\text{vertical common-size income statement ratios} = \frac{\text{income statement account}}{\text{sales}}$$

- Balance sheet accounts can also be converted to common-size ratios by dividing each balance sheet item by total assets.

$$\text{vertical common-size balance-sheet ratios} = \frac{\text{balance sheet account}}{\text{total assets}}$$

Example: Constructing common-size statements

The common-size statements in Figure 1 show balance sheet items as percentages of assets, and income statement items as percentages of sales.

- You can convert all asset and liability amounts to their actual values by multiplying the percentages listed below by their total assets of $57,100; $55,798; and $52,071, respectively for 2006, 2005, and 2004 (data is USD millions).
- Also, all income statement items can be converted to their actual values by multiplying the given percentages by total sales, which were $29,723; $29,234; and $22,922, respectively, for 2006, 2005, and 2004.

Figure 1: Vertical Common-Size Balance Sheet and Income Statement

Balance Sheet Fiscal year end	2006	2005	2004
Assets			
Cash & cash equivalents	0.38%	0.29%	0.37%
Accounts receivable	5.46%	5.61%	6.20%
Inventories	5.92%	5.42%	5.84%
Deferred income taxes	0.89%	0.84%	0.97%
Other current assets	0.41%	0.40%	0.36%
Total current assets	13.06%	12.56%	13.74%
Gross fixed assets	25.31%	23.79%	25.05%
Accumulated depreciation	8.57%	7.46%	6.98%
Net gross fixed assets	16.74%	16.32%	18.06%
Other long term assets	70.20%	71.12%	68.20%
Total assets	100.00%	100.00%	100.00%
Liabilities			
Accounts payable	3.40%	3.40%	3.79%
Short term debt	1.00%	2.19%	1.65%
Other current liabilities	8.16%	10.32%	9.14%
Total current liabilities	12.56%	15.91%	14.58%
Long term debt	18.24%	14.58%	5.18%
Other long term liabilities	23.96%	27.44%	53.27%
Total liabilities	54.76%	57.92%	73.02%
Preferred equity	0.00%	0.00%	0.00%
Common equity	45.24%	42.08%	26.98%
Total liabilities & equity	100.00%	100.00%	100.00%

Income Statement Fiscal year end	2006	2005	2004
Revenues	100.00%	100.00%	100.00%
Cost of goods sold	59.62%	60.09%	60.90%
Gross profit	40.38%	39.91%	39.10%
Selling, general & administrative	16.82%	17.34%	17.84%
Depreciation	2.39%	2.33%	2.18%
Amortization	0.02%	3.29%	2.33%
Other operating expenses	0.58%	0.25%	-0.75%
Operating income	20.57%	16.71%	17.50%
Interest and other debt expense	2.85%	4.92%	2.60%
Income before taxes	17.72%	11.79%	14.90%
Provision for income taxes	6.30%	5.35%	6.17%
Net income	11.42%	6.44%	8.73%

Even a cursory inspection of the income statement in Figure 1 can be quite instructive. Beginning at the bottom, we can see that the profitability of the company has increased nicely in 2006 after falling slightly in 2005. We can examine the 2006 income statement values to find the source of this greatly improved profitability. Cost of goods sold seems to be stable, with an improvement (decrease) in 2006 of only 0.48%. SG&A was down approximately one-half percent as well.

These improvements from (relative) cost reduction, however, only begin to explain the 5% increase in the net profit margin for 2006. Improvements in two items, "amortization" and "interest and other debt expense," appear to be the most significant factors in the firm's improved profitability in 2006. Clearly the analyst must investigate further in both areas to learn whether these improvements represent permanent improvements or whether these items can be expected to return to previous percentage-of-sales levels in the future.

We can also note that interest expense as a percentage of sales was approximately the same in 2004 and 2006. We must investigate the reasons for the higher interest costs in 2005 to determine whether the current level of 2.85% can be expected to continue into the next period. In addition, over 3% of the 5% increase in net profit margin in 2006 is due to a decrease in amortization expense. Since this is a noncash expense, the decrease may have no implications for cash flows looking forward.

This discussion should make clear that common-size analysis doesn't tell an analyst the whole story about this company, but can certainly point the analyst in the right direction to find out the circumstances that led to the increase in the net profit margin and to determine the effects, if any, on firm cash flow going forward.

Another way to present financial statement data that is quite useful when analyzing trends over time is a horizontal common-size balance sheet or income statement. The divisor here is the first-year values, so they are all standardized to 1.0 by construction. Figure 2 illustrates this approach.

Figure 2: Horizontal Common-Size Balance Sheet Data

	2004	2005	2006
Inventory	1.0	1.1	1.4
Cash and marketable sec.	1.0	1.3	1.2
Long-term debt	1.0	1.6	1.8
PP&E (net of depreciation)	1.0	0.9	0.8

Trends in the values of these items as well as the relative growth in these items are readily apparent from a horizontal common-size balance sheet.

Professor's Note: We have presented data in Figure 1 with information for the most recent period on the left and in Figure 2 we have presented the historical values from left to right. Both presentation methods are common and on the exam you should pay special attention to which method is used in the data presented for any question.

We can view the values in the common-size financial statements as ratios. Net income is shown on the common-size balance sheet as net income/revenues, which is the net profit margin, and tells the analyst the percentage of each dollar of sales that remains for shareholders after all expenses related to the generation of those sales are deducted.

One measure of financial leverage, long-term debt to total assets, can be read directly from the vertical common-size financial statements. Specific ratios commonly used in financial analysis and interpretation of their values are covered in detail in this review.

A stacked column graph (also called a stacked bar graph) shows the changes in items from year to year in graphical form. Figure 3 presents such data for a hypothetical corporation.

Figure 3: Stacked Column (Stacked Bar) Graph

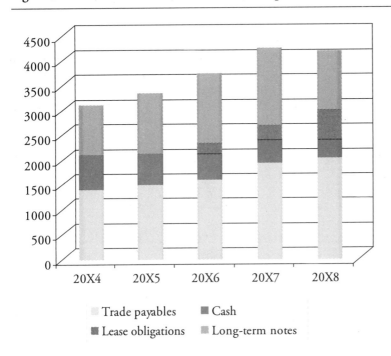

Another alternative for graphic presentation of data is a line graph. Figure 4 presents the same data as Figure 3, but as a line graph. The increase in trade payables and the decrease in cash are evident in either format and would alert the analyst to potential liquidity problems that require further investigation and analysis.

Figure 4: Line Graph

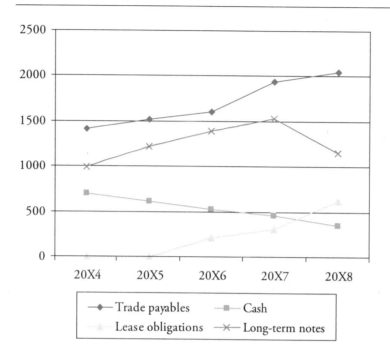

LOS 41.b: Describe the limitations of ratio analysis.

You must be aware of the **limitations of financial ratios.** Ratios are used for internal comparisons and comparisons across firms. They are often most useful in identifying questions that need to be answered rather than for answering questions directly. Their limitations are:

- Financial ratios are not useful when viewed in isolation. They are only valid when compared to those of other firms or to the company's historical performance.
- Comparisons with other companies are made more difficult because of different accounting treatments. This is particularly important when analyzing non-U.S. firms.
- It is difficult to find comparable industry ratios when analyzing companies that operate in multiple industries.
- Conclusions cannot be made from viewing one set of ratios. All ratios must be viewed relative to one another.
- Determining the target or comparison value for a ratio is difficult, requiring some range of acceptable values.

In conducting your analysis, you must always be aware of the limitations of ratios. Ask yourself these questions:

- Do the firms being compared have similar accounting practices?
- When comparing divisions within a firm, are the ratios comparable?
- Do the ratios being used give consistent readings?
- Do the ratios yield a reasonable figure for the industry?

LOS 41.c: Explain and demonstrate the classification of financial ratios.

LOS 41.d: Calculate and interpret activity, liquidity, solvency, profitability, and valuation ratios.

Financial ratios can be segregated into different classifications by the type of information about the company they provide. One such classification scheme is:

Activity ratios. This category includes several ratios also referred to asset utilization or turnover ratios (e.g., inventory turnover, receivables turnover, and total assets turnover). They often give indications of how well a firm utilizes various assets such as inventory and fixed assets.

Liquidity ratios. Liquidity here refers to the ability to pay cash expenses in the short term as they come due.

Solvency ratios. Solvency ratios give the analyst information on the firm's financial leverage and ability to meet its longer-term obligations.

Profitability ratios. Profitability ratios provide information on how well the company generates operating profits and net profits from its sales.

Valuation ratios. Sales per share, earnings per share, and price to cash flow per share are examples of ratios used in comparing the relative valuation of companies.

 Professor's Note: We examine valuation ratios in another LOS concerning equity analysis later in this review.

It should be noted that these categories are not mutually exclusive. An activity ratio such as payables turnover may also provide information about the liquidity of a company, for example. There is no one standard set of ratios for financial analysis. Different analysts use different ratios and different calculation methods for similar ratios. Some ratios are so commonly used that there is very little variation in how they are defined and calculated. We will note some alternative treatments and alternative terms for single ratios as we detail the commonly used ratios in each category.

ACTIVITY RATIOS

- A measure of accounts receivable turnover is *receivables turnover:*

$$\text{receivables turnover} = \frac{\text{annual sales}}{\text{average receivables}}$$

 Professor's Note: In most cases when a ratio compares a balance sheet account (such as receivables) with an income or cash flow item (such as sales), the balance sheet item will be the average of the account instead of simply the end-of-year balance. Averages are calculated by adding the beginning-of-year account value to the end-of-year account value, then dividing the sum by two.

It is considered desirable to have a receivables turnover figure close to the industry norm.

- The inverse of the receivables turnover times 365 is the *average collection period*, or *days of sales outstanding*, which is the average number of days it takes for the company's customers to pay their bills:

$$\text{days of sales oustanding} = \frac{365}{\text{receivables turnover}}$$

It is considered desirable to have a collection period (and receivables turnover) close to the industry norm. The firm's credit terms are another important benchmark used to interpret this ratio. A collection period that is too high might mean that customers are too slow in paying their bills, which means too much capital is tied up in assets. A collection period that is too low might indicate that the firm's credit policy is too rigorous, which might be hampering sales.

- A measure of a firm's efficiency with respect to its processing and inventory management is *inventory turnover:*

$$\text{inventory turnover} = \frac{\text{cost of goods sold}}{\text{average inventory}}$$

 Professor's Note: Pay careful attention to the numerator in the turnover ratios. For inventory turnover, be sure to use cost of goods sold, not sales.

- The inverse of the inventory turnover times 365 is *the average inventory processing period*, or *days of inventory on hand*:

$$\text{days of inventory on hand} = \frac{365}{\text{inventory turnover}}$$

As is the case with accounts receivable, it is considered desirable to have days of inventory on hand (and inventory turnover) close to the industry norm. A processing period that is too high might mean that too much capital is tied up in inventory and could mean that the inventory is obsolete. A processing period that is too low might indicate that the firm has inadequate stock on hand, which could hurt sales.

- A measure of the use of trade credit by the firm is the *payables turnover* ratio:

$$\text{payables turnover} = \frac{\text{purchases}}{\text{average trade payables}}$$

- The inverse of the payables turnover ratio multiplied by 365 is the *payables payment period* or *number of days of payables*, which is the average amount of time it takes the company to pay its bills:

$$\text{number of days of payables} = \frac{365}{\text{payables turnover ratio}}$$

 Professor's Note: We have shown days calculations for payables, receivables, and inventory based on annual turnover and a 365-day year. If turnover ratios are for a quarter rather than a year, the number of days in the quarter should be divided by the quarterly turnover ratios in order to get the "days" form of these ratios.

- The effectiveness of the firm's use of its total assets to create revenue is measured by its *total asset turnover:*

$$\text{total asset turnover} = \frac{\text{revenue}}{\text{average total assets}}$$

Different types of industries might have considerably different turnover ratios. Manufacturing businesses that are capital-intensive might have asset turnover ratios near one, while retail businesses might have turnover ratios near 10. As was the case with the current asset turnover ratios discussed previously, it is desirable for the total asset turnover ratio to be close to the industry norm. Low asset turnover ratios might mean that the company has too much capital tied up in its asset base. A turnover ratio that is too high might imply that the firm has too few assets for potential sales, or that the asset base is outdated.

- The utilization of fixed assets is measured by the *fixed asset turnover* ratio:

$$\text{fixed asset turnover} = \frac{\text{revenue}}{\text{average net fixed assets}}$$

As was the case with the total asset turnover ratio, it is desirable to have a fixed asset turnover ratio close to the industry norm. Low fixed asset turnover might mean that the company has too much capital tied up in its asset base or is using the assets it has inefficiently. A turnover ratio that is too high might imply that the firm has obsolete equipment, or at a minimum, that the firm will probably have to incur capital expenditures in the near future to increase capacity to support growing revenues. Since "net" here refers to net of accumulated depreciation, firms with more recently acquired assets will typically have lower fixed asset turnover ratios.

- How effectively a company is using its working capital is measured by the *working capital turnover* ratio:

$$\text{working capital turnover} = \frac{\text{revenue}}{\text{average working capital}}$$

Working capital (sometimes called *net* working capital) is current assets minus current liabilities. The working capital turnover ratio gives us information about the utilization of working capital in terms of dollars of sales per dollar of working capital. Some firms may have very low working capital if outstanding payables equal or exceed inventory and receivables. In this case the working capital turnover ratio will be very large, may vary significantly from period to period, and is less informative about changes in the firm's operating efficiency.

LIQUIDITY RATIOS

Liquidity ratios are employed by analysts to determine the firm's ability to pay its short-term liabilities.

- The *current ratio* is the best-known measure of liquidity:

$$\text{current ratio} = \frac{\text{current assets}}{\text{current liabilities}}$$

The higher the current ratio, the more likely it is that the company will be able to pay its short-term bills. A current ratio of less than one means that the company has negative working capital and is probably facing a liquidity crisis. Working capital equals current assets minus current liabilities.

- The *quick ratio* is a more stringent measure of liquidity because it does not include inventories and other assets that might not be very liquid:

$$\text{quick ratio} = \frac{\text{cash + marketable securities + receivables}}{\text{current liabilities}}$$

The higher the quick ratio, the more likely it is that the company will be able to pay its short-term bills. Marketable securities are short-term debt instruments, typically liquid and of good credit quality.

- The most conservative liquidity measure is the *cash ratio*:

$$\text{cash ratio} = \frac{\text{cash + marketable securities}}{\text{current liabilities}}$$

The higher the cash ratio, the more likely it is that the company will be able to pay its short-term bills.

The current, quick, and cash ratios differ only in the assumed liquidity of the current assets that the analyst projects will be used to pay off current liabilities.

- The *defensive interval ratio* is another measure of liquidity that indicates the number of days of average cash expenditures the firm could pay with its current liquid assets:

$$\text{defensive interval} = \frac{\text{cash} + \text{marketable securities} + \text{receivables}}{\text{average daily expenditures}}$$

Expenditures here include cash expenses for costs of goods, SG&A, and research and development. If these items are taken from the income statement, noncash charges such as depreciation should be added back just as in the preparation of a statement of cash flows by the indirect method.

- The *cash conversion cycle* is the length of time it takes to turn the firm's cash investment in inventory back into cash, in the form of collections from the sales of that inventory. The cash conversion cycle is computed from days sales outstanding, days of inventory on hand, and number of days of payables:

$$\text{cash conversion cycle} = \left(\begin{array}{c} \text{days sales} \\ \text{outstanding} \end{array} \right) + \left(\begin{array}{c} \text{days of inventory} \\ \text{on hand} \end{array} \right) - \left(\begin{array}{c} \text{number of days} \\ \text{of payables} \end{array} \right)$$

High cash conversion cycles are considered undesirable. A conversion cycle that is too high implies that the company has an excessive amount of capital investment in the sales process.

SOLVENCY RATIOS

- A measure of the firm's use of fixed-cost financing sources is the *debt-to-equity* ratio:

$$\text{debt-to-equity} = \frac{\text{total debt}}{\text{total shareholders' equity}}$$

Increases and decreases in this ratio suggest a greater or lesser reliance on debt as a source of financing.

Total debt is calculated differently by different analysts and different providers of financial information. Here, we will define it as long-term debt plus interest-bearing short-term debt.

Some analysts include the present value of lease obligations and/or non-interest-bearing current liabilities, such as trade payables.

- Another way of looking at the usage of debt is the *debt-to-capital* ratio:

$$\text{debt-to-capital} = \frac{\text{total debt}}{\text{total debt} + \text{total shareholders' equity}}$$

Capital equals all long-term debt plus preferred stock and equity. Increases and decreases in this ratio suggest a greater or lesser reliance on debt as a source of financing.

- A slightly different way of analyzing debt utilization is the *debt-to-assets* ratio:

$$\text{debt-to-assets} = \frac{\text{total debt}}{\text{total assets}}$$

Increases and decreases in this ratio suggest a greater or lesser reliance on debt as a source of financing.

- Another measure that is used as an indicator of a company's use of debt financing is the *financial leverage* ratio (or leverage ratio):

$$\text{financial leverage} = \frac{\text{average total assets}}{\text{average total equity}}$$

Average here means the average of the values at the beginning and at the end of the period. Greater use of debt financing increases financial leverage and, typically, risk to equity holders and bondholders alike.

- The remaining risk ratios help determine the firm's ability to repay its debt obligations. The first of these is the *interest coverage ratio*:

$$\text{interest coverage} = \frac{\text{earnings before interest and taxes}}{\text{interest payments}}$$

The lower this ratio, the more likely it is that the firm will have difficulty meeting its debt payments.

- A second ratio that is an indicator of a company's ability to meet its obligations is the *fixed charge coverage* ratio:

$$\text{fixed charge coverage} = \frac{\text{earnings before interest and taxes} + \text{lease payments}}{\text{interest payments} + \text{lease payments}}$$

Here, lease payments are added back to operating earnings in the numerator and also added to interest payments in the denominator. Significant lease obligations will reduce this ratio significantly compared to the interest coverage ratio. Fixed charge coverage is the more meaningful measure for companies that lease a large portion of their assets, such as some airlines.

©2008 Schweser

PROFITABILITY RATIOS

- The *net profit margin* is the ratio of net income to revenue:

$$\text{net profit margin} = \frac{\text{net income}}{\text{revenue}}$$

Analysts should be concerned if this ratio is too low. The net profit margin should be based on net income from continuing operations, because analysts should be primarily concerned about future expectations, and "below the line" items such as discontinued operations will not affect the company in the future.

Operating profitability ratios look at how good management is at turning their efforts into profits. Operating ratios compare the top of the income statement (sales) to profits. The different ratios are designed to isolate specific costs.

Know these terms:

gross profits	= net sales − COGS
operating profits	= earnings before interest and taxes = EBIT
net income	= earnings after taxes but before dividends
total capital	= long-term debt + short-term debt + common and preferred equity
Total capital	= total assets

How they relate in the income statement:

	Net sales
−	Cost of goods sold
	Gross profit
−	Operating expenses
	Operating profit (EBIT)
−	Interest
	Earnings before taxes (EBT)
−	Taxes
	Earnings after taxes (EAT)
+/−	Below the line items adjusted for tax
	Net income
−	Preferred dividends
	Income available to common

The *gross profit margin* is the ratio of gross profit (sales less cost of goods sold) to sales:

$$\text{gross profit margin} = \frac{\text{gross profit}}{\text{revenue}}$$

An analyst should be concerned if this ratio is too low.

- The *operating profit margin* is the ratio of operating profit (gross profit less selling, general, and administrative expenses) to sales. Operating profit is also referred to as earnings before interest and taxes (EBIT):

$$\text{operating profit margin} = \frac{\text{operating income}}{\text{revenue}} \text{ or } \frac{\text{EBIT}}{\text{revenue}}$$

Strictly speaking, EBIT includes some nonoperating items, such as gains on investment. The analyst, as with other ratios with various formulations, must be consistent in his calculation method and know how published ratios are calculated. Analysts should be concerned if this ratio is too low. Some analysts prefer to calculate the operating profit margin by adding back depreciation and any amortization expense to arrive at earnings before interest, taxes, depreciation, and amortization (EBITDA).

Sometimes profitability is measured using earnings before tax (EBT), which can be calculated by subtracting interest from EBIT or from operating earnings. The *pretax margin* is calculated as:

$$\text{pretax margin} = \frac{\text{EBT}}{\text{revenue}}$$

Another set of profitability ratios measure profitability relative to funds invested in the company by common stockholders, preferred stockholders, and suppliers of debt financing.

The first of these measures is the *return on assets* (ROA). Typically, ROA is calculated using net income:

$$\text{return on assets (ROA)} = \frac{\text{net income}}{\text{average total assets}}$$

This measure is a bit misleading, however, because interest is excluded from net income but total assets include debt as well as equity. Adding interest adjusted for tax back to net income puts the returns to both equity and debt holders in the numerator. This results in an alternative calculation for ROA:

$$\text{return on assets (ROA)} = \frac{\text{net income} + \text{interest expense} (1 - \text{tax rate})}{\text{average total assets}}$$

A measure of return on assets that includes both taxes and interest in the numerator is the *operating return on assets*:

$$\text{operating return on assets} = \frac{\text{operating income}}{\text{average total assets}} \text{ or } \frac{\text{EBIT}}{\text{average total assets}}$$

- The *return on total capital* (ROTC) is the ratio of net income before interest expense to total capital:

$$\text{return on total capital} = \frac{\text{EBIT}}{\text{average total capital}}$$

Total capital includes short- and long-term debt, preferred equity, and common equity. Analysts should be concerned if this ratio is too low. Total capital is the same as total assets. The interest expense that should be added back is gross interest expense, not net interest expense (which is gross interest expense less interest income).

An alternative method for computing ROTC is to include the present value of operating leases on the balance sheet as a fixed asset and as a long-term liability. This adjustment is especially important for firms that are dependent on operating leases as a major form of financing. Calculations related to leasing were discussed in Study Session 9.

- The *return on equity* (ROE) is the ratio of net income to average total equity (including preferred stock):

$$\text{return on equity} = \frac{\text{net income}}{\text{average total equity}}$$

Analysts should be concerned if this ratio is too low. It is sometimes called return on total equity.

- A similar ratio to the return on equity is the *return on common equity:*

$$\text{return on common equity} = \frac{\text{net income} - \text{preferred dividends}}{\text{average common equity}}$$

$$= \frac{\text{net income available to common}}{\text{average common equity}}$$

This ratio differs from the return on total equity in that it only measures the accounting profits available to, and the capital invested by, common stockholders, instead of common and preferred stockholders. That is why preferred dividends are deducted from net income in the numerator. Analysts should be concerned if this ratio is too low.

The return on common equity is often more thoroughly analyzed using the DuPont decomposition, which is described later in this topic review.

LOS 41.e: Demonstrate how ratios are related and how to evaluate a company using a combination of different ratios

Example: Using ratios to evaluate a company

A balance sheet and income statement for a hypothetical company are shown below for this year and the previous year.

Using the company information provided, calculate the current year ratios. Discuss how these ratios compare with the company's performance last year and with the industry's performance.

Sample Balance Sheet

Year	Current year	Previous year
Assets		
Cash and marketable securities	$105	$95
Receivables	205	195
Inventories	310	290
Total current assets	620	580
Gross property, plant, and equipment	1,800	$1,700
Accumulated depreciation	360	340
Net property, plant, and equipment	1,440	1,360
Total assets	$2,060	$1,940
Liabilities		
Payables	$110	$90
Short-term debt	160	140
Current portion of long-term debt	55	45
Current liabilities	325	$275
Long-term debt	610	$690
Deferred taxes	105	95
Common stock	300	300
Additional paid in capital	400	400
Retained earnings	320	180
Common shareholders equity	1,020	880
Total liabilities and equity	$2,060	$1,940

©2008 Schweser

Sample Income Statement

Year	Current year
Sales	$4,000
Cost of goods sold	3,000
Gross profit	1,000
Operating expenses	650
Operating profit	350
Interest expense	50
Earnings before taxes	300
Taxes	100
Net income	200
Common dividends	60

Financial Ratio Template

	Current Year	Last Year	Industry
Current ratio		2.1	1.5
Quick ratio		1.1	0.9
Days of sales outstanding		18.9	18.0
Inventory turnover		10.7	12.0
Total asset turnover		2.3	2.4
Working capital turnover		14.5	11.8
Gross profit margin		27.4%	29.3%
Net profit margin		5.8%	6.5%
Return on total capital		21.1%	22.4%
Return on common equity		24.1%	19.8%
Debt-to-equity		99.4%	35.7%
Interest coverage		5.9	9.2

Answer:

- current ratio = $\dfrac{\text{current assets}}{\text{current liabilities}}$

  current ratio = $\dfrac{620}{325} = 1.9$

The current ratio indicates lower liquidity levels when compared to last year and more liquidity than the industry average.

- quick ratio = $\dfrac{\text{cash + receivables + marketable securities}}{\text{current liabilities}}$

  quick ratio = $\dfrac{(105 + 205)}{325} = 0.95$

The quick ratio is lower than last year and is in line with the industry average.

- DSO (days of sales outstanding) = $\dfrac{365}{\text{revenue}/\text{average receivables}}$

  DSO = $\dfrac{365}{4{,}000 / [(205 + 195)/2]} = 18.25$

The DSO is a bit lower relative to the company's past performance but slightly higher than the industry average.

- inventory turnover = $\dfrac{\text{cost of goods sold}}{\text{average inventories}}$

  inventory turnover = $\dfrac{3{,}000}{(310 + 290) / 2} = 10.0$

Inventory turnover is much lower than last year and the industry average. This suggests that the company is not managing inventory efficiently and may have obsolete stock.

- total asset turnover = $\dfrac{\text{revenue}}{\text{average assets}}$

  total asset turnover = $\dfrac{4{,}000}{(2{,}060 + 1{,}940) / 2} = 2.0$

Total asset turnover is slightly lower than last year and the industry average.

- working capital turnover = $\dfrac{\text{revenue}}{\text{average working capital}}$

  beginning working capital = 580 − 275 = 305

  ending working capital = 620 − 325 = 295

  working capital turnover = $\dfrac{4{,}000}{(305 + 295)\,/\,2} = 13.3$

Working capital turnover is lower than last year, but still above the industry average.

- gross profit margin = $\dfrac{\text{gross profit}}{\text{revenue}}$

  gross profit margin = $\dfrac{1{,}000}{4{,}000} = 25.0\%$

The gross profit margin is lower than last year and much lower than the industry average.

- net profit margin = $\dfrac{\text{net income}}{\text{revenue}}$

  net profit margin = $\dfrac{200}{4{,}000} = 5.0\%$

The net profit margin is lower than last year and much lower than the industry average.

- return on total capital = $\dfrac{\text{EBIT}}{\text{short- and long-term debt + equity}}$

  beginning total capital = 140 + 45 + 690 + 880 = 1,755

  ending total capital = 160 + 55 + 610 + 1,020 = 1,845

  return on total capital = $\dfrac{350}{(1{,}755 + 1{,}845)\,/\,2} = 19.4\%$

The return on total capital is below last year and below the industry average. This suggests a problem stemming from the low asset turnover and low profit margin.

- return on common equity = $\dfrac{\text{net income} - \text{preferred dividends}}{\text{average common equity}}$

return on common equity = $\dfrac{200}{(1{,}020 + 880) \,/\, 2} = 21.1\%$

The return on equity is lower than last year but better than the industry average. The reason it is higher than the industry average is probably because of greater use of leverage.

- debt-to-equity ratio = $\dfrac{\text{total debt}}{\text{total equity}}$

debt-to-equity ratio = $\dfrac{610 + 160 + 55}{1{,}020} = 80.9\%$

Note that preferred equity would be included in the denominator if there were any, and that we have included short-term debt and the current portion of long-term debt in calculating total (interest-bearing) debt.

The debt-to-equity ratio is lower than last year but still much higher than the industry average. This suggests the company is trying to get its debt level more in line with the industry.

- interest coverage = $\dfrac{\text{EBIT}}{\text{interest payments}}$

interest coverage = $\dfrac{350}{50} = 7.0$

The interest coverage is better than last year but still worse than the industry average. This, along with the slip in profit margin and return on assets, might cause some concern.

LOS 41.f: Demonstrate the application of DuPont analysis (the decomposition of return on equity).

The **DuPont system of analysis** is an approach that can be used to analyze return on equity (ROE). It uses basic algebra to break down ROE into a function of different ratios, so an analyst can see the impact of leverage, profit margins, and turnover on shareholder returns. There are two variants of the DuPont system: The original three-part approach and the extended five-part system.

For the **original approach**, start with ROE defined as:

return on equity = $\left(\dfrac{\text{net income}}{\text{equity}} \right)$

Average or year-end values for equity can be used. Multiplying ROE by (revenue/revenue) and rearranging terms produces:

$$\text{return on equity} = \left(\frac{\text{net income}}{\text{revenue}}\right)\left(\frac{\text{revenue}}{\text{equity}}\right)$$

The first term is the profit margin and the second term is the equity turnover:

$$\text{return on equity} = \left(\frac{\text{net profit}}{\text{margin}}\right)\left(\frac{\text{equity}}{\text{turnover}}\right)$$

We can expand this further by multiplying these terms by (assets/assets), and rearranging terms:

$$\text{return on equity} = \left(\frac{\text{net income}}{\text{sales}}\right)\left(\frac{\text{sales}}{\text{assets}}\right)\left(\frac{\text{assets}}{\text{equity}}\right)$$

 Professor's Note: For the exam, remember that (net income / sales) × (sales / assets) = return on assets (ROA).

The first term is still the profit margin, the second term is now asset turnover, and the third term is a financial leverage ratio that will increase as the use of debt financing increases:

$$\text{return on equity} = \left(\frac{\text{net profit}}{\text{margin}}\right)\left(\frac{\text{asset}}{\text{turnover}}\right)\left(\frac{\text{leverage}}{\text{ratio}}\right)$$

This is the original DuPont equation. It is arguably the most important equation in ratio analysis, since it breaks down a very important ratio (ROE) into three key components. If ROE is relatively low, it must be that at least one of the following is true: The company has a poor profit margin, the company has poor asset turnover, or the firm has too little leverage.

 Professor's Note: Often candidates get confused and think the DuPont method is a way to calculate ROE. While you can calculate ROE given the components of either the original or extended DuPont equations, this isn't necessary if you have the financial statements. If you have net income and equity, you can calculate ROE. The DuPont method is a way to decompose ROE, to better see what changes are driving the changes in ROE.

Example: Decomposition of ROE with original DuPont

Staret Inc. has maintained a stable and relatively high ROE of approximately 18% over the last three years. Use traditional DuPont analysis to decompose this ROE into its three components and comment on trends in company performance.

Staret Inc. Selected Balance Sheet and Income Statement Items (Millions)			
Year	2003	2004	2005
Net Income	21.5	22.3	21.9
Sales	305	350	410
Equity	119	124	126
Assets	230	290	350

Answer:

ROE 2003: 21.5/119 = 18.1%

2004: 22.3/124 = 18.0%

2005: 21.9/126 = 17.4%

DuPont 2003: 7.0% × 1.33 × 1.93

2004: 6.4% × 1.21 × 2.34

2005: 5.3% × 1.17 × 2.78

(some rounding in values)

While the ROE has dropped only slightly, both the total asset turnover and the net profit margin have declined. The effects of declining net margins and turnover on ROE have been offset by a significant increase in leverage. The analyst should be concerned about the net margin and find out what combination of pricing pressure and/or increasing expenses have caused this. Also, the analyst must note that the company has become more risky due to increased debt financing.

Example: Computing ROE using original DuPont

A company has a net profit margin of 4%, asset turnover of 2.0, and a debt-to-assets ratio of 60%. What is the ROE?

Answer:

Debt-to-assets = 60%, which means equity to assets is 40%; this implies assets to equity (the leverage ratio) is 1 / 0.4 = 2.5

$$ROE = \left(\frac{\text{net profit}}{\text{margin}}\right)\left(\frac{\text{total asset}}{\text{turnover}}\right)\left(\frac{\text{assets}}{\text{equity}}\right) = (0.04)(2.00)(2.50) = 0.20, \text{ or } 20\%$$

The **extended (5-way) DuPont equation** takes the net profit margin and breaks it down further.

$$ROE = \left(\frac{\text{net income}}{\text{EBT}}\right)\left(\frac{\text{EBT}}{\text{EBIT}}\right)\left(\frac{\text{EBIT}}{\text{revenue}}\right)\left(\frac{\text{revenue}}{\text{total assets}}\right)\left(\frac{\text{total assets}}{\text{total equity}}\right)$$

Note that the first term in the 3-part DuPont equation, net profit margin, has been decomposed into three terms:

$\dfrac{\text{net income}}{\text{EBT}}$ is called the *tax burden* and is equal to $(1 - \text{tax rate})$.

$\dfrac{\text{EBT}}{\text{EBIT}}$ is called the *interest burden*.

$\dfrac{\text{EBIT}}{\text{revenue}}$ is called the *EBIT margin*.

We then have:

$$ROE = \left(\genfrac{}{}{0pt}{}{\text{tax}}{\text{burden}}\right)\left(\genfrac{}{}{0pt}{}{\text{interest}}{\text{burden}}\right)\left(\genfrac{}{}{0pt}{}{\text{EBIT}}{\text{margin}}\right)\left(\genfrac{}{}{0pt}{}{\text{asset}}{\text{turnover}}\right)\left(\genfrac{}{}{0pt}{}{\text{financial}}{\text{leverage}}\right)$$

An increase in interest expense as proportion of EBIT will increase the interest burden. Increases in either the tax burden or the interest burden will tend to decrease ROE.

EBIT in the second two expressions can be replaced by operating earnings. In this case, we have the operating margin rather than the EBIT margin. The interest burden term would then show the effects of nonoperating income as well as the effect of interest expense.

Note that in general, high profit margins, leverage, and asset turnover will lead to high levels of ROE. However, this version of the formula shows that more leverage *does not always* lead to higher ROE. As leverage rises, so does the interest burden. Hence, the positive effects of leverage can be offset by the higher interest payments that accompany more debt. Note that higher taxes will always lead to lower levels of ROE.

Example: Extended DuPont analysis

An analyst has gathered data from two companies in the same industry. Calculate the ROE for both companies and use the extended DuPont analysis to explain the critical factors that account for the differences in the two companies' ROEs.

Selected Income and Balance Sheet Data

	Company A	Company B
Revenues	$500	$900
EBIT	35	100
Interest expense	5	0
EBT	30	100
Taxes	10	40
Net income	20	60
Total assets	250	300
Total debt	100	50
Owners' equity	$150	$250

Answer:

EBIT = EBIT / revenue
   Company A: EBIT margin = 35 / 500 = 7.0%
   Company B: EBIT margin = 100 / 900 = 11.1%

asset turnover = revenue / assets
   Company A: asset turnover = 500 / 250 = 2.0
   Company B: asset turnover = 900 / 300 = 3.0

interest burden = EBT / EBIT
   Company A: interest burden = 30 / 35 = 85.7%
   Company B: interest burden = 100 / 100 = 1

financial leverage = assets / equity
   Company A: financial leverage = 250 / 150 = 1.67
   Company B: financial leverage = 300 / 250 = 1.2

tax burden = net income / EBT
   Company A: tax burden = 20 / 30 = 66.7%
   Company B: tax burden = 60 / 100 = 60.0%

Company A: ROE = 0.667 × 0.857 × 0.07 × 2.0 × 1.67 = 13.4%

Company B: ROE = 0.608 × 1.0 × 0.111 × 3.0 × 1.2 = 24%

Company B has a higher tax burden but a lower interest burden (a lower ratio indicates a higher burden). Company B has better EBIT margins and better asset utilization (perhaps management of inventory, receivables, or payables, or a lower cost basis in its fixed assets due to their age), and less leverage. Its higher EBIT margins and asset turnover are the main factors leading to its significantly higher ROE, which it achieves with less leverage than Company A.

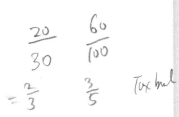
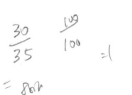

LOS 41.g: Calculate and interpret the ratios used in equity analysis, credit analysis, and segment analysis.

Valuation ratios are used in analysis for investment in common equity. The most widely used valuation ratio is the *price-to-earnings* (P/E) ratio, the ratio of the current market price of a share of stock divided by the company's earnings per share. Related measures based on price per share are the *price-to-cash flow*, the *price-to-sales*, and the *price-to-book value* ratios.

 Professor's Note: The use of the above valuation ratios is covered in detail in the review of equity valuation in Study Session 14.

Per-share valuation measures include *earnings per share* (EPS). *Basic EPS* is net income available to common divided by the weighted average number of common shares outstanding.

Diluted EPS is a "what if" value. It is calculated to be the lowest possible EPS that could have been reported if all firm securities that can be converted into common stock, and that would decrease basic EPS if they had been, were converted. That is, if all dilutive securities had been converted. Potentially dilutive securities include convertible debt and convertible preferred stock, as well as options and warrants issued by the company. The numerator of diluted EPS is increased by the after-tax interest savings on any dilutive debt securities and by the dividends on any dilutive convertible preferred stock. The denominator is increased by the common shares that would result from conversion or exchange of dilutive securities into common shares.

 Professor's Note: Refer back to our review of the income statement in Study Session 8 for details and examples of how to calculate basic and diluted EPS.

Other per-share measures include: *cash flow per share*, *EBIT per share*, and *EBITDA per share*. Per-share measures for different companies cannot be compared. A firm with a $100 share price can be expected to generate much greater earnings, cash flow, EBITDA, and EBIT per share than a firm with a $10 share price.

Dividends

Dividends are declared on a per-common-share basis. Total dividends on a firm-wide basis are referred to as *dividends declared*. Neither EPS nor net income is reduced by the payment of common stock dividends. Net income minus dividends declared is retained earnings, the earnings that are used to grow the corporation rather than being distributed to equity holders. The proportion of a firm's net income that is retained to fund growth is an important determinant of the firm's *sustainable growth rate*.

To calculate the sustainable growth rate for a firm, the rate of return on resources is measured as the return on equity capital, or the ROE. The proportion of earnings reinvested is known as the retention rate (RR).

- The formula for the *sustainable growth rate*, which is how fast the firm can grow without additional external equity issues while holding leverage constant, is:

$$g = RR \times ROE$$

- The calculation of the *retention rate* (RR) is:

$$\text{retention rate} = \frac{\text{net income available to common} - \text{dividends declared}}{\text{net income available to common}}$$

$$= 1 - \text{dividend payout ratio}$$

where :

$$\text{dividend payout ratio} = \frac{\text{dividends declared}}{\text{net income available to common}}$$

Example: Calculating sustainable growth

The following figure provides data for three companies.

Growth Analysis Data

Company	A	B	C
Earnings per share	$3.00	$4.00	$5.00
Dividends per share	1.50	1.00	2.00
Return on equity	14%	12%	10%

Calculate the sustainable growth rate for each company.

Answer:

RR = 1 – (dividends / earnings)

Company A: RR = 1 – (1.50 / 3.00) = 0.500
Company B: RR = 1 – (1.00 / 4.00) = 0.750
Company C: RR = 1 – (2.00 / 5.00) = 0.600

g = RR × ROE

Company A: g = 0.500 × 14% = 7.0%
Company B: g = 0.750 × 12% = 9.0%
Company C: g = 0.600 × 10% = 6.0%

Some ratios have specific applications in certain industries.

Net income per employee and *sales per employee* are used in the analysis and valuation of service and consulting companies.

Growth in same-store sales is used in the restaurant and retail industries to indicate growth without the effects of new locations that have been opened. It is a measure of how well the firm is doing at attracting and keeping existing customers and, in the case of locations with overlapping markets, may indicate that new locations are taking customers from existing ones.

Sales per square foot is another metric commonly used in the retail industry.

Business Risk

The standard deviation of revenue, standard deviation of operating income, and the standard deviation of net income are all indicators of the variation in and the uncertainty about a firm's performance. Since they all depend on the size of the firm to a great extent, analysts employ a size-adjusted measure of variation. The **coefficient of variation** for a variable is its standard deviation divided by its expected value.

 *Professor's Note: We saw this before as a measure of portfolio risk in Quantitative Methods.*

Certainly, different industries have different levels of uncertainty about revenues, expenses, taxes, and nonoperating items. Comparing coefficients of variation for a firm across time, or among a firm and its peers, can aid the analyst is assessing both the relative and absolute degree of risk a firm faces in generating income for its investors.

$$\text{CV sales} = \frac{\text{standard deviation of sales}}{\text{mean sales}}$$

$$\text{CV operating income} = \frac{\text{standard deviation of operating income}}{\text{mean operating income}}$$

$$\text{CV net income} = \frac{\text{standard deviation of net income}}{\text{mean net income}}$$

Banks, insurance companies, and other financial firms carry their own challenges for analysts. Part of the challenge is to understand the commonly used terms and the ratios they represent.

Capital adequacy typically refers to the ratio of some dollar measure of the risk, both operational and financial, of the firm to its equity capital. Other measures of capital are also used. A common measure of capital risk is *value-at-risk,* which is an estimate of the dollar size of the loss that a firm will exceed only some specific percent of the time, over a specific period of time.

Banks are subject to minimum *reserve requirements.* Their ratios of various liabilities to their central bank reserves must be above the minimums. The ratio of a bank's liquid assets to certain liabilities is called the *liquid asset requirement.*

The performance of financial companies that lend funds is often summarized as the *net interest margin,* which is simply interest income divided by the firm's interest-earning assets.

Credit Analysis

Credit analysis is based on many of the ratios that we have already covered in this review. In assessing a company's ability to service and repay its debt, analysts use interest coverage ratios (calculated with EBIT or EBITDA), return on capital, and debt-to-assets ratios. Other ratios focus on various measures of cash flow to total debt.

Ratios have been used to analyze and predict firm bankruptcies. Altman (2000)[1] developed a Z-score that is useful in predicting firm bankruptcies (a low score indicates high probability of failure). The predictive model was based on a firm's working capital to assets, retained earnings to assets, EBIT to assets, market to book value of a share of stock, and revenues to assets.

Segment Analysis

A **business segment** is a portion of a larger company that accounts for more than 10% of the company's revenues or assets, and is distinguishable from the company's other lines of business in terms of the risk and return characteristics of the segment. **Geographic segments** are also identified when they meet the size criterion above and the geographic unit has a business environment that is different from that of other segments or the remainder of the company's business.

Both U.S. GAAP and IFRS require companies to report segment data, but the required disclosure items are only a subset of the required disclosures for the company as a whole. Nonetheless, an analyst can prepare a more detailed analysis and forecast by examining the performance of business or geographic segments separately. Segment profit margins, asset utilization (turnover), and return on assets can be very useful in gaining a clear picture of a firm's overall operations. For forecasting, growth rates of segment revenues and profits can be used to estimate future sales and profits and to determine the changes in company characteristics over time.

Figure 5 illustrates how Boeing broke down its results into business segments in its 2006 annual report (source: Boeing.com).

---

1. Edward I. Altman, "Predicting Financial Distress of Companies: Revisiting the Z-Score and Zeta® Models," July 2000.

Figure 5: Boeing Inc. Segment Reporting

(Dollars in millions) Year ended December 31	2006	2005	2004
Revenues:			
Commercial Airplanes	$28,465	21,365	19,925
Integrated Defense Systems:			
Precision Engagement and Mobility Systems	14,350	13,510	12,835
Network and Space Systems	11,980	12,254	13,023
Support Systems	6,109	5,342	4,881
Total Integrated Defense Systems	32,439	31,106	30,739
Boeing Capital Corporation	1,025	966	959
Other	299	657	275
Accounting differences/eliminations	(698)	(473)	(498)
Total revenues	$61,530	$53,621	$51,400
Earnings from operations:			
Commercial Airplanes	$2,733	$1,431	$745
Integrated Defense Systems:			
Precision Engagement and Mobility Systems	1,238	1,755	1,697
Network and Space Systems	958	1,399	577
Support Systems	836	765	662
Total Integrated Defense Systems	3,032	3,919	2,936
Boeing Capital Corporation	291	232	183
Other	(738)	(363)	(546)
Unallocated expense	(1,733)	(2,407)	(1,311)
Settlement with U.S. Department of Justice, net of accruals	(571)		
Earnings from operations	3,014	2,812	2,007
Other income, net	420	301	288
Interest and debt expense	(240)	(294)	(335)
Earnings before income taxes	3,194	2,819	1,960
Income tax expense	(988)	(257)	(140)
Net earnings from continuing operations	$2,206	$2,562	$1,820
Income from discontinued operations, net of taxes of $6			10
Net gain/(loss) on disposal of disposal of discontinued operations, net of taxes of $5, $(5) and $24	9	(7)	42
Cumulative effect of accounting change, net of taxes of $10		17	
Net earnings	$2,215	$2,572	$1,872

LOS 41.h: Describe how the results of common-size and ratio analysis can be used to model and forecast earnings.

Both common-size financial statements and ratio analysis can be used in preparing pro forma financial statements that provide estimates of financial statement items for one or more future periods. The preparation of pro forma financial statements and related forecasts is covered in some detail in the next Study Session, Corporate Finance. Here, some examples will suffice.

A forecast of financial results that begins with an estimate of a firm's next-period revenues might use the most recent COGS, or an average of COGS, from a common-size income statement. On a common-size income statement, COGS is calculated as a percentage of revenue. If the analyst has no reason to believe that COGS in relation to sales will change for the next period, the COGS percentage from a common-size income statement can be used in constructing a pro forma income statement for the next period based on the estimate of sales.

Similarly, the analyst may believe that certain ratios will remain the same or change in one direction or the other for the next period. In the absence of any information indicating a change, an analyst may choose to incorporate the operating profit margin from the prior period into a pro forma income statement for the next period. Beginning with an estimate of next-period sales, the estimated operating profit margin can be used to forecast operating profits for the next period.

Rather than point estimates of sales and net and operating margins, the analyst may examine possible changes in order to create a range of possible values for key financial variables.

Three methods of examining the variability of financial outcomes around point estimates are: *sensitivity analysis, scenario analysis*, and *simulation*. Sensitivity analysis is based on "what if" questions such as: What will be the effect on net income if sales increase by 3% rather than the estimated 5%? Scenario analysis is based on specific scenarios (a specific set of outcomes for key variables) and will also yield a range of values for financial statement items. Simulation is a technique in which probability distributions for key variables are selected and a computer is used to generate a distribution of values for outcomes based on repeated random selection of values for the key variables.

KEY CONCEPTS

1. Common-size financial statements allow an analyst to compare performance across firms, evaluate a single firm across time, and quickly view certain financial ratios.

2. Vertical common-size ratios are stated in terms of sales (for income statements) or total assets (for balance sheets). Horizontal common-size financial sheet data index each item to its value in a base year.

3. Stacked column graphs and line graphs can illustrate the changes in financial statement values over time.

4. Limitations of ratio analysis:
   • Ratios are not useful when viewed in isolation.
   • Different companies use different accounting treatments.
   • Comparable ratios can be hard to find for companies that operate in multiple industries.
   • Ratios must be analyzed relative to one another.
   • Determining the range of acceptable values for a ratio can be difficult.

5. Financial ratios can be classified as activity, liquidity, solvency, profitability, and valuation ratios.

6. Activity ratios include receivables turnover, days of sales outstanding, inventory turnover, days of inventory on hand, payables turnover, payables payment period, and turnover ratios for total assets, fixed assets, and working capital.

7. Liquidity ratios include the current, quick, and cash ratios, the defensive interval, and the cash conversion cycle.

8. Solvency ratios include the debt-to-equity, debt-to-capital, debt-to-assets, financial leverage, interest coverage, and fixed charge coverage ratios.

9. Profitability ratios include net, gross, and operating profit margins, pretax margin, return on assets, operating return on assets, return on total capital, return on total equity, and return on common equity.

10. An analyst should use an appropriate combination of different ratios to evaluate a company over time and relative to comparable companies.

11. The DuPont system of analysis breaks return on equity into components for analysis. The basic DuPont equation is:

$$\text{return on equity} = \left(\frac{\text{net income}}{\text{sales}}\right)\left(\frac{\text{sales}}{\text{assets}}\right)\left(\frac{\text{assets}}{\text{equity}}\right)$$

The extended DuPont equation is:

return on equity =

$$\left(\frac{\text{net income}}{\text{EBT}}\right)\left(\frac{\text{EBT}}{\text{EBIT}}\right)\left(\frac{\text{EBIT}}{\text{revenue}}\right)\left(\frac{\text{revenue}}{\text{total assets}}\right)\left(\frac{\text{total assets}}{\text{total equity}}\right)$$

12. Ratios used in equity analysis include price-to-earnings, price-to-cash flow, price-to-sales, and price-to-book value ratios, basic and diluted earnings per share. Other ratios are relevant to specific industries such as retail and financial services.

13. A firm's sustainable growth rate can be calculated by multiplying its earnings retention rate by its return on equity

14. Coefficients of variation measure the risk related to a firm's sales, operating income, and net income.

15. Credit analysis emphasizes interest coverage ratios, return on capital, debt-to-assets ratios, and ratios of cash flow to total debt.

16. Business segments and geographic segments can be analyzed separately to provide more detail about a company's financial performance.

17. Common-size financial statements and ratio analysis can be used to construct pro forma financial statements based on a forecast of sales growth and assumptions about the behavior of a firm's financial ratios.

CONCEPT CHECKERS

1. To study trends in a firm's cost of goods sold (COGS), the analyst should
    standardize the cost of goods sold numbers to a common-sized basis by
    dividing COGS by:
    A. assets.
    B. sales.
    C. net income.
    D. the prior year's COGS.

2. Which of the following is *least likely* a limitation of financial ratios?
    A. Data on comparable firms are difficult to acquire.
    B. Ratios are not meaningful when viewed in isolation.
    C. Determining the target or comparison value for a ratio requires judgment.
    D. Different accounting treatments require the analyst to adjust the data
       before comparing ratios.

3. An analyst who is interested in a company's long-term solvency would *most
    likely* examine the:
    A. return on total capital.
    B. defensive interval ratio.
    C. fixed charge coverage ratio.
    D. number of days of payables.

4. RGB, Inc.'s income statement indicates cost of goods sold of $100,000. The
    balance sheet shows an average accounts payable balance of $12,000. RGB's
    payables payment period is *closest* to:
    A. 28 days.
    B. 37 days.
    C. 44 days.
    D. 52 days.

5. RGB, Inc. has a gross profit of $45,000 on sales of $150,000. The balance
    sheet shows average total assets of $75,000 with an average inventory balance
    of $15,000. RGB's total asset turnover and inventory turnover are *closest* to:

	Asset turnover	Inventory turnover
A.	7.00 times	2.00 times
B.	2.00 times	7.00 times
C.	0.50 times	0.33 times
D.	10.00 times	0.60 times

6. If RGB, Inc. has annual sales of $100,000, average accounts payable of
    $30,000, and average accounts receivable of $25,000, RGB's receivables
    turnover and average collection period are *closest* to:

	Receivables turnover	Average collection period
A.	1.8 times	203 days
B.	2.1 times	174 days
C.	3.3 times	111 days
D.	4.0 times	91 days

7. A company's current ratio is 1.9. If some of the accounts payable are paid off from the cash account, the:
   A. numerator and the current ratio would remain unchanged.
   B. numerator would decrease by a greater percentage than the denominator, resulting in a lower current ratio.
   C. denominator would decrease by a greater percentage than the numerator, resulting in a higher current ratio.
   D. numerator and denominator would decrease proportionally, leaving the current ratio unchanged.

8. A company's quick ratio is 1.2. If inventory were purchased for cash, the:
   A. numerator and the quick ratio would remain unchanged.
   B. numerator would decrease more than the denominator, resulting in a lower quick ratio.
   C. denominator would decrease more than the numerator, resulting in a higher current ratio.
   D. numerator and denominator would decrease proportionally, leaving the current ratio unchanged.

9. All other things held constant, which of the following transactions will increase a firm's current ratio if the ratio is greater than one?
   A. Accounts receivable are collected and the funds received are deposited in the firm's cash account.
   B. Fixed assets are purchased from the cash account.
   C. Accounts payable are paid with funds from the cash account.
   D. Inventory is purchased on account.

10. RGB, Inc.'s receivable turnover is ten times, the inventory turnover is five times, and the payables turnover is nine times. RGB's cash conversion cycle is *closest* to:
    A. 69 days.
    B. 104 days.
    C. 150 days.
    D. 170 days.

11. RGB, Inc.'s income statement shows sales of $1,000, cost of goods sold of $400, pre-interest operating expense of $300, and interest expense of $100. RGB's interest coverage ratio is *closest* to:
    A. 1 time.
    B. 2 times.
    C. 3 times.
    D. 4 times.

12. Return on equity using the traditional DuPont formula equals:
    A. (net profit margin) (interest component) (solvency ratio).
    B. (net profit margin) (total asset turnover) (tax retention rate).
    C. (net profit margin) (total asset turnover) (financial leverage multiplier).
    D. (tax rate) (interest expense rate) (financial leverage multiplier).

13.   RGB, Inc. has a net profit margin of 12%, a total asset turnover of 1.2 times, and a financial leverage multiplier of 1.2 times. RGB's return on equity is *closest* to:
        A. 12.0%.
        B. 14.2%.
        C. 17.3%.
        D. 18.9%.

14.   Use the following information for RGB, Inc.:
        *   EBIT/sales = 10%
        *   Tax retention rate = 60%
        *   Sales/assets = 1.8 times
        *   Current ratio = 2 times
        *   Interest/assets = 2%
        *   Assets/equity = 1.9 times

        RGB, Inc.'s return on equity is *closest* to:
        A. 10.50%.
        B. 11.32%.
        C. 12.16%.
        D. 18.24%.

15.   Which of the following equations *least accurately* represents return on equity?
        A. (net profit margin)(equity turnover).
        B. (net profit margin)(total asset turnover)(assets/equity).
        C. (ROA)(interest burden)(tax retention rate).
        D. [(operating profit margin)(total asset turnover) – interest expense rate)] (financial leverage multiplier)(tax retention rate).

16.   Paragon Co. has an operating profit margin (EBIT/S) of 11%; an asset turnover (S/A) of 1.2; a financial leverage multiplier (A/E) of 1.5 times; an average tax rate of 35%; and an interest expense rate (I/A) of 4%. Paragon's return on equity is *closest* to:
        A. 0.09.
        B. 0.10.
        C. 0.11.
        D. 0.12.

17.   A firm has a dividend payout ratio of 40%, a net profit margin of 10%, an asset turnover of 0.9 times, and a financial leverage multiplier of 1.2 times. The firm's sustainable growth rate is *closest* to:
        A. 5.5%.
        B. 6.5%.
        C. 7.5%.
        D. 8.0%.

18.   An analyst who needs to model and forecast a company's earnings for the next three years would be *least likely* to:
    A. begin with an estimate of revenue growth.
    B. assume that key financial ratios will remain unchanged for the forecast period.
    C. use common-size financial statements to estimate expenses as a percentage of net income.
    D. examine the variability of the predicted outcomes by performing a sensitivity or scenario analysis.

COMPREHENSIVE PROBLEMS

A.   The following table lists partial financial statement data for Alpha Company:

Alpha Company

Sales	$5,000
Cost of goods sold	2,500
Average	
Inventories	$600
Accounts receivable	450
Working capital	750
Cash	200
Accounts payable	500
Fixed assets	4,750
Total assets	$6,000
Annual purchases	$2,400

Calculate the following ratios for Alpha Company:
- Inventory turnover.
- Days of inventory on hand.
- Receivables turnover.
- Days of sales outstanding.
- Payables turnover.
- Number of days of payables.
- Cash conversion cycle.

Use the following information for problems B through E.

Beta Co. has a loan covenant requiring it to maintain a current ratio of 1.5 or better. As Beta approaches year-end, current assets are $20 million ($1 million in cash, $9 million in accounts receivable, and $10 million in inventory) and current liabilities are $13.5 million.

B.   Calculate Beta's current ratio and quick ratio.

C.   Which of the following transactions would Beta Co. *most likely* enter to meet its loan covenant?
   • Sell $1 million in inventory and deposit the proceeds in the company's checking account.
   • Borrow $1 million short term and deposit the funds in their checking account.
   • Sell $1 million in inventory and pay off some of its short-term creditors.

D.   If Beta sells $2 million in inventory on credit, how will this affect its current ratio?

E.   If Beta sells $1 million in inventory and pays off accounts payable, how will this affect its quick ratio?

ANSWERS – CONCEPT CHECKERS

1. **B** With a common-size income statement, all income statement accounts are divided by sales.

2. **A** Company and industry data are widely available from numerous private and public sources. The other statements describe limitations of financial ratios.

3. **C** Fixed charge coverage is a solvency ratio. Return on total capital is a measure of profitability, the defensive interval ratio is a liquidity measure, and the number of days of payables is an activity ratio.

4. **C** Payables turnover = (COGS / avg. AP) = 100 / 12 = 8.33. Payables payment period = 365 / 8.33 = 43.8 days

5. **B** total asset turnover = (sales / total assets) = 150 / 75 = 2 times

   inventory turnover = (COGS / avg. inventory) = (150 – 45) / 15 = 7 times

6. **D** receivables turnover = (S / avg. AR) = 100 / 25 = 4

   average collection period = 365 / 4 = 91.25 days

7. **C** Current ratio = (cash + AR + inv) / AP. If cash and AP decrease by the same amount and the current ratio is greater than 1, then the denominator falls faster (in percentage terms) than the numerator, and the current ratio increases.

8. **B** Quick ratio = (cash + AR) / AP. If cash decreases, the quick ratio will also decrease. The denominator is unchanged.

9. **C** Current ratio = current assets / current liabilities. If CR is > 1, then if CA and CL both fall, the overall ratio will increase.

10. **A** (365 / 10 + 365 / 5 – 365 / 9) = 69 days

11. **C** Interest coverage ratio = EBIT / I = (1000 – 400 – 300) / 100 = 3 times

12. **C** This is the correct formula for the three-ratio DuPont model for ROE.

13. **C** return on equity = $\left(\dfrac{\text{net income}}{\text{sales}}\right)\left(\dfrac{\text{sales}}{\text{assets}}\right)\left(\dfrac{\text{assets}}{\text{equity}}\right)$ = (0.12)(1.2)(1.2) = 0.1728 = 17.28%

14. **D** ROE = [(EBIT / S)(S / A) – (I / A)](A / EQ)(1 – t) = [(0.1)(1.8) – (0.02)](1.9)(0.6) = 0.1824 = 18.24%

15. **C** (ROA)(interest burden)(tax retention rate) is not one of the DuPont models for calculating ROE.

16. **A** ROE = [(EBIT / S)(S / A) – (I / A)](A / E)(1 – t) = [(0.11)(1.2) – (0.04)](1.5)(0.65) = 0.0897

LOS 42.b: Prepare a basic projection of a company's future net income and cash flow.

A forecast of future net income and cash flow often begins with a forecast of future sales. Over shorter horizons, the "top down" approach to forecasting sales is used. The analyst begins with a forecast of GDP growth, often supplied by outside research or an in-house economics group. Historical relationships can be used to estimate the relationship between GDP growth and the growth of industry sales. If the subject firm's market share is expected to remain the same, the growth of firm sales will be the same as the growth in industry sales. If the analyst has reason to believe the firm's market share will increase or decrease next period, the market share can be adjusted for this change and then multiplied by estimated industry sales for the next period to get the forecast of firm sales for the period.

In a simple forecasting model, some historical average or trend-adjusted measure of profitability (operating margin, EBT margin, or net margin) can be used to forecast earnings. In complex forecasting models, each item on an income statement and balance sheet can be estimated based on separate assumptions about its growth in relation to revenue growth. For multi-period forecasts, the analyst typically employs a single estimate of sales growth at some point that is expected to continue indefinitely.

To estimate cash flows, the analyst must make assumptions about future sources and uses of cash. The most important of these will be increases in working capital, capital expenditures on new fixed assets, issuance or repayments of debt, and issuance or repurchase of stock. A typical assumption is that noncash working capital as a percentage of sales remains constant. A first-pass model might indicate a need for cash in future periods, and these cash requirements can then be met by projecting necessary borrowing in future periods. For consistency, interest expense in future periods must also be adjusted for any increase in debt.

Figure 1 illustrates this method. This projection assumes the company's sales increase 5% per year, its cost of goods sold is 35% of sales, and operating expenses are 55% of sales. It also assumes noncash working capital stays constant at 85% of sales and fixed capital requirements will be 5% of sales in each year. Net income is projected to increase over the forecast period, but the analysis reveals that cash is expected to decrease, suggesting a need for financing.

Figure 1: Income and Cash Flow Projection

	20X0	20X1	20X2	20X3	20X4
Sales @ +5% per year	86,145	90,452	94,975	99,724	104,710
Cost of goods sold @ 35% of sales	30,151	31,658	33,241	34,903	36,648
Operating expenses @ 55% of sales	47,380	49,749	52,236	54,848	57,590
Pretax income	8,614	9,045	9,497	9,972	10,471
Taxes @ 35%	3,015	3,166	3,324	3,490	3,665
Net income	5,599	5,879	6,173	6,482	6,806
Cash (Borrowing)	8,615	6,311	3,891	1,350	(1,317)
Noncash working capital @ 85% of sales	73,223	76,884	80,729	84,765	89,003
Current assets	81,838	83,195	84,620	86,116	87,686
Net income	5,599	5,879	6,173	6,482	6,806
– Investment in working capital	3,478	3,661	3,844	4,036	4,238
– Investment in fixed capital @ 5% of sales	4,307	4,523	4,749	4,986	5,235
Change in cash	(2,186)	(2,304)	(2,420)	(2,541)	(2,668)
Beginning cash	10,801	8,615	6,311	3,891	1,350
Ending cash	8,615	6,311	3,891	1,350	(1,317)

LOS 42.c: Describe the role of financial statement analysis in assessing the credit quality of a potential debt investment.

Traditionally, credit analysts have spoken of the "three C's," "four C's," or even the "five C's" of credit analysis. One version of the three C's includes: Character, Collateral, and Capacity to repay. Character refers to firm management's professional reputation and the firm's history of debt repayment. The ability to pledge specific collateral reduces lender risk. It is the third C, the capacity to repay, that requires close examination of a firm's financial statements and ratios. Since some debt is for periods of 30 years or longer, the credit analyst must take a very long-term view of the firm's prospects.

Credit rating agencies such as Moody's and Standard and Poor's employ formulas that are essentially weighted averages of several specific accounting ratios and business characteristics. The specific items used in the formula and their weights vary from industry to industry, but the types of items considered can be separated into four general categories:

1. *Scale and diversification.* Larger companies and those with more different product lines and greater geographic diversification are better credit risks.

2. *Operational efficiency.* Such items as operating ROA, operating margins, and EBITDA margins fall into this category. Along with greater vertical diversification, high operating efficiency is associated with better debt ratings.

3. *Margin stability.* Stability of the relevant profitability margins indicates a higher probability of repayment (leads to a better debt rating and a lower interest rate). Highly variable operating results make lenders nervous.

4. *Leverage.* Ratios of operating earnings, EBITDA, or some measure of free cash flow to interest expense or total debt make up the most important part of the credit rating formula. Firms with greater earnings in relation to their debt and in relation to their interest expense are better credit risks.

LOS 42.d: Discuss the use of financial statement analysis in screening for potential equity investments.

In many cases an analyst must select portfolio stocks from the large universe of potential equity investments. Whether the object is to select growth stocks, income stocks, or value stocks, accounting items and ratios can be used to identify a manageable subset of available stocks for further analysis.

Some investment strategies even have financial ratios in their names, such as low price/earnings and low price/sales investing. Multiple criteria are used because a screen based on a single factor can include firms with other undesirable characteristics. For example, a company with a low P/E may also have operating losses, declining sales prospects, or very high leverage.

Analysts should be aware that their equity screens will likely include and exclude many or all of the firms in particular industries. A screen to identify firms with low P/E ratios will likely exclude growth companies from the sample. A low price-to-book or high dividend screen will likely include an inordinate proportion of financial services companies.

LOS 42.e: Determine and justify appropriate analyst adjustments to a company's financial statements to facilitate comparison with another company.

Because different companies choose different accounting methods, an analyst must be prepared to adjust the financial statements of one company to make them comparable to those of another company or group of companies. Differences in accounting methods chosen by firms subject to the same standards, as well as differences in accounting methods due to differences in local accounting standards, can make comparisons between companies problematic.

Consider two companies in the same industry that have different depreciation schedules. One company has selected straight-line depreciation even though physical assets in its industry tend to lose most of their productive value early in their economic lives. The analyst would need to adjust the depreciation of that firm so that the net income figures for the firms are comparable. A change in a firm's financial statement depreciation would lead to changes in gross profit, operating profit, and so on down to net profit and earnings per share.

Differences between U.S. GAAP and IFRS require an analyst to adjust the financial statements of firms from different countries before comparing their financial results. Important differences between the two include their treatments of the effect of exchange rate changes, certain securities held by the firm, and inventory cost flows. Differences in accounting standards are covered in more detail in the next topic review.

We have already covered other adjustments for certain accounting methods and estimates. The analyst may need to convert financial statements for LIFO-based firms to FIFO, or vice-versa. Analysts would likely increase both liabilities and assets for a firm with significant operating leases, or for one with take-or-pay contracts.

KEY CONCEPTS

1. Trends in a company's financial ratios and differences between its financial ratios and those of its competitors or industry averages can reveal important aspects of its business strategy.

2. A company's future income and cash flows can be projected by making assumptions about its sales growth and sources and uses of cash.

3. Credit analysis uses a firm's financial statements to assess its credit quality. Indicators of a firm's creditworthiness include its scale and diversification, operational efficiency, margin stability, and leverage.

4. Potential equity investments can be screened using criteria such as financial statement ratios to identify a subset of available stocks with specific characteristics for further analysis.

5. For companies that use different accounting methods and estimates, analysts must adjust the financial statements to make their data comparable.

CONCEPT CHECKERS

1. The table below shows selected data from a company's financial statements.

	20X6	20X7	20X8	20X9
Sales	8,614	9,217	9,862	10,553
COGS	5,304	5,622	6,072	6,679
Purchases	5,257	5,572	6,018	6,620
Inventory	2,525	2,475	2,421	2,362
Accounts receivable	3,491	3,728	3,928	4,352
Accounts payable	1,913	2,102	2,311	2,539

Based on these results, what was this company's *most likely* strategy for improving its operating activity during this period?
A. Increase its rate of growth in sales.
B. Improve its inventory management.
C. Change its credit and collections policies with its customers.
D. Change the degree to which it uses trade credit from suppliers.

2. An analyst who is projecting a company's net income and cash flows is *least likely* to assume a constant relationship between the company's sales and its:
A. interest expenses.
B. cost of goods sold.
C. noncash working capital.
D. selling, general, and administrative expenses.

3. Credit analysts are likely to consider a company's credit quality to be improving if the company reduces its:
A. scale and diversification.
B. operating efficiency.
C. margin stability.
D. leverage.

4. Which of the following stock screens is *most likely* to identify stocks with high earnings growth rates?
A. Dividend payout ratio > 30%.
B. Price to cash flow per share ratio < 12.
C. Operating income to revenues ratio > 20%.
D. Book value to market value ratio < 25%.

5.   An analyst needs to compare the financial statements of Firm X and Firm Y. Which of the following differences in the two firms' financial reporting is *least likely* to require the analyst to make an adjustment?

	Firm X	Firm Y
A.	LIFO inventory cost	FIFO inventory cost
B.	Straight line depreciation	Accelerated depreciation
C.	Direct method cash flows	Indirect method cash flows
D.	IFRS financial reporting	U.S. GAAP financial reporting

ANSWERS – CONCEPT CHECKERS

1. **B**   To analyze this company's operating strategy, calculate its activity ratios:

	20X7	20X8	20X9
Inventory turnover	2.25	2.48	2.79
Receivables turnover	2.55	2.58	2.55
Payables turnover	2.78	2.73	2.73
Days of inventory on hand	162	147	131
Days of sales outstanding	143	142	143
Number of days of payables	132	134	134

The ratios that have changed most significantly are the ones related to inventory. Receivables and payables performance has remained steady, suggesting no change in the company's use of supplier credit or extension of customer credit. Sales increased at the same 7% rate in each of the years shown.

2. **A**   Projections of net income and cash flows are typically based on assumptions that cost of goods sold, operating expenses, and noncash working capital remain a constant percentage of sales. The projections then show whether additional borrowing is needed during the forecast period. If so, the analyst will adjust the interest expense to reflect the additional debt.

3. **D**   Lower leverage improves a company's creditworthiness. Larger scale, more diversification, higher operating efficiency, and more stable margins also tend to indicate better credit quality.

4. **D**   Firms with high growth rates will tend to have high market values relative to the book value of their equity. High operating profit margins are a not necessarily an indicator of earnings growth. Low price to cash flow ratios would tend to identify value stocks rather than growth stocks. Screening for high dividend payout ratios would tend to identify mature firms with relatively few growth opportunities.

5. **C**   Cash flows are the same under either method. Differences in depreciation methods, inventory cost, and IFRS versus U.S. GAAP reporting can all require an analyst to adjust financial statements to make them comparable.

INTERNATIONAL STANDARDS CONVERGENCE

Study Session 10

EXAM FOCUS

The convergence of U.S. GAAP and international accounting standards is an ongoing process. The exact differences between the two can be expected to change over time as the governing bodies work toward convergence. Here you should gain an understanding of the key differences, including upward revaluations and the prohibition of LIFO inventory accounting under international standards. The process of restating a company's financials to make them comparable with another company's or those of a group of peer companies is the important lesson here, along with the effects of restatement on key financial ratios.

LOS 43.a: Identify and explain the major international accounting standards for each asset and liability category on the balance sheet and the key differences from U.S. generally accepted accounting principles (GAAP).

The elements of the balance sheet (assets, liabilities, and equity) are defined in the IASB's conceptual framework. According to the framework, for an item to be recognized on the balance sheet as an asset (liability), it must be probable that a future economic benefit (expense) will flow to or from the firm *and* the item's cost can be reliably measured. Conceptually, equity is simply assets minus liabilities.

Marketable Investment Securities

Marketable investment securities are initially recorded on the balance sheet at cost; that is, the fair value at the date of acquisition. The main issue involves whether to adjust the balance sheet to reflect subsequent changes in fair value. The adjustments depend on the classification of the securities.

As discussed in the topic review on understanding the balance sheet, marketable investment securities are classified as either held-to-maturity, trading, or available-for-sale under SFAS No. 115. Under IFRS, the accounting for marketable investment securities is virtually the same. One difference is that trading securities are known as "held-for-trading" securities under IFRS.

Held-to-maturity securities are debt securities acquired with the intent and ability to own them until they mature. Held-to-maturity securities are reported on the balance sheet at amortized cost. Amortized cost is equal to the face (par) value less any unamortized discount or plus any unamortized premium. Subsequent changes in fair value are ignored unless the security is sold or otherwise disposed of.

Held-for-trading securities are debt and equity securities, including derivatives, acquired with the intent to profit from near-term price fluctuations. Held-for-trading securities are reported on the balance sheet at fair value. Unrealized gains and losses (changes in market value before the securities are sold) are recognized in the income statement.

Available-for-sale securities are debt and equity securities that a firm does not expect to hold until maturity nor expect to trade in the near term. Like held-for-trading securities, available-for-sale securities are reported on the balance sheet at fair value. However, any unrealized gains or losses are not recognized in the income statement. Rather, any unrealized gains or losses are reported as other comprehensive income.

Regardless of a security's classification, dividend income, interest income, and any realized gains and losses (actual gains or losses relative to carrying values realized when securities are sold) are recognized in the income statement.

Figure 1 summarizes the differences among the treatments of the three categories of marketable securities on the balance sheet and income statement.

Figure 1: Summary of Marketable Investment Security Classifications

	Held-for-trading	Available-for-sale	Held-to-maturity
Balance sheet	Fair value	Fair value	Amortized cost
Income statement	Unrealized G/L	No effect	No effect

Example: Classification of investment securities

Triple D Corporation purchased a 6% bond, at par, for $1,000,000 at the beginning of the year. Interest rates have recently increased, and the market value of the bond declined $20,000. Determine the bond's treatment on the financial statements under each classification of securities.

Answer:

If the bond is classified as a *held-to-maturity* security, the bond is reported on the balance sheet at $1,000,000 and interest income of $60,000 [$1,000,000 × 6%] is reported in the income statement.

If the bond is classified as a *held-for-trading* security, the bond is reported on the balance sheet at $980,000 and the $20,000 unrealized loss and $60,000 of interest income are both recognized in the income statement.

If the bond is classified as an *available-for-sale* security, the bond is reported on the balance sheet at $980,000 and $60,000 of interest income is recognized in the income statement. The $20,000 unrealized loss is not recognized in the income statement; rather, it is reported as other comprehensive income and decreases stockholders' equity.

The performance of held-for-trading securities is more transparent since both unrealized gains and unrealized losses are recognized in the income statement. Conversely, there is asymmetric treatment with available-for-sale securities since the unrealized gains and losses bypass the income statement and are reported as a direct adjustment to equity. By bypassing the income statement, the performance of available-for-sale securities can be misinterpreted by analysts. If a firm owns an equity security classified as available-for-sale, continuing decreases in share prices do not affect the income statement as long as the security is not sold.

Firms that follow IFRS are required to make qualitative and quantitative disclosures about credit risk, liquidity risk, and market risk. Qualitative disclosures provide information about managing the risks and quantitative disclosures deal with the amount of risk.

Inventory

Under IFRS, the choice of inventory method is based on the physical flow of the inventory; that is, whether the inventory that is purchased or produced first, is sold first. Two acceptable methods are the first-in, first-out (FIFO) method and the average cost method. Recall in the topic review on understanding the income statement that the last-in, first-out (LIFO) method is allowed under U.S. GAAP but is not permitted under IFRS.

Under IFRS and U.S. GAAP, inventory is reported on the balance sheet at the lower of cost or net realizable value. In the United States, once an inventory write-down occurs, any subsequent recovery of value is ignored. Under IFRS, subsequent recovery in the value of inventory can be included in inventory values.

Property and Equipment

Under IFRS and U.S. GAAP, property and equipment, sometimes referred to as fixed assets, are reported on the balance sheet at original cost less accumulated depreciation. U.S. GAAP does not permit upward revaluations of property and equipment.

Under IFRS, property and equipment can be revalued upward. In this case, the property and equipment are reported at fair value at the revaluation date less the accumulated depreciation since revaluation.

The increase in value is reported in the income statement to the extent that a previous downward valuation was *included in net income*. Otherwise, the increase in value is reported as a *direct adjustment to equity.* This results in consistent treatment in the income statement. Similarly, a decrease in value is reported in the income statement to the extent that a previous upward valuation was included in net income. Otherwise, the decrease in value is reported as a direct adjustment to equity.

Intercorporate Investments

When a firm makes an equity investment in another firm, the accounting treatment depends on the firm's ability to influence or control the policies and actions of the investee. The classification of marketable equity securities as held-for-trading and available-for-sale only applies to **passive investments**. An investment is considered passive if the investor cannot significantly influence or control the investee. As a practical guideline, an ownership interest of less than 20% is considered passive.

If an ownership interest is between 20% and 50%, the investor can usually significantly influence the investee. Under IFRS, **significant influence** is defined as the power to participate in the financial and operating policy decisions of the investee without control or joint control over those policies.[1]

For investments over which they have significant influence, firms must use the **equity method** of accounting. Under the equity method, a pro-rata share of the investee's net income is added to the firm's assets. Any dividends received from the investment reduce the investor's assets.

If an ownership interest is greater than 50%, the investor can usually control the investee. In this case, the **consolidation method** must be used, and the firm reports *all* of the assets and liabilities, as well as the net income, of the investee in its own financial statement items.

In the case of joint control of an investee, such as an ownership interest in a joint venture, IFRS recommends the use of the **proportionate consolidation method.** Under proportionate consolidation, the investor reports its pro-rata share of the assets, liabilities, and net income of the investee. Alternatively, the equity method can be used, but proportionate consolidation is preferred.

Under U.S. GAAP, the equity method is usually required for joint ventures. Proportionate consolidation is permitted under IFRS only.

Figure 2 summarizes the accounting treatment for intercorporate investments.

Figure 2: Accounting Treatment for Intercorporate Investments

Method	Ownership	Degree of Influence
Market	Less than 20%	No significant influence
Equity	20% – 50%	Significant influence
Consolidation	More than 50%	Control
Proportionate Consolidation (IFRS only)	Shared	Joint control (venture)

Goodwill

Recall from the topic review on understanding the balance sheet that goodwill is the excess of purchase price over the fair value of the identifiable assets and liabilities acquired in a business acquisition. Goodwill is an unidentifiable intangible asset that cannot be separated from the firm.

Goodwill is not systematically amortized in the income statement but is tested at least annually for impairment. If impaired, goodwill is written down on the balance sheet and the consequent loss is recognized on the income statement. The impairment of

---

1. International Accounting Standard No. 31.

goodwill does not affect cash flows, but does affect certain financial ratios. In periods after a write-down, ratios such as ROA, ROE, and asset turnover will improve because the denominator of each is reduced.

Judgment is involved in determining whether goodwill is impaired. Of course, when judgment is involved, there are opportunities for the firm to manipulate earnings.

For comparability, analysts often make the following adjustments:

- Completely eliminate goodwill when computing ratios.
- Exclude goodwill impairment charges from the income statement when analyzing trends.
- Evaluate future acquisitions in terms of the price paid relative to the earning power of the acquired assets.

Two other issues affect the comparability of the financial statements of the acquiring firm in a business acquisition.

1. The assets and liabilities of the acquired firm are recorded at fair value at the date of acquisition. As a result, the acquiring firm reports assets and liabilities with a mixture of bases for valuation; old assets continue to be reported at historical cost while acquired assets are carried at their fair value.

2. The revenues and expenses of the acquired firm are included in the acquiring firm's income statement *from* the acquisition date. There is no restatement of prior-period income statements. Without restatement, acquisitions may create an illusion of growth.

Identifiable Intangible Assets

Under U.S. GAAP and IFRS, purchased intangible assets are reported on the balance sheet at their cost less accumulated amortization. The costs of internally developed intangibles are generally expensed as incurred. U.S. GAAP does not permit upward revaluations of intangible assets.

As with property and equipment, IFRS does allow upward revaluations of identifiable intangible assets. Intangible assets are then reported at their fair value as of the revaluation date, less the accumulated amortization since revaluation.

As with property and equipment, any increase in value is reported in the income statement to the extent that a previous downward revaluation reduced net income. Any upward revaluation in excess of prior downward revaluation is reported as a direct adjustment to equity. Under the same principle, a decrease in value is reported in the income statement to the extent that a previous upward revaluation was included in net income, and any decrease in value in excess of prior upward revaluation is reported as a direct adjustment to equity.

Analysts must be aware that not all intangible assets are reported on the balance sheet. Some intangibles are expensed as incurred. These unrecorded assets must still be considered when valuing a firm. A valuable brand name such as Coke®, the software developed by Microsoft Corporation, or the patents and manufacturing expertise of a large pharmaceutical firm may not be recorded as firm assets.

Provisions

Provisions are nonfinancial liabilities that are uncertain as to their timing or amount. Examples include warranty obligations and contingencies. According to IAS No. 37, a firm should recognize a liability when it has a present obligation that is a result of a past event and the firm can reliably estimate the cost to settle the obligation.

U.S. GAAP does not use the term "provisions." Under U.S. GAAP, if a contingency is probable and can be reasonably estimated, a loss is recognized in the income statement and a liability is recorded on the balance sheet.

LOS 43.b: Identify and explain the major international accounting standards for major revenue and expense categories on the income statement, and the key differences from U.S. GAAP.

The definitions of revenue and the criteria for revenue recognition under U.S. GAAP and IFRS differ slightly. The main principles are the same but U.S. GAAP provides more industry-specific guidance than IFRS.

Construction Contracts

Under U.S. GAAP, the percentage-of-completion method of revenue recognition is appropriate for contracts that extend beyond one accounting period if the outcome of the project can be reasonably estimated. Accordingly, revenue, expense, and therefore profit are recognized as the work is performed. If the outcome of project cannot be reasonably estimated, the completed-contract method is required.

Under IFRS, if the firm cannot reliably measure the outcome of the project, revenue is recognized to the extent of contract costs and profit is only recognized at project completion.

Cost of Goods Sold

IFRS does not permit LIFO inventory accounting. LIFO firms that follow U.S. GAAP must disclose the LIFO reserve in the footnotes to their financial statements. The change in the LIFO reserve over a period of time is equal to the difference between COGS calculated under LIFO and COGS calculated under FIFO. Disclosure of the LIFO reserve allows users to adjust the LIFO COGS to FIFO COGS. This adjustment enhances the comparability U.S. and IFRS firms.

Operating Expenses

U.S. GAAP differentiates between expenses and losses, but IFRS does not. Under IFRS, losses not related to a firm's primary business operations are included in operating expenses.

Depreciation

Tangible assets (excluding land) are depreciated, intangible assets (except goodwill) are amortized, and natural resources are depleted. All three terms describe the allocation of an asset's cost over its useful life. The allocation process requires the use of estimates such as useful life and salvage value. Estimates often change as new information is acquired. A change in an estimate is put into effect prospectively; that is, no cumulative adjustment is made for prior period depreciation, just as with U.S. GAAP.

In choosing an appropriate allocation method (e.g., straight-line, accelerated), IFRS requires that the method reflect the pattern of expected consumption and the allocation must be made on a systematic basis over the asset's useful life.

Interest Expense

Borrowing costs are generally expensed in the year incurred. Under IFRS, firms can *choose* to capitalize interest that is related to the acquisition, construction, or production of an asset that will take a substantial time to complete. The capitalized interest is simply added to the cost of the asset and is eventually recognized in the income statement as the asset is depreciated.

Firms that follow U.S. GAAP *must* capitalize construction interest.

Income Taxes

Both U.S. GAAP and IFRS require firms to recognize temporary differences between financial reporting standards and tax reporting standards. These differences can create both deferred tax assets and deferred tax liabilities.

The differences between IFRS and U.S. GAAP in accounting for income taxes relate primarily to differences and exceptions in financial accounting principles between U.S. GAAP and IFRS.

Nonrecurring Items

Analysts often ignore nonrecurring items when forecasting future earnings because recurring earnings are usually viewed as more sustainable. Over the past several years, there has been convergence between U.S. GAAP and IFRS in reporting discontinued operations and changes in accounting principles. However, their treatments of extraordinary items still differ.

Under U.S. GAAP, an extraordinary item is a material transaction that is both unusual in nature and infrequent in occurrence. Extraordinary items are reported in the income statement, net of tax, below income from continuing operations.

IFRS does not permit firms to treat items as "extraordinary" in the income statement. The analyst, however, can use required IFRS disclosures to separate recurring and non-recurring earnings.

LOS 43.c: Identify and explain the major differences between international and U.S. GAAP accounting standards concerning the treatment of interest and dividends on the cash flow statement.

Under U.S. GAAP, dividends paid to the firm's shareholders are reported as CFF and interest paid is reported as CFO. Interest received and dividends received from investments are also reported as CFO.

IFRS allows more flexibility in the classification of interest and dividend cash flows. Under IFRS, interest and dividends received may be classified as either operating or investing activities (CFO or CFI). Dividends paid to the firm's shareholders and interest paid on the firm's debt may be classified as either CFO or CFF.

LOS 43.d: Interpret the effect of differences between international and U.S. GAAP accounting standards on the balance sheet, income statement, and the statement of changes in equity for some commonly used financial ratios.

When comparing firms that follow different accounting standards, the analyst must make adjustments to the specific balance sheet and income statement accounts that differ. This is done by recasting the financial statements of one of the firms so that the financial statements of both firms can be compared.

As an example, consider a U.S. firm that reports its inventory under LIFO and an IFRS firm that reports its inventory under FIFO. The income statements and balance sheets of the two firms cannot be compared without recasting the IFRS firm's financial statements to U.S. GAAP or vice versa. Because LIFO firms are required to disclose the LIFO reserve in the financial statement footnotes, it is usually easier to convert the LIFO firm statements to a FIFO basis.

In an inflationary environment, a LIFO firm will report higher COGS and lower inventory as compared to a FIFO firm. Higher COGS will result in lower profitability (gross profit, operating profit, taxable profit, and net profit). Lower taxable profit will result in lower income taxes. Lower net profit will also result in lower equity (lower retained earnings).

The LIFO reserve is the difference between LIFO and FIFO inventory. By adding the LIFO reserve to the U.S. firm's inventory balance, the analyst can state the U.S. firm's inventory on a FIFO basis to make it comparable with the IFRS firm.

In addition, it is necessary to convert LIFO COGS to FIFO COGS. This can be accomplished by subtracting the increase in the LIFO reserve over the period from LIFO COGS.

Example: LIFO adjustments for comparison purposes

Brownfield Company is a LIFO firm. At the end of last year, Brownfield reported inventory of $2 million and cost of goods sold of $6.4 million. Brownfield's LIFO reserve was $600,000 at the beginning of the year and $900,000 at year-end. Calculate Brownfield's COGS and ending inventory on a FIFO basis.

Answer:

The LIFO reserve increased $300,000 over the year [$900,000 – $600,000]. By subtracting the increase in the LIFO reserve from LIFO COGS, COGS on a FIFO basis is $6.1 million [$6.4 million – $300,000].

By adding the LIFO reserve of $900,000 to Brownfield's LIFO inventory of $2 million, inventory on a FIFO basis is $2.9 million [$2 million + $900,000].

Adjustments to LIFO inventory and LIFO COGS (in an inflationary environment) to their FIFO equivalents will result in:

- Higher gross profit margin [(revenue – COGS) / revenue] because of lower COGS.
- Higher operating profit margin [operating profit / revenue] because of higher gross profit.
- Higher net profit margin [net income / revenue] because of higher operating profit.
- Higher current ratio [current asset / current liabilities] because of higher current assets (inventory).
- Lower total asset turnover ratio [revenue / average total assets] because of higher total assets (inventory).
- Lower inventory turnover ratio [COGS / average inventory] because of lower COGS and higher inventory.
- Lower debt-to-equity ratio because of higher equity.

64 – v.5

KEY CONCEPTS

1. Held-for-trading securities are reported at fair value on the balance sheet and any unrealized gains and losses are recognized in the income statement.

2. Under IFRS, inventory is reported on the balance sheet at the lower of cost or net realizable value, but unlike under U.S. GAAP, any subsequent recovery of value subsequent to a writedown is recognized under IFRS.

3. Under IFRS, the value of property and equipment can be revalued upward, but upward revaluation is not permitted under U.S. GAAP.

4. The equity method is used when the investor can significantly influence the investee (between 20% and 50% ownership interest) and a proportional amount of the investee's net income is added to the investor's assets.

5. The consolidation method is used when the investor can control the investee (greater than 50% ownership interest).

6. In the case of joint control, the proportionate consolidation method is preferred to the equity method under IFRS, but the equity method is required under U.S. GAAP.

7. Business acquisitions affect the comparability of financial information.

8. Under IFRS, identifiable intangible assets can be revalued upward. Upward revaluation is not permitted under U.S. GAAP.

9. Revenue recognition based on costs incurred is allowed under IFRS when the firm cannot reliably estimate the outcome of the project; under U.S. GAAP, however, revenue is only recognized at completion in these circumstances.

10. LIFO is prohibited under IFRS.

11. IFRS requires that the depreciation method reflects the pattern of consumption and that the amount is allocated on a systematic basis over an asset's useful life.

12. IFRS does not permit firms to treat items as "extraordinary" in the income statement.

13. Under IFRS, interest and dividends received may be classified as either operating *or* investing activities. Dividends paid to the firm's shareholders and interest paid on the firm's debt may be classified as either operating *or* financing activities.

14. It is necessary to adjust the financial statements when comparing firms that use different accounting methods.

CONCEPT CHECKERS

1. Are held-for-trading securities and influential securities reported on the balance sheet at fair value?

	Held-for-trading	Influential
A.	Yes	No
B.	Yes	Yes
C.	No	Yes
D.	No	No

2. According to the International Accounting Standards Board, should the costs of developing goodwill and the costs of acquiring goodwill be capitalized?

	Developing goodwill	Acquiring goodwill
A.	Yes	No
B.	Yes	Yes
C.	No	Yes
D.	No	No

3. At the end of 20X6, Toreador Inc. owned equipment that became impaired. At the time of impairment, the market value of the equipment was $150,000 and a $25,000 expense was recognized. At the end of 20X7, the market value of the equipment increased $40,000. Which of the following *best* describes the effect of the recovery on Toreador's 20X7 financial statements according to the International Accounting Standards Board?
   A. Neither net income nor shareholders' equity are affected.
   B. Net income increases $25,000 and shareholder's equity increases $40,000.
   C. Net income increases $25,000 and shareholders' equity increases $15,000.
   D. Net income increases $40,000.

4. Bledsoe Construction Company is in the second year of a 3-year contract to build a new hotel. Due to a labor strike, Bledsoe is unable to reliably estimate the total cost of the project. Can Bledsoe recognize revenue in the first year of the project according to U.S. accounting standards and international accounting standards?

	U.S. accounting standards	International accounting standards
A.	Yes	Yes
B.	Yes	No
C.	No	Yes
D.	No	No

5. According to the International Accounting Standards Board, where should a firm report interest received and dividends received in the cash flow statement?
   A. Operating activities or investing activities.
   B. Operating activities only.
   C. Investing activities only.
   D. Neither operating activities nor investing activities.

6. At the end of the year, a firm reported LIFO inventory of $100,000 and cost of goods sold of $320,000. If the LIFO reserve was $30,000 at the beginning of the year and $80,000 at year-end, how much was FIFO COGS?
   A. $220,000.
   B. $240,000.
   C. $270,000.
   D. $370,000.

7. An analyst wants to compare the financial results of a U.S. firm and a European firm. The accounting standards followed by both firms are the same except that the European firm revalues its real property upward to reflect fair value. The U.S. firm's real property is reported at historical cost. The analyst decides to restate the European firm's real property by eliminating the unrealized gains. What effect will the restatement have on the European firm's total asset turnover and debt-to-equity ratios?

	Total asset turnover	Debt-to-equity
A.	Lower	Higher
B.	Lower	Lower
C.	Higher	Higher
D.	Higher	Lower

ANSWERS – CONCEPT CHECKERS

1. **A**   A held-for-trading security is reported on the balance sheet at fair value. An influential security is accounted for using the equity method. Under the equity method, the balance sheet account is not reported at fair value.

2. **C**   The costs associated with developing goodwill should be expensed as incurred. The cost of goodwill acquired in a business acquisition is capitalized.

3. **B**   The impairment loss of $25,000 was reported in 20X6 net income. Therefore, $25,000 of the $40,000 increase in market value is reported in 20X7 net income. The remainder of $15,000 is reported as a direct adjustment to shareholders' equity. Total shareholders' equity increases $40,000; $25,000 from net income (increases retained earnings) and $15,000 from the direct adjustment.

4. **C**   Since Bledsoe cannot reasonably estimate cost, the completed-contract method is required under U.S. GAAP and no revenues are recognized until project completion. Bledsoe can use the percentage-of-completion method under IFRS; however, revenue is recognized only to the extent that costs are incurred. No profit can be recognized until the project is complete.

5. **A**   Under IFRS, interest received and dividends received can be reported as either operating activities or investing activities. Under U.S. GAAP, interest received and dividends received are reported as operating activities in the cash flow statement.

6. **C** $320,000 LIFO COGS – ($80,000 ending reserve – $30,000 beginning reserve) = $270,000 FIFO COGS.

7. **C**   Removing the unrealized gain from assets will increase the total asset turnover ratio (lower assets). Removing the unrealized gain from equity will increase the debt-to-equity ratio (lower equity).

1. Which of the following would *least likely* be included in the Management Discussion and Analysis (MD&A) portion of the financial statements?
    A. Information on trends in sales and some categories of expenses.
    B. Information about expected capital expenditures and events with liquidity implications.
    C. Outlook for future results based on known trends.
    D. Discussion of depreciation methods or changes in method.

2. Contractors, Inc. has contracted to build a stadium for the City of Waston. The contract price is $100 million, costs are estimated to be $60 million, and the time to completion is three years. Compared to the completed contract method, the percentage-of-completion method will *most likely* result in a year 2 leverage ratio and year 3 cash flow from operations that are:

	Leverage ratios	Cash flow
A.	Higher	The same
B.	Higher	Lower
C.	Lower	The same
D.	Lower	Lower

3. Two firms are identical except that the first pays higher interest charges and lower dividends, while the second pays higher dividends and lower interest charges. Both prepare their financial statements under U.S. GAAP. Compared to the first, the second will have cash flow from financing (CFF) and earnings per share (EPS) that are:

	CFF	EPS
A.	The same	Higher
B.	The same	The same
C.	Lower	Higher
D.	Lower	The same

4. Which of the following is an analyst *least likely* to be able to find on or calculate from either a common-size income statement or a common-size balance sheet?
    A. Tax as a percentage of net income.
    B. Inventory turnover.
    C. Operating profit margin.
    D. Debt to equity ratio.

5. If a firm's inventory turnover and number of days of payables both increase, the effect on a firm's cash conversion cycle is to:
    A. shorten it.
    B. lengthen it.
    C. not affect it.
    D. either shorten or lengthen it.

6. The following information is summarized from Famous, Inc.'s financial statements for the year ended December 31, 200X:
   - Sales were $800,000.
   - Net profit margin was 20%.
   - Sales to assets was 50%.
   - Equity multiplier is 1.6.
   - Interest Expense was $30,000.
   - Dividends declared were $32,000.

   Famous, Inc.'s sustainable growth rate based on results from this period is *closest* to:
   A. 3.2%.
   B. 8.0%.
   C. 16.0%.
   D. 12.8%.

7. On January 1, Orange Computers issued employee stock options for 400,000 shares. Options on 200,000 shares have an exercise price of $18, and options on the other 200,000 shares have an exercise price of $22. The year-end stock price was $24, and the average stock price over the year was $20. The change in the number of shares used to calculate diluted earnings per share for the year due to these options is *closest* to:
   A. 20,000 shares.
   B. 22,000 shares.
   C. 67,000 shares.
   D. 100,000 shares.

8. Premier Corp.'s year-end LIFO reserve was $2,500,000 in 2006 and $2,300,000 in 2007. Premier's $200,000 decline in the LIFO reserve is *least likely* a result of:
   A. a LIFO liquidation.
   B. declining purchase prices.
   C. the LIFO reserve being amortized.
   D. cost of goods sold exceeding purchases.

9. If a firm issues par bonds with warrants attached rather than issuing an equal amount of par convertible bonds with the same coupon rate, it will tend to:
   A. increase net income over the early years after issuance.
   B. decrease income variability prior to conversion or warrant exercise.
   C. improve the firm's leverage ratios.
   D. decrease ROA prior to conversion or warrant exercise.

10. Train paid $8 million to acquire a franchise at the beginning of 20X5 that was expensed in 20X5. If Train had elected to capitalize the franchise as intangible asset and amortize the cost of the franchise over eight years, 20X5 cash flow from operations (CFO) and Train's 20X6 leverage ratios would have been:

	CFO	Leverage
A.	Higher	Higher
B.	Higher	Lower
C.	Lower	Lower
D.	Lower	Higher

SELF-TEST ANSWERS: FINANCIAL STATEMENT ANALYSIS

1. **D**   The MD&A is required to contain information on trends in sales and expenses, expected capital expenditures and other events affecting liquidity, and the outlook for the future based on known trends. Details of depreciation methods are contained in the footnotes to the financial statements.

2. **C**   The percentage-of-completion method recognizes a proportion of estimated project profits, which will increase net income, retained earnings, and equity and assets relative to the completed contract method. With increased equity and assets, both the debt/assets and debt/equity ratios are decreased. Cash flows are unaffected by the method selected to account for the project on the financial statements.

3. **C**   Interest paid is an operating cash flow, and dividends paid are a financing cash flow, so the firm that pays higher dividends will have lower CFF. The firm with lower interest expense will have higher EPS.

4. **B**   Inventory turnover involves sales (from the income statement) and average inventory (from the balance sheet) so it cannot be calculated from common-size statements. Tax as a percentage of net income can be calculated from income tax expense/sales divided by net income/sales. Debt to equity is debt/assets divided by equity/assets. Operating profits/sales can be read directly from the common-size income statement.

5. **A**   Cash conversion cycle = collection period + inventory period – payables period.

    An increase in inventory turnover will decrease the inventory period and shorten the cash conversion cycle. An increase in the payables period will also shorten the cash conversion cycle.

6. **D**   Famous, Inc.'s sustainable growth rate = (retention rate)(ROE).

    ROE is 0.20(800,000) / [(800,000/0.5)(1/1.6)] = 160,000/1,000,000 = 16%.

    Retention rate = (1 – Dividend Payout Ratio) = 1 – {32,000/[(0.20)(800,000)]} = 0.80.

    Growth = 0.80 (16%) = 12.8%.

7. **A**   Based on the average stock price, only the options at 18 are in the money (and therefore dilutive). Using the treasury stock method, the average shares outstanding for calculating diluted EPS would increase by [(20 – 18)/20] 200,000 = 20,000 shares.

8. **C**   LIFO reserves are not amortized. A decline in the LIFO reserve occurs when the increasing prices that created the reserve begin declining or when inventory is liquidated (i.e., fewer units in inventory at the end of the year than at the beginning).

9. **C**   With convertible bonds, the proceeds at issuance represent a balance sheet liability. For a bond with warrants attached, the fair market value of the warrants is recorded as equity, and the remainder of the proceeds is recorded as a liability, so liabilities to assets and liabilities to equity are both lower (improved). With interest expense the same on both issues, there is no effect on net income or ROA.

10. **B**   If the cost were amortized rather than expensed, the $8 million cost of the franchise would be classified as an investing cash flow rather than an operating cash flow, so CFO would increase (and CFI decrease). The asset created by capitalizing the cost would increase assets and equity, so debt to assets and debt to equity would both decrease.

11. **B**   If it becomes probable that a portion of a deferred tax asset will not be realized, a valuation allowance should be established. A valuation allowance serves to reduce the value of a deferred tax asset for the probability that it will not be realized (the difference between tax payable and income tax expense will not reverse in future periods).

12. **B**   Interest expense will be the market rate at issuance times the balance sheet liability each year. With the par bond, the liability remains constant and the interest expense equals the coupon payment since the yield at issuance is equal to the coupon rate. With the premium bond, for an equal amount of proceeds received, the interest expense will be the same in the first period (market yield times proceeds) as for the par bond. Since the premium is amortized over time, however, the liability will decrease toward par each period, so interest expense will decrease each year, and net income will increase over time as the premium is amortized.

   With the value of the bonds issued equal in either case, CFF in the first year will be the same (increased by the proceeds). There is no effect on CFF in the interim years, just when the issue is redeemed at maturity.

13. **C**   With a capital lease, only the interest portion of the lease payment is classified as CFO, so CFO will be greater than it would be with an equivalent operating lease. CFI will be less for a capital lease because the principal portion of each lease payment is classified as an investing cash flow (CFI). Operating income, EBIT, will be reduced only by the (equal) annual depreciation expense with a capital lease, so operating income will be greater for a capital lease than for an operating lease (for which the entire lease payment will be an operating expense). At inception, a capital lease will increase assets and liabilities by the same amount so there is no effect on equity. An operating lease has no effect on CFI so classification as a capital lease cannot reduce CFI variability.

14. **C**   At asset acquisition, a liability equal to the present value of the asset disposal costs (not the expected disposal cost) is created and an asset of equal value is created, so there is no initial effect on equity. The increase in the liability (accretion) each year is recorded as interest expense, so interest coverage ratios are lower each year when there are asset disposal costs. With asset disposal costs, net income will be reduced each year by both the interest expense on the liability and by depreciation of the offsetting asset that is created.

15. **D**   Impairment charges reduce operating income and net income in the period of the charge. Taxes are not affected because any loss in asset value will reduce taxes only when the asset is disposed of and the loss is actually realized. The debt to equity ratio increases in the period of the charge because equity is reduced.

INDEX

A

accelerated depreciation 56
accelerated depreciation methods 180
account format 86
accounting changes 60
accounting equation 11
accounts 20
accounts payable (trade payables) 89
accrual accounting 22
accrued liabilities 89
activity ratios 273
amortization 229
antidilutive securities 64
asset retirement obligation 190
assets 20, 84
audit 13
authorized shares 95
available-for-sale securities 94, 316
average age 187
average cost method 57, 137
average depreciable life 187
average inventory processing period 274
average receivables collection period 274

B

balance sheet 11
barter transaction 52
basic accounting equation 21
basic EPS 62
bonds 225
bonds with warrants 234
book value 178

C

capital leases 247
capitalized interest 168
capitalizing interest costs 169
cash collections 115
cash dividends 117
cash flow from financing activities (CFF) 107
cash flow from investing activities (CFI) 107
cash flow from operating activities (CFO) 107
cash flow statement 11
cash from bond issue 117
cash from sale of land 117

cash interest 116
cash paid to suppliers 116
cash ratio 97, 276
cash taxes 116
cash to reacquire stock 117
cash wages 116
change in accounting estimate 61
change in accounting principle 60
chart of accounts 20
classified balance sheet 86
common-size balance sheet 97
common-size income statement 71
common-size statements 267
comparability 36
completed-contract method 49
complex capital structure 61
comprehensive income 74
consolidation method 318
contra accounts 20
contributed capital 95
convertible bonds 234
cost recovery method 51
coverage ratios 125
current assets 87
current cost method 148
current liabilities 87
current portion of long-term debt 89
current ratio 97, 276

D

debt-to-equity ratio 98, 277
debt-to-total capital 278
declining balance method (DB) 56
deferred tax assets 202, 207
deferred tax liabilities 201, 204, 207
depreciable lives 185
depreciation 54
diluted EPS equation 66
dilutive securities 64
direct-financing lease 255
disclosure requirements 111
discontinued operations 59
double-declining balance 180
double-entry accounting 22
DuPont analysis, extended 289

©2008 Schweser

Notes

Notes

Notes

Notes

Notes